"It is an honor to have played a ⟨...⟩ Carmichael story. She is a masterful storyteller with a stinging wit that will make you LOL. Judy is one of a kind and reading this book is like hearing stories told in an after hours piano bar when jazz musicians come to relax and enjoy life and laughter. Brava, Judy!!"

—Felix Contreras (Host/Jazz Producer, NPR)

"Judy Carmichael's witty, ebullient pianism recalls us to the joy of spirit of classical jazz. More power to her!"

—E. L. Doctorow

"Guts, sass, humor and a phenomenal stride pianist and terrific singer too! All this is Judy Carmichael and so much more. She knows how to beguile on stage and in the pages of this book, which you'll lap up. This is her story, a brave young woman who rides the waves of her life with grace, spunk and resilience, even in choppy waters."

—Blythe Danner (Golden Globe, Tony, and Emmy-winning actress)

"Judy's personality leaps from the page; her humor, her vulnerability and her pain. This is a generous, entertaining autobiography by a wonderful jazz artist and courageous human being. I couldn't put it down and I look forward to the sequel, if I'm still around."

—Alan Broadbent (Multi-Grammy-winning jazz pianist/composer)

"Judy Carmichael's music accomplishes what all great art should—feelings of joy, delight, hope and the knowledge that what you are experiencing is very real and honest. Anyone who wants some real theatre should go to one of her concerts—lots of fun."

—F. Murray Abraham (*Homeland*)

"Judy Carmichael's page-turner of a memoir captures the thrills, laughs, perils, setbacks, and victories of a jazz life well-lived. It's the story of a woman who has followed her heart on a nonstop roller-coaster ride around the globe, making exciting music and weathering plenty of blows--some of them life-threatening--while never forgetting to have as much fun as she possibly could. *Swinger!* is an inspiring, moving, and vastly entertaining read."

—James Gavin (Author of *Is That All There Is?* The Strange Life of Peggy Lee and *Stormy Weather* The Life of Lena Horne)

"How can this slender and elegant woman play with the strength of a truck driver and the energy of a tom cat? Some mysteries are meant not to be revealed."

—Milton Glaser

"Judy Carmichael is an amazing combination of passion, pluck, and persistence, going against the common wisdom and all odds, where few have gone before. She didn't just choose a musical niche for herself, she carved out a new one. She, and her story, are a joy and an inspiration."

—Frank King, (Writer for *The Tonight Show*)

"The life of a jazz musician seems almost as fraught as climbing Mount Everest. Judy Carmichael's adventures are hilarious and inspiring."

—Paul Deegan (Everest mountaineer and author of *The Mountain Traveller's Handbook*)

"Many of the things one could say about Fats Waller's music could be applied equally to Judy Carmichael: Playful, Stylish, Mischievous, Virtuosic and with—as Fats said of himself—"A butterfly right hand and a paintbrush left" (and seriously saucy ankles activating those pedal extremities!) How lucky we are that Judy is around to keep the magic of Fats so gloriously alive and tickling."

—Tony Walton (Oscar, Tony and Emmy—winning costume and set designer)

Swinger!

A Jazz Girl's Adventures from Hollywood to Harlem

Judy Carmichael

C&D Productions
P.O. Box 360
Sag Harbor, NY
11963

For information on booking a reading or event with Judy Carmichael contact Jamie Roche at
Piercemgmt@aol.com or visit our website at www.judycarmichael.com.

Cover and book design: Kathleen Lynch/Black Kat Design kat@blackkatdesign.net

Bio page photo: Kenny James

Some names and identifying details of people portrayed in the book have been changed.

ISBN: 1979764417
ISBN 13: 9781979764414

I'm here with Michael Crichton and Ray Eames, two of my biggest inspirations, in Venice, CA, 1987.

For Gilda Block and Jill and John Walsh, in gratitude

Checkup

"**J**udy, I think you've got cervical cancer."

Well, that's not good. Didn't he tell me last year that cervical cancer isn't hereditary? I can't believe I got it anyway. Mom was twenty-six when she had it. Well . . . at least I lasted until forty-nine.

"You'll need surgery immediately and possibly chemo and radiation."

Let me think. Do I have any gigs I have to cancel? No, nothing for a while. Good. I won't have to tell anyone about this and hear how awful it was when their Aunt Minnie had cancer and how horrible her treatment was and how sad it was when her hair fell out.

I can hear it: "I hope you're not like my Uncle Nathan. He was throwing up nonstop from the chemo. Oh man, and my friend Hank got so depressed."

Yeah, don't tell anyone. If I'm not around for a while, everyone will figure I'm on the road. Oh, God! And I can't tell anyone in the business.

"Nope, we can't hire Judy Carmichael. Isn't she dying from cancer? Wait! Isn't she dead already?"

"Yeah, I think so. Let's get Dick Hyman."

"Is Dick still around? Damn, it's so hard when everyone's either really old or dead."

"Who do we know who's alive and young, but plays like Judy or Dick?"

Yeah. Don't tell anyone.

"Judy! Did you hear me?

"Oh, sorry, doctor. I was thinking about gigs."

"Gigs?"

"Yeah. I'm making sure I don't have any concerts I need to cancel."

"Listen, forget what I just said. Let's wait for your test results and decide then what needs to be done. I'm sorry I was so blunt with my diagnosis."

"Actually, I appreciated it. I'm tired of doctors obfuscating or saying, 'Let's wait for the results.'"

Silence.

"I must say you're taking this remarkably well, Judy."

"I'm a jazz musician, doctor. To tell you the truth, this isn't the worst thing that's ever happened to me."

— —

I drove to my favorite nursery, and parked in the almost empty lot. I rolled down my car windows and breathed in the sweet, cool air. Looking across acres of farmland and an endless expanse of flowers, just brought in for the start of the spring season, I pondered my diagnosis.

Is getting Mom's sense of humor, talent, and good hair worth growing up with her narcissism, irrational behavior, phobias, and history of cancer?

I smiled and thought: *Absolutely. She was nuts and a pain in the ass but thank God, never dull. And if I've come this far just to die, well, then there really isn't any meaning to life.*

I'm not going to die.

"*California is a great place to live . . . if you're an orange.*"

—Fred Allen

"*If you're one in a million, there are ten of you in New York.*"

—Ed Koch

"*As a jazz musician, if your phone rings, you're more likely to spend money than to make it.*"

—Judy Carmichael

1

California Girl

I was a bubbly, blonde, ex-beauty-queen teen with a thing for Fred Astaire when I dove into the macho world of jazz as a stride pianist in the 1980s. Few women at the time were jazz instrumentalists, and none played stride piano, a physically demanding style made famous by Fats Waller and Count Basie in the '20s and '30s. Many had played it in the early years of jazz, but those two brought stride to the masses.

Stride piano requires a deft left hand that alternates low bass notes with mid-keyboard chords rhythmically driving the music harder than any other solo jazz piano style. All early jazz pianists were influenced by stride, notably Art Tatum, Earl Hines, and Duke Ellington and later on, Nat Cole, Thelonious Monk, Oscar Peterson and other jazz greats.

An early review called me "the first important stride pianist to emerge in nearly thirty years." The most famous one up to that point had been Fats Waller, a three-hundred-pound black man who lived hard and fast and died in 1943 at the age of thirty-nine. I'm five-foot-five and weigh one hundred and fifteen. "Hard and fast" to me means a good day on a tennis court.

I grew up in Pico Rivera, California, twenty minutes south of downtown Los Angeles—"if there isn't any traffic," a caveat always added by the natives. It's where the 605 and 5 freeways cross, which I used to say made it easy to escape. I wasn't a big fan of the place, even as a kid.

"PR," as we locals called it, had a population of around fifty thousand in the 1960s, when I lived there. The number felt purely theoretical, though, since the city limits blurred into the bordering towns of Whittier, Montebello, and Downey, while their city limits blended into neighboring towns, forming an endless urban sprawl. I used to fantasize about what it would be like to live in a place surrounded by countryside and fresh air instead of asphalt and smog.

Most of Pico Rivera consisted of hardworking middle-class folks of various races who got along. But as with many of the cities in Los Angeles County in the '50s and '60s, there were Mexican gangs who regularly engaged in knife fights and other adventures, usually after football games or occasionally after school. A custom among the gang girls was to strategically place razor blades in their highly teased hairdos to slice the fingers of an opponent who tried a hair-grab mid-fight. It was an exciting time.

By the time we baby-boomer locals had reached high school, we took all this in stride, since our schoolmates were uniquely integrated. We rarely met someone whose parents were native Californians. My parents were from Illinois, someone else's came from Mexico, and another's hailed from Nebraska. We all had the same accent, and most of us had parents at a similar socioeconomic level. Whether we were Mexican, Asian, or white, we were all afraid of the gangs, and we stuck together. Eighty percent of my high-school graduating class was Mexican which seemed normal to me, since ours was the only high school in the city, and most of those in the surrounding cities had a similar demographic.

Like much of Southern California, Pico Rivera had once been a bucolic scene of farmland, orange groves, avocado trees, and a few clapboard-sided farmhouses and weathered barns. By the time I arrived on the scene in 1952, however, there was a rapid advance of tract homes and strip malls. We were lucky to have the single remaining rundown homestead behind our property, which I found terribly exotic. I was sure the barn was haunted. This one bit of something different in my neighborhood spurred my imagination and determination to travel beyond PR.

There were huge avocado trees in our front and back yards, the front ones great for playing airplane on the long, overhanging branches in the strong Santa Ana winds, the back ones perfect for the tree-houses my brother and I had. Mine was larger and better constructed because my father had put more effort into helping me build it. Its superiority was a continuing source of resentment from my brother Bob, who was two and a half years older than I and felt his seniority should have given him the better place.

"Dad likes you better," he'd say.

"Mom likes you better," I'd counter.

"Yeah, okay. You're right."

My earliest memory is the fragrance of freshly laundered cotton, the kind used in men's T-shirts, back when men and boys wore white, 100% cotton T's under their shirts. That particular cotton smelled delicious, right off the line, which is how my mom insisted on drying her wash.

My father wore those T's, and I'm sure my happy memory of their scent is from his hugging me close to his chest as a baby and my breathing in a combination of clean cotton and Old Spice. He was a hugger; and since Mom disappeared periodically in my early years with various mysterious ailments, I appreciated hugging.

Dad was also my first hairdresser, brushing my hair in the morning into two long golden ponytails on either side of my head, with a perfect part in the middle. This isn't a look I'd attempt now, but it was pretty cute then. People always commented on my hair, a combination of red and gold that sparkled in the sun.

My first instrument was the ukulele, which I started learning at three. I played "Five Foot Two, Eyes of Blue" and "Ain't She Sweet," already heading in a traditional direction, although who knows where I'd be had I been exposed to Don Ho. I abandoned the uke when the piano caught my eye, but resurrected it for a Hawaiian dance number I performed in Brownies, which made me the audience favorite.

Another lovely memory is my mother's piano playing, which I first heard in utero, her swollen belly getting me nice and close to the keyboard as she played. I was initially drawn to the piano, not just from that early memory, but from the sound of my mother's beautiful ballads and the image of her fingers sinking into the keys, which from my perspective as a three-year-old standing at the end of the keyboard was just about eye level. I loved the look of her graceful fingers disappearing into the keys, which looked like a long tray of ivory cream with licorice sticks floating on it. With my nose pushed up to the edge of the piano, I could smell the lemony fragrance of the polished wood, making it all seem like a yummy musical cake.

"You know my mom wrote 'Night and Day,' right?"

"Judy, I think that was Cole Porter."

"No, it's one of my favorites of hers. She also wrote 'Here's That Rainy Day.'"

"I think that's by Jimmy Van Heusen."

"I think he got it from my mother."

I was seven when I boasted about this to my new piano teacher, Mrs. Browning. Finding out Mom didn't actually write these songs was only slightly less shocking than my discoveries about the Easter Bunny and the Tooth Fairy.

Mom, who'd been a talented self-taught musician from a young age, did compose some wonderful melodies and lyrics and played her tunes along with the standards, so I assumed she'd written them all. I obviously showed good taste early on by choosing "Night and Day" as a favorite. I also particularly liked "For All We Know," although, sadly, she didn't write that either.

I was envious of her ability to play by ear and frequently asked her to reveal to me the secret of this mysterious gift. I'll never know if her withholding that information was a result of her continual competition with me or her genuinely not knowing how to explain it. She never did, which made me feel I wasn't musically talented, no matter how much people complimented my playing as a child. I had to unlock this puzzle on my own in my early twenties, a late date for a professional musician to learn music theory.

My mother wrote comedy numbers as well as ballads and composed a catchy ditty entitled "The Freudian Fight Song," subtitled "If Your Chin Is Up, You're Too Damn Tense," a hit Bob and I performed at family gatherings when we were kids, the bizarreness of which I only now appreciate.

The Freudian Fight Song

If your chin's up you're tense
Your wrinkles look immense
You're tired, you're sick, you're nervous, you're neurotic
Your upper lip's so stiff you look psychotic
So let your chins relax
And listen to the facts
Take your tranquilizers
And admit that it makes sense
If your chin is up you're too damn tense

Not exactly the Family Von Trapp.

My mom, Jeanne Boock, and dad, John Hohenstein, were attractive, talented standouts in their families. Mom had dark curly hair, big brown eyes, and two handsome older brothers she was mad about. The oldest, Bob, for whom my brother was named, enlisted in England's Royal Air Force's "Eagle Squadron," the troop of American flyers who joined the RAF before the United States entered World War II. Bob went missing in action over the English Channel in 1943, something that defined everything afterward for my mother and gave me an early connection with England. Her brother Jim returned from the war with shrapnel in his legs and demons in his head and never fully got his life together. He looked like the actor Tyrone Power. As a little girl, I had a huge crush on him.

Mom's younger sister was born in 1941, so she was closer to my age than Mom's, although my mom said she was thrilled to finally have a sister, even one so much younger.

My mother said people always commented that she looked like Maureen O'Sullivan, who had played Jane to Johnny Weissmuller's Tarzan in "Tarzan the Ape Man" in 1932. She had that classic 1940s can-do-babe look about her. The adult Shirley Temple, perky and cute.

Her family was upper-middle-class and well known in Springfield, Illinois, where she and Dad grew up. Her father was a self-made man, the only one of my grandparents to go to college. He went on to become a highly respected engineer, serving on various top-secret committees during World War II and heading Allis-Chalmers, then a farm equipment manufacturer and Springfield's largest employer.

My maternal grandmother went to finishing school (a common path after sixth grade for girls of the time who had enough money to do it) and business school for a year before she married my grandfather. She had the most privileged upbringing of all my grandparents.

Mom's dad was a drinker with a temper who beat her two older brothers and seldom said much to anyone once he came home from work. Mom was scared to death of him. Dad was the youngest of five and resembled a taller, friendlier version of James Cagney, with Irish good looks and a devilish glint in his eye, as if a good story or witticism were on the tip of his tongue.

My paternal grandmother's Irish emigrant parents were poor and troubled. They put my grandmother and her sister in an orphanage at a young age and only brought them home when their mother died, so that my grandmother could take care of her father until he drank himself to death a few years later. Like many of this generation, my grandfather left school after sixth grade to go to work and help support his family.

Dad was proud of our family name, which had been von Hohenstein until the "von" was dropped during World War I so it would sound less

German. von Hohenstein is an ancient, royal name dating from the Middle Ages. I only reveal my family name when I'm in Germany or Austria, where many towns and castles have the name Hohenstein attached to them. Locals recognize the history and importance of this name, which gives me an immediate connection with them. My German band mates referred to me as Baroness von Hohenstein for an entire tour of Germany I did a few years ago, which we all thought amusing until an actual Baroness von Hohenstein came to one of our concerts.

When I was in my twenties and trying to understand why my two gifted parents had wound up so unhappy, my father's older brother, Ed, told me that all my dad's siblings were musically and athletically talented but none so much as my father, adding, "He was much more stylish than the rest of us too. People noticed your dad."

Ed thought their father's constant criticism of Dad stemmed from his jealousy of him. Ed was tough and stood up to their father, but my dad was the youngest, a gentle, artistic soul, and his father's abuse damaged him. When Dad started taking operatic vocal lessons, his father ridiculed him and declared he must be a homosexual to focus on this kind of singing.

In her teens, my mother developed Raynaud's disease, a condition in which fingers and toes suddenly have decreased blood flow. This can be brought on by stress or extreme cold, and for my mother, Springfield had plenty of both. She and Dad jumped at this excuse to move to California.

Mom believed that it was never too early to appreciate sophisticated humor, making sure I had some Tom Lehrer songs in my early piano repertoire and giving me Oscar Levant's *Memoirs of an Amnesiac* to balance my Nancy Drew. At family parties my brother and I alternated between Lehrer's "Vatican Rag" and Mom's "The Freudian Fight Song" as our big party pieces, with the occasional "Poisoning Pigeons in the Park" or "Freddy the Freshman" to round things out.

My father loved words and clever wordplay and gave me a different word each morning to use during the day in conversation. He had me report my progress at dinnertime. The word of the day I remember most vividly was "ennui," an inspired choice for a nine-year-old.

I went most of the day with no chance to drop this word casually into my conversation, and was getting desperate. Finally, inspiration struck. I yawned and stretched my arms conspicuously sitting at my desk at the back of my class, until my teacher called on me.

"Are we keeping you awake, Judy, or is something bothering you?"

"Miss Johnson, this class fills me with ennui."

"I'll see if we can step things up." She did, and also sent me to the principal.

Around this same time, I announced that I wanted to move away from Pico Rivera because I felt it was "culturally bereft," which is probably why I was filled with ennui.

Dad was a wonderful singer in the virile, stentorian Robert Preston mode, and as a child I saw him perform musical-comedy numbers in various civic light-opera settings and the occasional P.T.A. production at my elementary school. This made me the envy of all my classmates, who wished their fathers were as humorous, talented, and lovable.

He also gave me the best advice I've ever gotten about performing. "Remember, when you walk on stage, the audience is more nervous than you are, worrying you'll make a mistake and make them feel awkward, or worse, bore them. Your first job is to let them know you have it under control, so they can relax and enjoy themselves."

＿ ＿

I took piano lessons between the ages of seven and eleven, quitting a few times out of frustration that my teacher wouldn't go deeper into the music. I learned to read music, but nothing of theory or how to play by ear. I didn't realize it then, but I had a great ear and rhythmic sense. I'd ask my teacher to play a piece through before I'd sight-read it; then I'd be able to read it more easily because I'd memorized the rhythm. This is common with children with good ears, so she should have seen through this. My teacher was a big woman who was proud of her time in the military. I can't remember her smiling or complimenting me, but do remember her yelling.

The piano is an instrument you can play without understanding the underlying harmony; in other words, you can learn that four flats in the key signature means you flat those notes every time they appear, without knowing that four flats in the key signature means you're in the key of Ab, which has its own set of rules. You've learned the words of the language without the grammar so you can't build your own sentences. Once, when my teacher referred to something theoretical and I asked her to explain what she meant, she snapped, "I already taught you that!" I never asked another question.

When I was in my twenties and gaining something of a reputation in my music career, I got a call from Mrs. Browning's son.

"Hi, this is Craig Browning. I don't know if you remember me."

"Of course I do. You're Mrs. Browning's son, right? I haven't seen you since I was eleven, I think, and you were nine?"

"Yes, I think that's about right. I just wanted to tell you how thrilled I am with your success and how much you've always meant to me."

When you've gained a bit of fame, people you barely knew from your past sometimes turn up and act like your best friend. I braced myself for something weird.

"Why do you say that? We haven't seen each other since we were kids."

"Well, I said I wanted a music career when I was a kid and my mother said I'd never amount to anything because I was 'just like Judy Hohenstein, always wanting to do my own thing.' I've followed your career and been inspired by your success. I now have my own business as a sound engineer. I just called to thank you."

It was a lovely surprise and reinforced the thought I'd had at every one of those piano lessons: The only thing worse than having this woman as a teacher would be having her as a mother. She did, however, help me learn a tune that served me well in launching my music career.

My paternal grandfather, a gruff, intimidating German-Scot, offered fifty dollars to the first of his grandchildren to learn "Maple Leaf Rag" and a hundred dollars to the first to learn "Cannonball Rag." This was a huge amount of money in 1963 especially for a man who had only made it through the sixth grade, worked for the post office, and raised five kids.

My cousins in Springfield, where my grandfather lived, were making very little progress on the piano, so he thought he was safe with this offer. I, on the other hand, was improving fast out west, and that fifty dollars was inspiring me further. I loved "Maple Leaf Rag," and for the first time I was seriously motivated at the keyboard.

Mrs. Browning had told me I wasn't good enough to learn "Maple Leaf." I begged her to help me anyway. The happy result is that I got the fifty dollars and quit taking piano lessons. I'm not the first person to quit taking lessons but I'm certainly the first to go into music for the money.

As my grandfather begrudgingly handed me the fifty dollars, he said, "Don't bother learning 'Cannonball Rag.' I'm not giving you that hundred dollars."

Musicians take note: Always get a deposit.

I tended to experience things intensely while growing up. Bob said I was melodramatic, histrionic, and a show-off, but I like to think I was artistically sensitive. My high-school best friend Christine once commented, "Judy, you do know that not *everything* is a big deal, right?" Of course, Christine's personality and outlook were the antithesis of mine. Her parents were stoic Austrians, and nothing was a big deal.

My theatrical view of things influenced my childhood dreams, which were always vivid, and frequently ended, movie like, with a swelling soundtrack and rolling credits:

Judy played by Judy

Judy's brother Bob played by Bob

Mom played by Mom

Dad played by Dad

Clementine the dog played by Clementine [my dog]

Years later, I mentioned these dreams to my therapist and he pretended they were normal, which I've always appreciated.

— —

There was a weekly television program in Los Angeles called the *Million Dollar Movie* that played classic films of the 1930s, '40s, and '50s. I was obsessed with these as a child. The same movie would play seven nights in a row and I would watch each showing and memorize the dialogue, songs, and dance routines, acting it all out until my family pleaded for relief.

"*Judy, stop doing Ann Miller!* You're tap-dancing in *flip-flops*! You're going to hurt yourself!"

"Mom, listen to this: *Why can't yooooooou behave? Oh, WHYYY can't YOOOU behaaaaave?*"

"I'm a Cole Porter fan too, Judy, but enough is enough!"

I loved showbiz stories about nobodies with talent who worked hard and became stars. I never understood *The Jolson Story*, where Jolson's love interest wanted him to give up the stage for a quiet life in the country. Jolson wanted her to give up a home life for the stage, which seemed a much more reasonable choice to me.

My dad was a movie buff, too. He'd discuss these films in depth with me and give me context and the backstory on the actors, since these were the films of his youth. I was sure I'd grow up to sing and dance my way through life in good lighting, dressed to the nines, with a handsome man on my arm romancing me with song and witty repartee. My life would be a *Thin Man* movie.

Mom and Dad reinforced this obsession by occasionally taking me to a revival house, so I could see the full extravaganza on the big screen. These outings were no small thing since, at the time, revival theaters in the Los Angeles area were far from Pico Rivera and in dangerous parts of town.

When I was ten, I had my first revival-house adventure, a double bill of *Gold Diggers of 1933* and *42nd Street*. Mom and I were the lone females in the theater, the other audience members being shady-looking guys with overcoats they kept on throughout the picture. This was Los Angeles in August, so overcoats were not a common look.

Our row was empty except for Dad on one side of me and Mom on the other, until a Peter Lorre lookalike sat a couple of seats to Mom's right. Mom kept leaning into me to put as much distance as possible between herself and our creepy-looking friend. She was practically in my lap when I asked her to stop crowding me. Reaching over, she grabbed Dad's arm and whispered desperately, "John! The man next to me is *playing with himself!*"

Dad, who was enjoying a Busby Berkeley moment onscreen and didn't want to be interrupted, replied, "Don't look at him."

For years, I thought men with overcoats had toys hidden in their inside pockets for a bit of spontaneous fun whenever the mood struck.

Around this same time, I asked my brother what French kissing was after hearing the term from one of my friends. He put me off, saying, "Ask Dad." I did, during a drive to the market. Dad explained, gesticulating artfully to illustrate the tongue action, which was impressive, considering he was driving in L.A. traffic.

Not surprisingly, I squealed, "*Yuck,* that's *disgusting!*"

"You'd be surprised," he replied. "It seems natural at the time."

I was a bit of a weirdo as a pre-teen. I remember having a good time at school, mainly because of sports. Before the boys got big and we all still played together, I was consistently among the first to be picked when teams were chosen, played anything with a ball well, and competed fiercely.

Dad and Bob were great athletes; and Bob, always knowing a good thing when he saw it, used me as his ace whenever neighborhood teams were gathered. "I'll make a sacrifice and have my little sister on my team," he would say, knowing I was fast, knew the plays, and, unlike my girlfriends, knew how to throw a football. Dad said everyone should know the proper way to throw a football. It was un-American not to throw a football well.

Dad also made sure I was good with a basketball. One of my family sports memories is of our outing to see the Harlem Globetrotters when I was eight. My folks paid extra for seats close to the action, hoping that Bob would be chosen as the kid to play with the team, a fun bit the Globetrotters always included. Seeing the cute red-haired boy, they shot over to grab Bob, but then spotted me and undoubtedly thought that a little golden-haired girl provided more comedic potential. They tossed me between them, handed me the ball, and dumped me head first into the basket with it. The team was surprised when I ran off dribbling, bouncing the ball between my legs, and threw in a basket on my own. I was already a showoff. My brother never forgave me for edging him out.

Years later, while Bob was in high school and I was still in junior high, he had a job at a pool hall and made extra money on the side hustling that artful game. His place of employment was dark, seedy, and frequented by scary sorts, and certainly no women.

Stories of this mysterious place fascinated me, so I begged to be taken there and taught how to play. Bob quickly discovered that I could hit the ball wherever he instructed with the required English to curve it left or right, fade backward, roll forward, or stop on a dime. Those piano lessons had not been wasted. Excellent hands.

Bob would lick his finger and mark the place on the felt in front of the spot where I should hit the ball. I'd do the deed and look like a professional.

Out of that ploy came the Bob and Judy Hustle.

"Hey, Bob, how about a game?"

"Hi, Kevin. Oh, man, I'd love to, but I'm stuck playing with my little sister. She wants to learn how to play, and it's taking forever!"

I'd hit the cue ball off the table with a bang.

"Bob, show me how to do it again. I keep missing."

"You're missing the *table*, Judy! Don't hit it so hard!"

"Come on," Kevin said. "Dump her and let's play. I've got some money."

"No, really, I can't. Well ... unless you get someone to play with you and I use Judy as my partner."

"Are you kidding? She's terrible."

"She won't be if I show her where to hit the ball."

"Well, if you're willing to lose money."

We made quite a bit on this scam until my mother found out and banished me from the pool hall, which I have to admit was a pretty dodgy scene. The place eventually burned down in an arson/murder scandal, so Mom's ire was understandable. Dad tried to act angry, but one of his favorite movies was *The Hustler*, so he was drawn to this sort of thing. In his own way, he was an early feminist; to him it made no difference if his son was a pool shark or his daughter.

— —

I've always loved sports, but in my time, girls were only allowed a chance to be unselfconscious sports hounds in elementary school. After that, it was all about avoiding gym so as not to mess up your hair and makeup, or, worse, be branded weird for actually liking sports. Cool girls acted out their excess energy by becoming a cheerleader or some other wimpy sports substitute. I say this as an ex-cheerleader.

Like most high schools in Los Angeles County during the baby-boom years, mine was huge, with three thousand students. It was a good school academically, but what made it famous was its tremendous football team. Pico Rivera had only recently incorporated, so most folks out of my immediate vicinity hadn't heard of it, although if I said, "I go to El Rancho High School," there was always an appreciative nod.

Our games were played in a stadium filled with thousands of people with the play-by-play announced by a professional. I still remember the smell of the grass field combined with the fog on those cold winter evenings. I sat in the stadium completely underdressed, since no one in Los Angeles admits that it gets cold. Throughout school I was either on drill team or cheerleading, wearing some sort of skimpy outfit, freezing.

Since this was before Title Nine, the federal law that mandated equal financing on girls' athletics, everything was about boys' sports. The one great sporting event for girls was the annual "Powder Puff" football game, a common activity in Southern California high schools, where girls would play an exhibition game of flag football—juniors against seniors—and everyone would laugh at girls running around in their shorts, throwing the ball badly, and running plays that were mostly improvised.

"Sarah, quick, run over there, and I'll toss you the ball."

Not at El Rancho. We had a training period that lasted for weeks, a time during which the football players tortured us with brutal versions of their exercises to get us in shape and watch us suffer. Also, we suited up in full gear—pads, helmets, the works—and played a night game in a packed stadium with the school's professional announcer.

The Head Cheerleader, i.e. the most popular girl in school, who of course dated the quarterback, would always get to be Powder Puff quarterback, whether she could play or not.

Every position was decided according to popularity, not ability. The less glamorous positions went to the "weird" girls, the ones who kept playing sports after elementary school because they didn't care about being cool or knew they would never be cool; or the ones so big and mean that they could beat up anyone who said they weren't cool. Mostly we had the popular girls and the big mean ones on our team.

And when I say big, I mean *big*, and angry, because everyone treated them as if they weren't cool. You remember high school.

While I won numerous awards, ran lots of committees and clubs, and had become well known in high school, I wasn't particularly popular, which was reflected in my getting offensive guard as my position.

This was flag football, where a Velcro flag hangs on either side of the belt around your waist, and grabbing it off is the equivalent of a tackle. That's the game in theory. Things usually got aggressive and ugly, because the athletic girls resented the cheerleaders getting the prime spots and the cheerleaders resented spending time with girls of a lower social standing. Seniors always won, since they'd had one year to figure things out, but not in my junior year. It was an upset of massive proportions.

Powder Puff was a perfect marriage of my two passions: sports and theater. The one thing that dampened my spirits was the obvious: I was a five-foot-five, 115-pound offensive guard, and the defensive line was made up of aggressive, angry, gigantic females. Compared to these social outcasts, even I was popular, so being gentle with the midget offensive guard was not in their playbook.

Many of the girls looked upon this as a social rather than a sporting event, so a few of us were getting impatient. We were heading toward defeat, with the cheerleader/quarterback in charge, so the girls who knew I could actually throw a football forced a switch, not only putting me in the position I wanted but probably saving my life.

I had secretly prepared for this and had learned some real plays. I would call, "Thirty-four, trigger reverse," having taught my main teammates what that meant.

The other team would huddle and say, "You run that way, you over there. I'll run back and throw you the ball." Things immediately improved. I passed repeatedly, mostly to avoid being flattened. My plays became predictable, but I stayed in one piece.

The most memorable moment was when, after having advanced the field with a series of pass plays, I set up for another, only to notice the entire defense had dropped back to cover the receivers, leaving thirty lovely yards clear in front of me. The seniors figured I had no other moves except a pass, so ran off in anticipation. With no one to stop me, I ran for daylight, and scored a touchdown.

My teammates screamed, the crowd went wild, and the girls ran off the field. Our coach yelled at everyone, calling us back for the extra point, a play no one had taught us, since no one thought we'd need it. My team looked at me expectantly while I invented a play.

"OK. Everyone, no matter what your position, when I get the ball, push forward like a wall, knock everyone over and I'll crawl over the top. It will surprise them, piss them off, and hopefully work."

Incredibly, it did. It took a while for everyone to pile off of me and for me to realize we'd actually done it, but these were the points that won the game and became my most illustrious high-school moment. Years later, I found out this play is called the "quarterback sneak." I assume someone saw me do it and stole the idea.

My brother had to give up football in junior high because he had what was called Osgood Slaughter Knee. I remember that amazing name but not what it means. Since Bob couldn't realize his football dreams, he and Dad were particularly proud of my Powder Puff triumph. Those early throwing lessons had paid off. My football exploits became legendary in my family and, I fear, a bit exaggerated. I think Dad told a few people I won the Heisman, but that's not true, so don't believe it, even if you read it on Wikipedia.

2

Come Fly With Me

I always wanted to travel, see the world, speak lots of languages, and live in other countries. Even as a child, I knew I wanted to absorb a place, not just pass through it.

Some of my favorite childhood memories are of the cross-country trips we'd take to visit my grandparents and cousins in Illinois, where my parents grew up. Mom would map a different route every year and sometimes we'd take as long as five weeks to explore it. We referred to these adventures as going "back East," since everything is east of California. It wasn't until I moved to Manhattan that I realized that Illinois wasn't "the East."

We'd make scrapbooks of our travels, with postcards and little souvenirs taped onto the colorful paper that filled our binders. In mine, I'd draw Bob and me in cowboy gear, with Bob always pointing out something interesting.

"Look, Judy! Mount Rushmore!"

I remember smells, sounds, and the "wildlife" during these outings. When I was growing up in the cement-covered San Gabriel Valley, the main smell was smog, and the only animals running around were pets. Seeing my first squirrel on one of these vacations was a major event.

I have a vivid memory of coming home from one such trip, driving over the San Gabriel Mountains, and seeing the smog-covered valley into which we were about to descend and thinking: *Someday I'll live in a place as beautiful as anywhere I've visited. I'll look forward to coming home.* This was a major goal and motivating force in my early life.

We would picnic in lush parks along the way and stay in little roadside motels, always run by some weathered character, laconic and suspicious. I loved drifting off to sleep to the distant sound of a train whistle or catching the wonderful metallic fragrance of rain in the desert as it wafted through the windows.

My local park in Pico Rivera was surrounded by a chain-link fence and covered with dirt and patchy grass, with a few dried-out trees trying mightily to survive in the polluted air. The occasional drug dealer hanging about made staying past late afternoon a bad idea. All this made visiting a park with thriving flora and fauna like a trip to Oz.

Driving across wide-open spaces, where you could be surrounded by storms and see them close in on you, was exciting and poetic. I remember seeing my first full-on lightning storm and realizing that lightning could fork and be distinctly defined, not just the hazy flash I'd witnessed in the occasional thunderstorm in Southern California. Before that, I had thought dramatic lightning was a movie effect.

"We used to put our bathing suits on and play in the rain in the summer," my mom remembered.

"But wasn't it cold?" asked the California girl, who only knew rain in cold weather.

"No, in the Midwest it can be hot and rain at the same time."

This was extraordinary news.

I wasn't sure what I'd do for a living, but I knew I wanted to do it all over the world, so these trips reinforced that dream. I liked the idea of working for a traveling circus or leading safaris through Africa. An aunt worked for the CIA, so being a spy also sounded like a good way to see the world and do something interesting. I saw my first James Bond film when I was ten and this experience reinforced my spy and travel fantasies. I loved all those exotic locations and of course, Sean Connery.

I also thought it would be great to grow up to look like Ursula Andress and be sexy and kick-ass, i.e. to wear a bikini *and* a knife. By ten, my youthful ambitions were clear: do something adventurous in a foreign country, wear a bikini well, carry a knife like you mean it and look like Ursula Andress, but speak better English. To this day, I channel Ursula when I surface from an ocean swim and saunter onto the beach, especially if I happen to have a conch shell in my hand.

Honor Blackman's Pussy Galore was even more inspiring. She was gorgeous, smart—to be honest, Ursula didn't seem that bright—and could fly a plane and have her way with Bond. She also had that velvety alto voice. My nickname in elementary school was Froggy, since I already had an unusually low voice, especially for a kid, so Pussy let me know that was OK.

Another early inspiration was the British TV series *The Avengers,* whose main character was the sleek brunette Emma Peel, a dangerous, sophisticated gal in leather who drove a Lotus Elan. That show was yet another opportunity to enjoy foreign locales, witty repartee, and cool accents. I did my Emma Peel thing in college and got a Fiat 850 Spider that looked very similar to a Lotus Elan but sadly, had an engine like a Flintstones car.

Commercial air travel was for the privileged few back then, and these films showed it in all its glory—the beautiful flight attendants, spacious cabins, well-dressed passengers, all the things you can only experience now in first class on Emirates. Being a flight attendant seemed like a good way to travel all over, if the spy thing didn't pan out or I didn't make it to Africa.

An airline stewardess was a big deal in those days. Pan Am girls had to be at least 5'5", speak two languages, have a nursing degree and presumably a few karate moves to fend off unwanted advances from inebriated passengers. These were skills I thought useful in any field.

My folks knew my travel fantasies and treated me to my first plane ride, a solo trip, when I turned fourteen, as a reward for my good grades and a way of launching me into adulthood. I planned to spend the summer with friends who owned a horse farm outside Wichita, Kansas. I dressed for the big event in a crisp white blouse, double-breasted navy blue blazer, pencil skirt, navy pumps, and a white barrette in my hair, inadvertently looking like Flight Attendant Barbie. Air travel was obviously in my blood.

Mom drove me to the airport while dodging her way through hair-raising speedsters, a typical situation on the 405 freeway. Mom was agoraphobic and over-protective, so fighting L.A. traffic and letting me fly were two major accomplishments for her.

Mom saw the future as a series of disasters waiting to happen. "Don't climb the backyard trees without someone watching you," was a favorite command. "If you fell you'd hit the chain link fence beneath it, impale yourself or, if not that, scratch yourself on it, get tetanus, and develop lockjaw."

Bob and I joked about these things Mom would say, but they created crazy fears in both of us, especially me. Another favorite command of hers was, "Don't take a shower without someone in the house because you might fall, hit your head, pass out, and drown."

When I finally made it to Kansas there was a moment when I wanted to take a shower, but everyone was going out. I said to my friend's mom, "I can't take a shower if everyone is leaving." She asked why, and I said, "I could fall down, hit my head, pass out, and drown." She responded, "I'll risk it." To this day, I prefer company when taking a shower.

Back on the 405, Mom warned, "Now don't be nervous, honey. You'll be fine. It's going to be the trip of your life. You'll have so much fun on the farm. I'm sure nothing bad will happen. I know you'll be a good girl and everything will work out. I mean, horses aren't that dangerous if you're careful, although they *are* awfully big."

You could still see folks off on the tarmac in those days, so Mom stood with me and continued to blather on anxiously to delay my departure.

"Isn't this exciting?" she shouted over the roaring engines. "And this little breeze is nice too. It's helping with the fumes."

"Thanks, Mom, bye!" I yelled above the din as I left her waving at my back.

The flight was just as I imagined, very posh and a bit wild. The stewardesses looked chic and sophisticated, and so did the passengers. Everyone was talking, flirting, and moving around the cabin. No jeans, no sweats, no rules. I loved it.

I sat next to a nineteen-year-old beauty who thought I was her age. She offered me a cigarette. She lit her own and launched into her employment woes and relationship troubles and asked my advice on everything from how one keeps a guy interested to various sexual issues. I did my best to help out, but we hit a snag when the attendant offered us a drink and I demurred.

"Take the drink," she whispered. "They don't care how old you are."

"Yeah, but I'm only fourteen."

She choked on her screwdriver and turned pale.

I've gotten my wish and travel constantly. I have a white bikini (but no knife, since airport security frowns on this sort of thing) and a lover in MI6. Wait—I'm not supposed to mention that.

I got great early flying advice from one of my jazz mentors, who toured with Count Basie in the '60s, back when flying alternated between an elegant mile-high party and a terrifying, near-death experience. The Basie band traveled almost nonstop, so the guys were usually sleep-deprived; my pal had trained himself to sack out the minute he hit the seat.

He regaled me with stories of planes barely making it over the Andes and other frightening experiences, but my favorite was about the time he woke for some reason during taxiing, looked out the window, and saw the plane's gas cap off and fuel streaming over the wing. Being the cool jazz cat he is, he pressed the call button and waited politely for the stewardess. When she arrived, he directed her attention out the window and asked, "Is that supposed to be happening?"

Unlike my cool friend, she ran down the aisle shrieking, "*STOP THE PLANE!*"

My own cool was tested on a flight to India in the late '80s. Instead of the modulated voice of reason coming over the intercom informing us that there was a bit of a mechanical problem and we were changing course, the flight attendant shot down the aisle shouting, *"We've lost an engine! Buckle your seat belts now!"*

I was traveling with my sweetheart at the time, a rugged, good-looking cowboy type from Oklahoma, who immediately crossed himself, kissed his hand, and reached for mine.

"What are you doing?" I demanded. "You're not Catholic."

"Just in case."

"Just in case of what? I don't even think you did that cross right. Haven't you ever seen a real Catholic?"

"Did I do it wrong?"

"Oh, honestly, give me my hand back. I need to dig out my flight schedule and see what flights are possible to get me to my gig. Where did the captain say we're going instead of Bombay?"

"Judy, I can't believe you're looking at your flight schedule. What if we crash?"

"If we don't, I'll know which flight to run to when we land, and if we do, I won't make the gig anyway, so it won't matter. Get a grip on yourself. I thought you Oklahoma men were made of sterner stuff."

We were over what the captain called "unfriendly airspace" and looking for a place to land. They announced it would be Istanbul, but after a couple of hours of flying toward Turkey, they informed us that the "weather wasn't suitable in Istanbul"; we turned toward Athens, although we were told the airport there was closed.

Passengers sat in their seats crying, and many were saying goodbye to one another. Even my cowboy was melting down with worry. He looked like Gary Cooper but was acting like Woody Allen, sort of my Lotus/Fiat situation.

Flying has changed, of course, but it can still be enjoyable. I took a flight from Antigua to Miami recently and was welcomed aboard by the very fetching Captain, which I thought an especially friendly way to start the trip. To reciprocate his warmth (and thinking of Pussy) I offered to help out in the flying duties.

"Have you ever flown a plane before?" he asked.

"No, but my dad was a pilot so I know I can do it. Isn't it mostly automatic at this point? It can't be that hard. Is it?"

"I'm not sure. It's only my second day."

I love a man in uniform, especially if he has a sense of humor.

If nothing else, my flying attitude proved I was meant to be a jazz musician. I've experienced plenty of interesting times in the air since these initials adventures but have yet to see one of my bandmates panic. In fact, I usually have to wake them up to tell them something's going on.

3

Perfect Judy

I was the good face of my family, or at least the constantly smiling one. As long as I won every possible award, got straight A's, and was "happy," all was right with the world. I was told in ways implicit and explicit to be spectacular or else. My family nickname was "Perfect Judy."

One of the many ironies of my being the family's good face was that my brother Bob had by far the better face, one often compared to Robert Redford's. The mother of a friend was the first to comment that Bob looked like Redford. This was "Downhill Racer" Redford, a name so new to our young selves that when I told Bob that someone's mother thought he looked like "some actor named Robert Redford," he recognized the name but I didn't.

Even though we lived in modest circumstances—the lower end of middle class—Bob worked three jobs so he could dress beautifully. He was the only boy at our school with three suits, the other guys not owning even one. Bob also went through a couple of Corvettes between sophomore and senior year, not crashing them but buying up. He was a smooth-talking, suit-wearing, Corvette-driving Robert Redford lookalike.

Mom had style but abandoned me in my attempts to look good. I'm not clear whether this was her competitiveness or not. She was the center of attention in the family and probably wanted to keep it that way. Her moods, her illnesses, and her appearance were all important. She kept me in bobby socks and childish clothing well into my teens. And while my friends were piling on makeup and switching to push-up bras once they got to school, I was Perfect Judy, and wouldn't challenge my mother's style edicts.

On the surface, we were the happy, wholesome family everyone envied, a combination of *Ozzie and Harriet* and *Leave It to Beaver*, with my brother having the personality of Eddie Haskell and the face of Robert Redford, making him even more effective at charming adults and getting away with murder.

I was too honest and earnest to get away with anything. I behaved beautifully at all times, trying mightily to please everyone, especially my mother, whose mood swings were wide, deep, and unpredictable. I never knew which one would greet me when I came home from school. Her daily Valium helped, a little.

I was an overachieving student throughout elementary school, middle school, and high school. A special assembly was held my senior year in high school to give an award to the person who had won more honors, headed more committees, and done more citywide fundraising than anyone in the history of the school. As I sat in the auditorium with my friend Jeani, whom I'd known since kindergarten, listening to the list of achievements of this mystery person, I turned to her and said, "Whoever this is sounds like an asshole. They should have taken a day off." When we heard, "In addition to all these accomplishments, this individual also holds the only two beauty titles in our city," Jeani turned to me and said with amusement, "They're talking about you." Because of this exchange, I vowed to do nothing but study once I was in college and skip any extracurricular activities. Even I knew there was something wrong with my manic schedule.

My brother often talked about the future and how he and I would live in the world. Occasionally we'd dress up and he'd take me to dinner somewhere fancy to practice for a life beyond Pico Rivera. He encouraged me to be a Renaissance woman, and was a major reason I worked so hard at everything. We weren't sure what he was going to do besides be a stylish playboy. He was sure how he'd live, though.

"Someday my house is going to be as clean as a hospital," he said, with feeling. "Perfect, scrubbed."

"Our house isn't messy," I replied.

"No, Judy, it's *dirty*. Haven't you ever noticed that the only times the floors are cleaned is every other year when a relative visits and Mom goes crazy scrubbing for hours? Then her arthritic wrists swell up, and she says, 'See why I don't do this?'"

"I'm sick of her excuses too," I admitted. "Maybe you want your house to look like a hospital, since we've spent so much time in them visiting Mom."

In later years, I mentioned to Bob how much I admired his youthful bravery and the various risks he'd take—staying out with friends, drinking, getting arrested—as opposed to my always complying with others' wishes. His response was that as the boy, and Mom's favorite, he could do whatever he wanted. If he got caught he was barely chastised, whereas I was punished severely for the smallest infraction. This was an interesting bit of information I wish I'd had twenty years earlier.

Throughout my youth, my father would joke about my being "Perfect Judy," who obeyed without question from the time I could walk and talk. His favorite bit was quoting conversations with me as a little girl to visiting friends.

"Judy, sing me a song."

"Ahwight, Daddy."

"Judy, give me a hug."

"Ahwight, Daddy."

"Judy, walk off that cliff."

"Ahwight, Daddy!"

At this point all the adults would laugh. But even as a kid, I knew something was off.

— —

I'd already figured out that my dad was more loving to me than my mother, albeit less dependable. Dad was the one I went to for a hug. Mom was the one I called if I needed someone to show up.

My mother constantly competed with me while Dad was encouraging, so I couldn't understand his ridiculing my good behavior. I spent much of my childhood being fearful, never knowing what parental actions meant. Both were bright, funny, and loaded with talent, but all the merriment flew out the window if Mom was angry or felt put upon.

Mom was a hypochondriac and genuinely sick at times. She was also a master passive-aggressive manipulator, charming and cute, so she had a wide array of skills to get what she wanted. She was often completely irrational, so our house was a confusing and unsettling environment.

I won a prize for a limerick I wrote in fourth grade that was inspired by my mother giving me the title, "The Cat Named Pat."

There once was a cat named Pat
Who never looked where she sat
Until one day
She sat in some clay
And she looked where she sat after that

My proud papa asked me to recite my winning limerick at a dinner party he and Mom were having. When I finished, everyone applauded. Mom asked, "Judy, did you *really* write that all by yourself?"

"Yes."

"Really? Didn't you get some help?"

"No, I wouldn't cheat. I wrote it."

"Didn't I help you?"

By now I could see the adults squirming, but no one stopped her.

This went on until I broke down crying and ran from the room. I look back now and ache for a woman so insecure that she not only had to take credit for a title she gave her eight-year-old daughter but was willing to humiliate her to get it.

At the same time, Dad repeatedly told me, "You're smart, you're talented, you're pretty. You can do anything."

When my IQ was recorded at genius level, my mother made a point of telling me the high number with pride but followed with the caveat: "Don't get too excited about this. Girls' IQ scores often drop when they reach puberty." She built me up and took me down in rapid succession.

Dad also talked money with me and taught me details he thought would serve me well later in life. I got a weekly allowance and extra money for certain jobs around the house, so I had a little stash.

I think I was nine when he told me the key to success was having an understanding of the tax system. He explained that home ownership was a good way to get an excellent write-off. I bought some rental property when I was nineteen, sold it, and bought my first house when I was twenty-three. I told no one until the deed was done. My parents were stunned when they learned what I'd done.

"Where did you get the money?"

"I saved everything from my piano jobs and borrowed what I didn't have from a couple of friends. I'll pay them back in the next few months."

My male musician friends asked why I wanted to be tied down with a house, and my girlfriends couldn't imagine why I'd spend the money when I was sure to get married and be "taken care of." I already had the feeling that no one would take care of me. My parents were struggling with their own issues and talked about money woes more and more. I knew nothing would ever come from them, financially or otherwise.

My loan officer in Newport Beach, California was the most enthusiastic.

"This will make me look great and fill a little quiet quota we have going with mortgages," he told me.

"What's that?"

"Giving a home loan to a single female. We like to sneak a few in when we can, although it usually isn't possible. I've never given a home loan to a woman. And you're so young, and a musician. Most unusual."

I paid my own way in college. Later I told my brother that Mom had told me they could only afford to pay for one of us, and since he'd have to support a family, they'd pay for him. I could skip college if necessary, because I'd be supported by a husband.

"That's interesting," Bob replied. "I paid for my own college. I thought they paid for you."

— ⁓ —

When I was in high school, it was still considered better to have a date with a dope than to be alone or with your girlfriends on a weekend night. One particularly arrogant, doltish soul asked me out, and I told my mother I was going to say no. Aghast, she responded, "Say yes. He's just a bit odd."

"He's full of himself, Mom. And boring."

"It's your job to make him interesting. Ask good questions and make him feel special."

"Mom, if mothers would let their daughters say no to these guys, instead of pretending they're interesting, they'd be forced to develop a personality."

It was a big deal to be asked to the senior prom as a sophomore, and my mother urged me to go. I went with a guy everyone called Barney because he looked like Barney Rubble, or as my brother called him, "Barney No Neck," since he was a champion wrestler with serious muscles and, well, no visible neck.

"But Mom, it's Barney's senior prom. He should be with a girlfriend so at least it'd be romantic. I'm just a friend."

"This is a great opportunity for you. You should be flattered."

I decided I'd say yes but tell it to him straight how I felt.

"Barney, it's a big deal for a sophomore to be asked to the senior prom and I'd like to go, but I want to be honest. I'm not interested in you as a boyfriend and I think you should ask someone else."

"I want to go with you."

"I don't want to kiss or anything."

"I understand. I'm okay with that. Honest. I'm cool."

The big night came. Our prom photo shows me with an awkward smile and wary eyes, hair piled high, wearing a slinky mint-green silk gown. Barney is holding me in a death grip, madly smiling, looking slightly insane, anticipating the big evening ahead. Thank God he only looked like Barney Rubble and didn't carry a club. He was a wrestler, though, something I should have considered.

We got in the car and he immediately yanked me toward him and kissed me hard.

"Barney! I said I wouldn't kiss you! Stop it!"

"I don't know what came over me. I'm sorry. It won't happen again."

"Oh, man, I think the inside of my lip is bleeding."

"I really didn't mean to kiss you so hard, Judy."

In fairness to Barney, a number of guys split my lip in high school.

I'm happy to say that this period wasn't all wrestling and bruised lips. My best high-school kiss was from a beautiful boy named Doug, who starred in all the school musicals. I was sure he would go on to a successful acting career. Everyone had a crush on him, myself included.

I asked Doug to the girl-ask-boy formal, and it was heaven. He held me tenderly, danced beautifully, and sang softly into my ear the entire evening, proving that something besides injury was possible from a night out with someone of the opposite sex.

He walked me to my door at the end of our perfect evening, took me into his arms, gently brushed my hair back and gave me a slow, sensuous kiss that lasted at least a year, or maybe a few minutes. That dreamy moment carried me on with optimism to my college dating life and beyond.

Doug did go on to great success in Hollywood. Years later I ran into him at a little sidewalk café on Melrose, looking gorgeous as ever, happily married to another sensitive soul named Brian.

4

Miss Congeniality

As I got older, I realized I couldn't be an actor in a '30s movie, but I didn't give up on acting. I performed in plays and musicals throughout my school years. I had a naturally low voice, even as a child, and a propensity to lose it. Choral teachers didn't know what to do with a child singing tenor and constantly told me to sing higher, without teaching me how to do it properly, which led to serious vocal-cord damage. By high school, some level of laryngitis was almost a constant, which kept me from the lead singing roles. Only in recent years has the nature of my condition and my propensity for vocal cord cysts been fully understood.

Every child has vocal cords that meet at one end but not at the other. When they get older the opposing ends join as well. It's rare, but some girls' vocal cords never join on the opposite end, resulting in vocal cords that never vibrate smoothly, which can cause irritation and eventually cysts. This is what happened to me. I gave up trying to sing and focused on an acting career; at least, that was my plan. I adored acting, and when I turned seventeen, I started auditioning in Hollywood for professional roles.

Beauty contests were a typical way for aspiring young actresses to meet potential agents, so I did a number of them as a teenager. I've only recently started admitting I was a beauty queen because as a baby boomer-feminist I've played down the high heels and bathing suit period. I know Gloria Steinem has talked about being a Playboy bunny, but she's older than I am. By my time, we smart, motivated career girls were supposed to be beyond this sort of thing.

There isn't much good to say about beauty pageants, although in many ways they're excellent preparation for life. If you can walk around in a bathing suit and heels in front of a thousand people and look comfortable, you can pretty much do anything.

I won my first title in Pico Rivera. It was a little awkward being Miss Pico Rivera in a city with a largely Mexican population, since all the ribbon-cutting ceremonies were held in Spanish. After "Hola," I was pretty much done. The bilingual mayor was always at my side, madly translating, as I answered questions asked in Spanish with English, hoping I was responding appropriately.

Photo shoots were a big part of my queenly duties. One of the more memorable ones had me on the front page of our local newspaper in a paisley bikini, kneeling on the sidewalk with a frying pan in one hand and an egg in the other, with the caption, "Was it *really* hot enough to fry an egg on the sidewalk? Miss Pico Rivera finds out!"

The egg shoot took forever, because the old guy photographer talked constantly to lengthen our time together.

"Just one more, Judy. Lean in. Good, great! Perfect! Work that frying pan. Turn it toward me. It's reflecting the sun beautifully. Wonderful! Yes! That egg *loves* you, Judy."

I also won Pico Rivera's Junior Miss contest, which professed to be about IQ, talent, and poise instead of sex appeal. There was no bathing-suit competition, but we were repeatedly required to speak in front of an audience in response to surprise questions in order to display our verbal skills, grace, and high IQs.

The pageant's slogan was, "The Search for the Ideal High-School Senior Girl." The pageant organizers recruited me after having lowered the age limit to sixteen so I could compete, showing that the ideal high-school senior girl has connections.

I won Pico Rivera's Junior Miss pageant, and went on to the California Junior Miss contest, where the girls became even more "ideal" or, to my mind, more disingenuous, self-involved, and manipulative. One curvy redhead commented on the stunning thirty-year-old former winner, who was "Pageant Hostess" for the week.

"Isn't it sad to see her over the hill? I'm sure she was once pretty. Face it, we're the ones in our prime."

"If I thought sixteen was my prime, I'd kill myself," I answered, envying the thirty-year-old's clear complexion and confidence, since I possessed neither.

Everyone hated the extemporaneous speaking part of the contest, which was a large portion of our score. I've always been a talker so I looked forward to it, although I knew it would be tricky.

As the week progressed, I realized the judges wanted us to sound intelligent but not too intelligent. It was still a few years before Sigourney Weaver had kicked *Alien* ass onscreen, so we ideal high-school seniors were expected to be girls, not *girls*, at least in my little part of the world. Giggling was welcome, as were sighs, eye flutters, and anything said dreamily about marriage and kids when we were asked about future plans.

The emcee was a tall, dark, forty-something God. We were all smitten and rendered almost speechless when standing next to him, fidgeting in our gowns as if on an awkward prom date, nervously awaiting the big question that we'd answer with flair and intelligence, balanced with just the right amount of modesty and indecision.

I was already struggling to seem giggly, shy, and retiring; and my voice, frequently noted for its low un-Junior Miss timbre, sounded even sultrier after a week of pageant activities.

"Please welcome PICO RIVERA'S JUNIOR MISS!"

The band broke into the theme from "The Stripper," thinking that it suited my voice, walk, and cheeky sense of humor. I was always a favorite with musicians.

"Hi, Judy, how are you?" the emcee asked, revealing his perfectly capped teeth.

"Hi, Larry," I answered in my Lauren Bacall drawl. "I'm great. How are you? Are you enjoying the pageant?"

"Wait a minute, young lady. I'll ask the questions here."

The audience found his comment hilarious, which confused me, both because it wasn't and because I thought we were supposed to chat.

Eye on the ball, Judy. Win this thing. Follow his lead. He's obviously a little slow, so watch it.

"Tell me, Judy, it says here you're a quarterback. I didn't know girls could play football. What's your favorite play?"

"Thirty-four trigger reverse."

Silence. Turns out Larry knew nothing about football and expected me to say something like, "I, uh, you know, I mean, I like it when I, uh, toss the ball to the girl next to me and um, like, she runs toward, ah, uh, gosh. Is it called the 'goalie'?"

Meanwhile, back in a bathing suit, I moved on to the Miss Los Angeles County contest. I came in first runner-up, meaning that I'd jump in if the winner did something scandalous and had to be disqualified.

The title everyone says is most important (they lie) is "Miss Congeniality," which is voted on by the contestants. I think the girls chose me because I was by far the youngest and least jaded, and I was still pleasant to my fellow combatants—I mean, contestants. Most of the others were a scary, competitive, conniving bunch of world-weary girls who had been at this since childhood. Let me just say their minds were not preoccupied with world peace.

Their titles were "Miss Farm Equipment," "Miss Rodeo Romp," "Miss Poultry Princess," "Miss Pretty in Pink," and others too saccharine or inexplicable to list. I still occasionally get a card from "Miss Georgia Sweet Potato."

The newly crowned Miss L.A. County was a tall, lithe brunette who packed a bag as her "talent." She sauntered onstage with a suitcase and bag of clothes, placed them on a table center stage, turned dramatically to the crowd, and raised her eyes and intoned silkily, "Imagine we're taking a trip together." Right there she had the male judges, the straight ones thinking about the trip and the gay ones intent on learning packing tips. With the audience hushed and the spotlight focused, our pretty packer illustrated how to efficiently organize clothes for travel.

The competition included singers, a ballet dancer, a baton twirler, a tapper, and me, a ragtime pianist. Still, the girl who packed a bag won. Fifty percent of the score in the Miss America affiliated contests (like this one) comes from the talent portion, which is why aspiring actresses entered, so everyone was confused and pretty angry that filling luggage carried the day.

Backstage, among the pompoms, cardboard facades, abandoned glittery costumes, and a fragrant mix of perfume and lighter fluid, which Miss Fresno used for her flaming batons, I pondered how I'd been beaten by a packing princess.

Then two things happened.

The leader of the house band came over and said I was the band's favorite, that I should have won, and that the musicians thought the contest was fixed. The head of the pageant cornered me and said I was the judge's favorite, that I should have won, and that the contest was fixed. He begged me to compete the following year.

"The suitcase packer is the daughter of the orchestra conductor for the Miss California contest, which gives her a better chance of winning that title than you," he explained. "Connections, Judy. She's also ten years your senior and more experienced."

Back then, younger wasn't necessarily better.

"Is it because she's 36-24-36 and I'm only 34-24-34? Be honest. I can take it."

"You're 34-24-34? You look smaller."

He assured me that I'd win next year, because everyone had wanted me to win this year, but that they'd had to go with the girl with the dad at the state pageant who had "influence." I told him I had a dad at the phone company, but he wasn't impressed.

I said I'd think about it and was relieved to know it was nepotism, not bust size that had brought me down.

"See, none of the other girls use words like 'nepotism.' We love you!"

Against my better judgment, I entered the following year, again was named first runner-up, again was begged to compete again the following year, and was told about the disheveled, chunky winner:

"Of course she's not as talented as you, has to lose twenty pounds, cut her hair, learn to sing and improve her walk, but she was Miss Santa Barbara last year, so she's already competed at the state level and will have a better chance of winning than you. Experience is key."

"But did you talk to her? Her syntax verges on mind-disorder."

"There you go with that vocabulary. The other girls don't use words like 'syntax.'" What does it mean, by the way?"

Again, the leader of the band told me I was the band's favorite, prompting me to think maybe a career in jazz was the better choice. Jazz musicians are smart and use big words like *euphonium* and *Thelonious*. And besides, I knew that jazz musicians have to travel a lot, and now I knew how to pack.

I did manage to get an in with a commercial agent from my Miss Los Angeles County connection and arrange a meeting. I didn't have a portfolio put together, so I sent my 1970 high school yearbook picture, which was recent, since I'd just graduated. Surprisingly, that was enough to get me a call for a shampoo commercial for blondes. Since my high-school photo was black and white, the agent asked how blonde I was.

"Extremely," I replied. This was not exactly accurate.

He suggested I come by his office before the audition so we could get to know each other and discuss my future. I knew my big break was upon me. I could feel it. I stopped feeling it quite so strongly after waiting three hours in the agent's office and missing the audition. Finally, he called me in, looked up from the pile of papers on his desk, narrowed his eyes and recoiled, as if I were the female Elephant Man.

"My God, you're not even pretty!"

I'd read a lot about making it in Hollywood and knew you had to be ready for anything. It was all about getting in the door. I had, and although this guy thought I was repulsive, he hadn't actually thrown me out. I took this as a good sign.

He stood and leaned across the desk toward me. He scanned my face as he shook his head in disappointment.

"Your skin is terrible!"

"I'm on my period."

"No excuse. And I expected a blonde. What *is* that color? Red? gold? What do you call that?"

"I didn't wash my hair this morning. Usually it looks a lot blonder."

"I can't imagine why Hank recommended you to me. Why *did* he recommend you?"

"He heard me play ragtime in the Miss L.A. County contest and liked it."

"You play ragtime? Now that's interesting. None of my blondes—or dirty blondes in your case—plays ragtime. Can you ride a horse?"

Non-sequiturs are common in Hollywood.

"Oh, yes, I ride, quite well, in fact." (Not true.)

"Great. Can you barrel-race?"

"Funny you should say that. Barrel racing is my specialty." (Definitely not true.)

"Are you sure? I'm talking about barrel racing, the rodeo trick. It can be dangerous. And I need a girl who's fearless. I'm casting a Western, so I could work in your ragtime somewhere. This film could use a bar scene with a piano. We'll have to do something about your skin, though. Try not to be on your period when we do the shoot."

He told me to wear jeans, boots, and a T-shirt to the audition. Nothing fancy. We were going to ride a horse, after all.

The day of the shoot I arrived and surveyed the scene: a corral, a few horses, some barrels, and five of the tallest, most beautiful women I'd ever seen, all at least a few years older than I. I was used to being the youngest, but these gals were lookers. Like me, they were in jeans and T's, although this was my first introduction to the fact that not all jeans and T's are created equal. Mine were Levis, and everyone else's were sleek designer numbers, perfectly cut to display their long legs and perfect bottoms. Their T's were a size too small, with just the right amount of breast action and belly peeking through. I think I'd borrowed one of Bob's. I had a lot to learn.

The casting director rode up to us on his mighty steed, dismounted, walked over with a nice, macho gait, and proceeded to examine us as an Army General would a line of cadets, except that this guy's focus was clearly on bust line and pretty much nothing else.

He stopped at 38D and asked her to follow him, pointing to the horse next to his that she would ride. She smiled shyly, and walked to the right (wrong) side of the horse. Ever Miss Congeniality, I rushed over to her and led her to the correct side. A collective gasp came from the other girls, who were aghast at the thought that I might help the competition.

Macho Man and 38D rode unsteadily to the far end of the corral, talked a bit, and rode back to us.

"Thank you, girls, that will be all for today."

I turned to one of the others and said, "Doesn't she have to show she can barrel race?"

"I have a feeling she has other skills."

I started to lose my enthusiasm for an acting career when I went through a few more auditions like this, or photo shoots where someone handed me a dress that looked like cellophane. "You know this is completely see-through," I called out from the dressing room to one photographer as I looked at myself in the mirror. "Really?" he responded innocently.

— —

I thought there must be a better way into acting, so I went out on "sideline" auditions during the first year I started playing piano professionally. I was nineteen at the time and still in college. Sideline work refers to a Musician's Union requirement that movies hire professional musicians to portray musicians in movies, although the musicians don't have to play the instrument being portrayed, since that's recorded separately.

So even though I'm a pianist, I went out on calls as a trumpet player, saxophonist, singer—everything.

The first time I went for a sideline tryout, the call was at three p.m., a time I assumed they thought comfortable for working jazz musicians to arrive and be relatively awake. I'm an early riser, so I'd already been up for a while, gotten in a game of tennis, showered, and dolled up for the audition. The other guy had had a late gig the previous night, drunk too much, overslept, hadn't shaved, and arrived late. The casting director finally came out, looked at me, looked at the other guy, looked back at me, and said:

"What are you doing here? I need a jazz musician."

"I *am* a jazz musician."

"No," he said, pointing to the other guy, who'd fallen asleep with a cigarette dangling from his hand. "*That's* a jazz musician. I've got a part for a cigarette girl, though, if you want to read for that. Stand up, let me see your legs."

L.A. sideline work never panned out, but I did give it one more shot when I moved to New York City. My friend Vince Giordano, the jazz bandleader who has done a lot of the music for Martin Scorsese, called to ask if I'd like to be in the band for the movie "Cotton Club."

"Thanks for thinking of me, Vince. I'd love to do it. Let me know if they want me."

Vince called back the next day with the bad news.

"I tried, Judy. They were into it until they asked me if you were good looking and I said, 'Yeah, she's beautiful.'"

"Sorry, we can't use her. We need someone ugly who won't show up the singer."

"Well, she's not *that* great. And her hair's a weird color. Does that help?"

5

The Girl in the Middle

$\mathcal{I}$ decided to go to California State College, Fullerton, because it was close, my brother was going there, and it was cheap, which was key since I would be footing the bill. I was seventeen, still living at home, and determined to focus on academics and nothing else. I couldn't put my finger on it, but I knew things were getting worse at home. I felt progressively isolated, as if Mom, Dad, and Bob knew things that they wouldn't share with me. I decided I wouldn't date, wouldn't join clubs, and would exclusively think about studying. I wore overalls to schools and tried to be invisible. I was trying to control a situation that wouldn't be controlled.

I majored in German with a minor in French. I hadn't considered music because, while I played a few ragtime tunes well, I was not a literate, educated musician. I wouldn't have been accepted into the music program just for playing well. In my first semester I took German, French, anthropology, and sociology. This was a ridiculously dense schedule. Language courses require hours in the language lab on top of class time.

My tonsils had been infected throughout high school, so we finally scheduled a tonsillectomy at the end of my college freshman year. My tonsils were still in terrible shape, but I was healthier than I'd been in high school, so this was my chance to get them out. The doctor said I'd feel a huge difference in my energy level in six months because it would take that long for all the poison to leave my system. I was in the hospital for three days. A week later I started a six-week summer program, which equaled a semester in credits, and took two general education classes. I can't remember why I felt compelled to do this intense, accelerated schedule but it accomplished little except to exhaust me.

When summer school ended, I went in for the first of my vocal-cord surgeries to remove a nodule. They called everything a nodule back then, although my current vocal doctor thinks I had the same thing I have now, a cyst.

This was delicate surgery, and not something that should have been performed a few weeks after a previous procedure, my tonsillectomy. Fortunately, the operation was successful and I left the hospital with an order not to speak for two weeks, followed by vocal therapy to learn to use my voice in a way that wouldn't result in laryngitis. No one understood my particular issues at the time and hadn't yet ascertained that my vocal weakness was not solely a result of the way I spoke, but also of my unusual vocal cords.

I started my sophomore year a week later, physically weakened from a summer of two surgeries and a full class schedule. I also had a job as a cashier at a movie theater and was now heading to school as a language major with an order not to speak.

My German teacher told me I had to take the following summer off and go to Germany.

"Judy, you're the top in the department, our best student. You have a talent for languages but you're killing yourself learning all this from a book. You must spend time in the country of the language you're studying."

"If I continue like this and don't go to Europe, will I be fluent when I graduate?"

"You'll have the vocabulary of a native four-year-old."

This was disappointing, and not enough for me. I didn't have the money to go to Europe. I didn't have the money to go anywhere.

A violist in my French class and I had become pals and occasionally played together. Josh was a music major and needed a practice partner and asked if I wanted to give it a go. I enjoyed this chance to accompany him on some classical pieces and also amuse him with my few ragtime tunes. Josh was always encouraging and one day mentioned a summer job he'd heard about playing the two relief nights for a pianist/organ-ist on an old ferry boat called the Pavilion Queen, which did cocktail cruises in Newport Beach.

"You play great. I'm sure you could get the gig."

"I only know five tunes, and four of them are 'Maple Leaf Rag.'"

"Your 'Maple Leaf' is so good he won't ask you to play a second tune. Watch, I'll bet you can get the gig with one tune."

I hadn't thought seriously about pursuing a music career, but had gotten pretty smooth with "Maple Leaf Rag," since I kept pulling it out for beauty pageants and the occasional acting audition. At this point, I still didn't know which key I was in when I played anything. "Maple Leaf" had scored me that fifty dollars from Gramps, though, so I decided to give it a shot.

The pianist/organist who had the job was a big, friendly guy named Gus. The Pavilion Queen had been a ferry off Coronado Island, near San Diego, and looked a bit like a Mississippi river boat. It cruised eve-nings in the inlet between Balboa Island and the Balboa Peninsula, an exquisitely picturesque area of small islands with impossibly quaint and sometimes grand houses, built mostly in the 1920s, '30s, and '40s. These islands were densely landscaped to give maximum privacy to the privileged residents. On Linda Isle, the least known and most exclusive, each home faced a shared park on one side and water on the other. Some islands, like Linda, were exclusive, some less so, but all were charming, with a human scale that encouraged walking, biking, and boating.

The Pavilion Queen was docked next to the Balboa Pavilion, a historic restaurant, bar, and party space built in 1906. The Pavilion was originally the southern terminus for the Pacific Electric Railway, which connected the beach with downtown Los Angeles. In 1973, its bar, the Tale of the Whale, would become my piano-playing home for five years.

The enormous room above the bar had a spectacular view of the water on all sides. At various times it had been a ballroom, a skating rink, and a dance hall, and was now a popular spot for wedding receptions and class reunions. Occasionally, I amused myself on my breaks by grabbing a nametag to join in a wedding or reunion. The reaction to people trying to reconcile the twenty-year-old "Sally Hallock" in front of them with the one they'd known twenty years earlier was always interesting.

"Wow, Sally, I don't remember you looking like this in high school. You look fabulous. And so young!"

"Please don't say anything. I've had a little work."

I played my big audition number for Gus on the Pavilion Queen and hoped he wouldn't request a second.

"Wow! 'Maple Leaf Rag' is a hard tune. I can't play it. I'm impressed."

"Thank you."

"Can you start in two days?"

"Sure!"

"And you play organ too, right?"

"Well, it's not primarily what I do." (A tricky way to hide that I didn't play it at all.)

"OK, focus on the piano, but play a little organ if they request it."

"Of course."

"The job pays thirty dollars a night."

"I'm afraid I never work for less than fifty dollars."

I'm not sure how I had the nerve, but Gramps had set the bar at fifty dollars for "Maple Leaf," so somehow I squeaked out that demand.

"OK. We've never paid that much, but I know this crowd will love you."

I launched into my summer of '72, my first steady gig and my first time living away from home. My mother was very strict, and escaping from her demands was huge.

I had a week to learn enough tunes to cover the ninety-minute cruise. I had about ten minutes worth of material. When I started, I would make up stories about the movie stars who lived in the area and ones who didn't (pretending they did) and point out their homes. The more songs I learned, the less I talked, but this was also the beginning of my developing comedy routines onstage.

I only played ragtime, but for some reason my new boyfriend, Randy, a knowledgeable jazz fan and Gus's son, was determined to give me a jazz education and believed that I'd develop into a jazz musician. Randy and I had met when he happened to be at my audition for his dad, so I got the gig *and* a boyfriend. I've always had excellent timing.

Randy not only loaned me his albums, he also took me to my first jazz club, a famous spot in Hermosa Beach called the Lighthouse, which was dark, shabby, pretentious, and claustrophobic. Yusef Lateef, a celebrated multi-instrumentalist in his most abstract and least accessible mode, was featured, which was an inauspicious choice for my jazz initiation. I hated it all and swore I'd never go to another jazz club.

$\sim$ $\sim$

I was still going on acting calls and participating in beauty contests, but the honesty of music appealed to me and was taking more of my energy. With sophisticated music, no amount of lighting, makeup, or nepotism will make you sound better.

At the same time, I was beginning to tire of my image as a young, pretty girl playing ragtime. I wanted the music to satisfy me, and didn't want to feel dependent on the response of the audience to make me feel like a success. If I had an empty house, I still wanted to enjoy myself, and my ragtime performances weren't fun unless I had an enthusiastic crowd. I loved ragtime, but I wasn't excited about it, and I knew that I wouldn't stick with music without a deeper passion for it. I was painfully aware of my lack of a music education and still felt I was bluffing my way through it. Various people kept encouraging me, though, and insisting I had a future as a professional musician. I wasn't convinced.

When I was seventeen, my piano tuner took me to a meeting of a ragtime association in Los Angeles called the Maple Leaf Club. The composer-pianist Eubie Blake was the featured guest. Eubie had returned to the scene in his eighties after years of obscurity. He'd written hit Broadway tunes in the 1920s and beyond, including "I'm Just Wild About Harry" and "Memories of You," and had been an important pianist stylistically, a link between ragtime and jazz. After years away from the entertainment world, he was now touring and appearing on talk shows and had become quite well known again. He was a dapper, witty character with enormous energy and enthusiasm.

The club had someone play "Maple Leaf Rag" at every meeting, which was my spot on the bill. This wasn't just my grandfather's favorite tune, but the most famous ragtime composition ever written and number one "pop" tune of its day, which made its composer, Scott Joplin, ragtime's king. This was my first public performance in front of a room full of musicians, and I was scared to death. I played it faster than the usual tempo and swung it, much to the dismay of purists. The audience barely applauded. I was devastated and looked it as I walked off stage. Eubie was the star of the night and about to go on, but before he did, he rushed over and took me aside.

"These people know nothing! That was great. Listen, I knew Scott Joplin. You play the way we did in those days, with your own interpretation, great time, and feeling. I loved it. Here, shake my hand. My hand has touched Scott Joplin's, and now I've touched yours. We're connected."

A month after the "Maple Leaf Club" appearance, the same man who recommended me to the Hollywood agent asked if I'd like to appear in a show celebrating the Special Olympics at UCLA's Royce Hall, an impressive venue and an exciting opportunity for me.

"The bill will be you, Edgar Bergen, Jo Stafford, and Paul Weston."

These names meant nothing to me, but my parents were thrilled. These were huge stars of their era. Edgar Bergen was an actor, comedian, and radio performer, best known as a ventriloquist with his characters Charlie McCarthy and Mortimer Snerd. Jo Stafford was one of the greatest popular singers of the '40s, '50s, and '60s. Her husband,

Paul Weston, had his own celebrated career as a pianist, arranger, and composer.

Edgar Bergen, Jo Stafford, Paul Weston, and Judy Hohenstein.

My acting agent had told me I had to get a new name. This was before Hollywood had begun accepting names like Renee Zellweger. I wanted to keep Judy and use a last name that sounded like it could be mine, not like a stage name.

For the Royce Hall concert, I played my big tune, "Maple Leaf Rag," which got a wonderful reception, unlike the dreary reaction I'd received at the Maple Leaf Club. I walked off stage and was greeted by a smiling Paul Weston, who shook my hand and enthusiastically said, "I haven't heard 'Maple Leaf Rag' played like that since Hoagy Carmichael's mother got up out of the audience at a club I was playing in the thirties and sat in and played it." I didn't know who Hoagy Carmichael was, but by now I knew Paul Weston was a big deal, so Hoagy Carmichael must have been one too, or at least his mother was. I was mainly thinking, *Carmichael. That's a good name. Judy Carmichael.*

Thirteen years later, Hoagy Carmichael's son, Hoagy Bix Carmichael, came to hear me at Hanratty's, my steady gig in New York, with a mutual friend. Before I played, our friend had introduced us. "Judy, meet Hoagy Carmichael." I had become a huge Hoagy Carmichael fan by then and knew this wasn't Hoagy Carmichael. I inferred he was someone named Carmichael who used the nickname Hoagy. I responded, "Yeah, people call me Hoagy too."

I played my set and joined "Hoagy" and my friend for the break. Hoagy said with great emotion, "That was wonderful! My father would have loved you. I've got to send you some of Dad's music. Let's figure out if we're related." To my horror I realized he was Hoagy's son and that I'd been cavalier about the meeting because it had never occurred to me that he was. Our mutual friend said, "I thought you'd be nervous playing for Hoagy's son, but you were very cool, Judy."

"I'm afraid we're not related, although I definitely feel a connection to your dad. I don't usually tell people this, but my name isn't Carmichael, it's Hohenstein."

"Where did you get the name Carmichael?"

"I did a show with Paul Weston when I was seventeen where I played 'Maple Leaf Rag' and he told me he hadn't heard it played like that since Hoagy Carmichael's mother—"

"—got up out of the audience and played it," he said, finishing my sentence.

"How did you know that?"

"It was her big tune. She was known for it. That was a quite a compliment from Paul."

Genuinely talented people, at least in my experience, are happy to find other talented people pursuing their art in a thoughtful, serious way. Many times when I've felt defeated, a great artist like Paul Weston or Eubie Blake would step forward and say something that kept me going.

— —

I continued to get more ragtime work but still wasn't enthusiastic about music. That changed when one of my regular audience members at the Balboa Pavilion handed me a cassette of Count Basie in 1932, back when he was "Bill Basie" playing "Prince of Wails" with Benny Moten's band.

That cassette changed my life. I liked ragtime, but I loved this. When I heard Basie with Moten, I knew I wanted to learn how to play like that. This was joyful, exciting, rhythmically driving music—ragtime on steroids with a swing feel. I later learned that this was stride piano. Basie was one of the best practitioners of this madly swinging style.

It was an amped-up jazz version of the music I'd heard in those '30s and '40s movies I'd loved as a kid. The seeds of this style were in my bones and Basie was the next level. I was instantly smitten and determined to learn this way of playing. I didn't know it was jazz. In fact, it was radically different from the jazz I'd heard at the Lighthouse, so I didn't associate the two. I loved Basie's playing and was intent on teaching myself how to play this kind of piano, which I did, note by note by ear, from that cassette. I still didn't know music theory, so I couldn't hear a chord and know the notes that were in it. I didn't recognize harmonic patterns.

I literally learned the piece by picking out each note. Slowly, the patterns were revealed. I was twenty-two, old for a professional to just be figuring these things out.

The movie *The Sting* came out in 1973 and started a ragtime revival that was perfect timing for me. There was a chain of pizza parlors in California called Shakey's Pizza that featured ragtime pianists; so did an indoor shopping center in Torrance called Old Towne Mall that was made to look like a town in the late 1800s, just like Main Street USA at Disneyland. I worked two nights on the Pavilion Queen in Newport Beach, three nights at Shakey's in La Habra, and five days a week at Old Towne Mall, totaling five days and seven nights a week of playing. Each place was an hour or more from where I lived in Pico Rivera, so every minute of the day I was driving, playing the piano, or practicing. Eventually, the Tale of the Whale bar at the Balboa Pavilion replaced Shakey's with a five-night-a-week residency for me, although I continued to do occasional club gigs in Los Angeles and at spots in Orange County.

I loved playing as part of a duo, and became known for odd musical combinations. I had duos with guitar, banjo, bass sax, every kind of reed instrument, and a few memorable gigs with a great musician, Lee Westenhofer, on sousaphone and double-bell euphonium. I billed these duos as the Judy Carmichael Orchestra, since anything more than solo piano seemed huge to me.

In my early twenties I became friends with Rod Miller, the main Coke Corner pianist at Disneyland. His ragtime and "honky-tonk" playing, as we called it, were big influences on me. There are different definitions of honky-tonk piano, but in his case it meant Gay Nineties songs— "Take Me Out to the Ball Game," "In the Good Old Summertime," and others of that ilk—played in a ragtime style.

I was offered the Coke Corner ragtime job a number of times during this period, but didn't want to take it. I had friends who worked there who told me stories that made me resistant to the Magic Kingdom.

Coke Corner is an outdoor café at the end of Main Street, USA, whose buildings are designed at three-quarter scale—something you don't consciously notice, but that makes you feel cozy. I once spotted Magic Johnson walking along this promenade, and his scale made Main Street seem like toy town.

Coke Corner specializes in cokes and hotdogs, and is an extravaganza of red-and-white stripes everywhere you look. The curtains, the umbrellas over the tables and chairs, the piano bench, and the piano are all red, white or both. Sadly, so was my costume.

The piano sat between the café's indoor and outdoor areas at the edge of the first central square that leads to Disneyland's themed areas— Adventure Land, Fantasy Land, Frontier Land, and Tomorrow Land. All the parades and visitors pass Coke Corner. When I worked there, everyone who passed me was gleeful with anticipation at the beginning of the day and exhausted and spent by the end of it.

I first heard the Coke Corner pianist in high school, when I spent the afternoon listening to Rod Miller, known as "Ragtime Rod." He made that spot famous among ragtime lovers. Rod was an Iowa farm boy who had gotten the gig at a young age and stayed for thirty-nine years. He formed the position and it formed him.

Disney offered me the job because I was young, sounded a lot like Rod, and could smile for hours while playing nonstop ragtime at breakneck speed. Disney wanted a Rod clone and I was a female version, which Rod said was appropriate, since he's gay.

Before we became close, he could be a bit competitive.

"Just so you know, I've heard you referred to as the Queen of Ragtime, Judy, but *I'm* the Queen of Ragtime."

"I'm fine with that, Rod. I was a beauty queen, so I know queens. If you say you're the Queen of Ragtime, I concur."

Rod became a good friend and mentor. No one has a better attitude about life. He's relentlessly positive.

Rod played ten a.m. to five p.m. and I played five p.m. to midnight five days a week with occasional changes in schedule, depending on the time of year; two others played our days and nights off during the summer. When we did the changeover from his shift to mine, Rod would announce, "There's my sister Judy Carmichael. Glenn *Miller* is my father and Hoagy *Carmichael* is hers, but we share the same mother."

"Mother" was a drag queen we knew who called us her kids. The crowd didn't know about this particular Mother and believed Rod's ridiculous story. Rod amused himself with these sorts of pranks, and it was incredible how often people believed him.

Calling Mother a drag queen isn't completely accurate. Rudy de la Mor, a.k.a. "Mother," looked like a Mexican Fats Waller, if Fats had worn boas and outrageous hats. I never saw Mother wear makeup, so the ensemble was even more surprising and appealing. He was a classically trained pianist who found his natural métier in comedy. Mother had a substantial following in Hollywood and in gay clubs across the country.

Rod and Mother were big supporters from the time I got the Pavilion gig at nineteen until I moved to New York fulltime in 1985. Even after I moved, I'd see them both when I visited California, and was always hearing of their proud pronouncements about my success through other people. Both introduced me to interesting characters in the business. Mother had a number of parties to showcase young talents she thought significant; the guest lists included gays, straights, and the occasional movie star from a bygone era.

The singer and comic actress Martha Raye was in attendance at one of these soirées, and for a '30s-and-'40s film nut like me, this was big. Raye's first feature film was with Bing Crosby, another hero of mine, so I was one nervous twenty-two-year-old when my turn at the piano came. After I played, Mother called me over to introduce me to Martha.

"I'm a huge fan, Miss Raye," I said. "It's wonderful to meet you."

"You're a great talent, young lady."

"That's sweet of you. Thank you."

She was sitting in a one of Rudy's beautiful antique, rattan chairs, looking regal. Martha was known for her big personality, but she was only five-foot-three and slight; and on this particular evening she stayed focused on all of us who played for her, not on yucking it up and being the center of attention. If anything, she was a bit subdued, until she responded to my words of thanks.

"*Wait!* Judy, come here!"

She grabbed my hand and pulled me to her with surprising force, placing us nose to nose.

"It isn't 'sweet' of me to say this. Listen to me: You're a *great* talent. Don't mess around with this. You have things to do. Get serious."

Ragtime Rod could play effortlessly, seven hours a day, five days a week; smile constantly; flirt with his listeners; joke around; and stay positive no matter what. It was his domain and he loved it. This all looked like fun when I saw him for the first time on a high-school outing with a trumpet-playing boyfriend. I was there to hear my boyfriend but wound up spending the entire day listening to Rod.

When I was offered the Coke Corner job, I was living with a musician who played banjo and guitar in a revue at Disneyland. My sweetie's stories of long hours, huge crowds, humiliating costumes, and crazy guests made me reluctant to take the gig. It looked like fun at seventeen, but now I was twenty-four and less interested in ragtime. I didn't know if Disney was for me. Other musicians could joke it all away, but I'm a sensitive type and was afraid that working there would be too depressing. But I needed the money, always a great motivator.

The head of entertainment gave me the lay of the land. "Judy, you'll be playing ragtime piano at Coke Corner, and you'll also do sets of classical music on a harpsichord, which is on a balcony overlooking the Blue Bayou restaurant in New Orleans Square."

This was a surprise, and not a happy one.

He continued. "The Blue Bayou has low lighting and is elegant and romantic, so you'll play background music, not the flashy things you'll do at Coke Corner. You do play harpsichord, right?

"Well, it's not primarily what I do." (Never touched one.)

Rod had long ago gotten out of the harpsichord part of the job, but the rest of us were expected to be skilled at both ragtime and Bach. I played ragtime most of my Disney days, but snuck in stride whenever I could get away with it. On Rod's days off I alternated with another pianist who was a pot-smoking, Bill Evans-influenced, laid-back dude who'd sink into the music and ignore the daily craziness around him. He was the anti-Rod. I'm not even sure he knew any ragtime. He preferred playing the harpsichord sets because its placement was hidden from view and he could get high and jam on Mozart or "Waltz for Debby." This was perfect for me, since I didn't play harpsichord, Mozart, or "Waltz for Debby." I did his sets at Coke Corner and he did mine at the Blue Bayou. Any time a supervisor came around, which was often—working for Disney is like working for IBM, except in costume—we'd both say, "Oh, she/he just left. You should have heard the set. Wonderful." Incredibly, we got away with this for five years.

— ~

I was the first female instrumentalist ever hired by Disneyland and remained the only one during my tenure. I was surrounded by male musicians, something that seemed normal to me since I was always the only female instrumentalist in any jazz gathering. Because there were no women's dressing rooms, I shared a dressing room with ten men. One of them was a crazy, Bible-thumping washboard player who thought my daily presence unseemly and tried to get me tossed. Happily, he was outvoted in a skirmish that was the talk of the park for weeks.

There were many unusual aspects of working at Disneyland. For example, since Disney promoted from within, most of my supervisors had previously portrayed Mickey, Minnie, Donald, or other characters that required an unusually short person to play the part. I towered over every boss I had. These folks often had odd personalities as well. They'd spent a lifetime being discriminated against for being short, only to become the most famous, beloved characters imaginable. People hugged and kissed them all day, then they shed their costumes and some still thought they were Mickey, Minnie, or Donald.

One of my favorite amusements was to play for the characters and do spontaneous skits with them under the red-and-white-striped umbrellas in front of my white upright. The characters weren't allowed to talk, so I would recite all the lines, interpreting their gestures, which were broad and hilarious. Chip and Dale often came by since Chip could play piano, and we could wow the crowd with a duet.

"And here he is: *THELONIOUS CHIPMONK*!"

He had only three fingers, which helped tremendously in getting Monk's sound. "Blue Monk" was a real crowd-pleaser.

One memorable afternoon, I played Fats Waller's "Vipers Drag," a regular request from Br'er Fox and Br'er Bear. The temperature was about ninety degrees, so inside their costumes it was well over a hundred and-- with all their dancing--getting hotter by the minute. Both were frantically giving me the signal to end the tune. I perversely kept going until Br'er Bear feigned a faint. Br'er Fox ran around in a pretend panic and beckoned me to help. I jumped up and yelled, *"DR. JAZZ TO THE RESCUE!"*

I ran from the piano and gave mouth-to-mouth respiration to my supine sufferer. Br'er Bear is one of the tall characters, so he sees out of a small screen-covered opening at his neck with his head towering above. From that sensitive spot I heard his irritated whisper, "I'll get you for this, Carmichael!" These guys aren't supposed to talk, so I, of course, ignored him.

"HIS HEART HAS STOPPED! I'LL HAVE TO TAKE DRASTIC MEASURES!" I pounded his chest, vibrating the costume and giving him a good shaking, about a five on the Richter scale.

Adults were laughing, but a few kids started crying.

"Mommy, is Br'er Bear dead?

"He's alive, he's alive!" I reported happily as I stood and surveyed the scene. Then I whispered into his furry throat, "Quick! I see our supervisor!" I grabbed a paw to help him up.

"Hi, Mr. Anderson," I said to the famously intimidating head of entertainment. "Thanks for coming to see our set." I lowered myself into a semi-curtsy in an effort to make him feel taller.

"That was a funny bit, Judy, but don't let it happen again or you'll be playing piano at Knott's Berry Farm."

This is the worst thing a Disney executive can say to you.

There were always postings in "The Zoo," as the character dressing room was called, saying: "DON'T VISIT JUDY CARMICHAEL!" I'm happy to say that I still got daily visits from the entire menagerie. I got especially close to the Seven Dwarfs, jazz fans all. Snow White was a bit of a snob and more into classical music, so we never clicked. I think she was also a little jealous of my thing with the Dwarfs.

Hours were long at Disneyland and more fun for band musicians, who had one another for company. I was a soloist and it was a lonely slog playing seven hours a day, five days a week, and trying to stay sane. I developed killer chops and got in some great practice time, but I still had to devise ways to keep from losing my mind.

Early on, I became a mascot of sorts to the older musicians, who encouraged me, sat in with me, and supported me when there was nonsense from any quarter. The Disneyland Band—the marching band that performed at parades and concerts—was made up of ex-studio players who had taken the gig when Disneyland opened in 1955. They had years of seniority, a spectacular dressing room, and basically did whatever they wanted.

One of the major rules at Disneyland was that you must not wander out of your area, since your costume wouldn't match contextually. This was only acceptable when all the bands passed by my piano to go backstage and gather at the start of Main Street for the daily parade. I asked every passerby to play with me, making for interesting combinations of men in lederhosen, space suits, cowboy gear, knickers, brightly colored outfits with huge buttons all over them, and me in my turn-of-the-century red-and-white stripes, puffed sleeves and bustle. These jam sessions brought more threats of Knott's Berry Farm from a number of my supervisors.

I was widely ridiculed for my costume, which added a good twenty pounds to my appearance and hid anything I had going for me. Once when I was walking backstage, having changed into short shorts and a T-shirt, one of the crusty old musicians called after me, "Hey, *Carmichael!* If I'd known you had a great body, I would have hit on you!"

Kids periodically snuck up and hit me and were surprised when I didn't stop playing. "Hey, Mom, she's *real!*" they'd yell. "I thought she was audio-animatronic, like the guy in 'Great Moments with Mr. Lincoln,' but she stopped playing when I tried to push her over."

They kept designing costumes for me, each less attractive than the last. One of my outfits had the same pattern as a child's flannel nightgown and became a favorite source of ridicule from my fellow "cast members," which is what we Disney workers were called. Mickey and I periodically visited children's hospitals to entertain, and once a child in the front row was wearing a nightgown that was an exact duplicate of my costume. Mickey danced out on stage, spotted her, started laughing, danced back off and grabbed me in the wings, barely able to contain himself.

"Little girl in wheelchair at twelve o'clock. Brace yourself."

Back out he went. I followed to the piano and the child screamed with delight,

"The piano player is wearing my pajamas!"

We all pay our dues in different ways.

— ⌣

Many of the guys did drugs to get them through the day. Disneyland, for me, was a continual out-of-body experience, so no drugs were needed. Also, a number of the older musicians had engaged me in serious discussions about my future in the music business and told me not to get used to this steady income. I didn't want to dull the pain of the place with drugs and lose my motivation to leave.

I loved the bizarre juxtapositions Disneyland allowed, and some of my dating experiences reflected that. I had a little thing with a Polynesian fire dancer; we used to hook up in his dressing room among the grass skirts and spears, me in my high-neck ruffles and endless slips, he shirtless and wearing a sarong, all the while hearing authentic sounding jungle noises crackling around us, since our dressing rooms were behind the Jungle Cruise ride. There was a rumor that the jungle excursion was so authentic that leeches had spontaneously generated, but I didn't believe it.

Another memorable moment involved a sax-playing, lederhosen-wearing pal named Frank, who one evening asked that I accompany him to "experience something interesting behind the Matterhorn."

The Matterhorn was the centerpiece of Disneyland when I was a kid, and it continued to be throughout the years I worked there. You could see it towering above the landscape from the freeway as you whizzed by. Seeing a snow-covered mountain from the Santa Ana Freeway shooting up above Anaheim was just another interesting part of the Southern California landscape.

The backstage area, behind the mighty mountain, was a large field covered in beautiful wild grass with gently sloping mounds in various spots and tall pines. The treetops could be seen from inside the park, but if you were in the midst of them backstage you'd swear you were in a Northern California forest. It was darker than any part of the park, and there was a delicious scent of pine in the air. Above it all loomed the Matterhorn.

When I worked at Disney no planes were allowed to fly over the area, and strategically placed rides, buildings, and landscaping made it impossible to see anything outside the park. The experience was controlled, creating a fantastic visual environment. Once inside, it was all the Disney fantasy. Back then they changed the flowerbeds and did repair work overnight, so you never saw anyone doing maintenance or landscaping. You'd see a flowerbed covered with daisies on Monday. Tuesday it would be a bed of petunias.

Frank had found a good spot to watch the nightly fireworks but didn't tell me that was the plan. He took me into the Matterhorn forest and said, "Lie down."

"Right, Frank. Come on."

"Seriously. Trust me. We have to be right here leaning into this mound, so you're laying back and sitting up just a little."

I lay back and contemplated the stars on this unusually clear summer evening and felt the warm breeze, scented with evergreen. I looked up at the Matterhorn with the lights highlighting it and focused on the spot where Tinker Bell jumps off and flies down to set off the pyrotechnics. Suddenly, I heard the trumpets that cue the fireworks. The orchestra soundtrack was magnificent, in perfect stereo, while fireworks shot up over the mountain and burst directly above us. It was spectacular. Frank had found the exact spot between the giant speakers where we could hear the music in surround sound, with our placement making it seem as if the fireworks were falling right over us.

"Pretty amazing, huh?"

We lay side by side and soaked in the show.

"Okay, you did it. I have to say, this is one of my best Disney moments."

"I know all the spots. Come on. I'll show you where Tinker Bell lands. She flies down on a wire from the top of the Matterhorn and crashes into a mattress face first. I don't know how she survives it. You know she's an old lady, right? Used to be in the circus or something."

The best part of the Disney experience was hearing the big bands that played every week in the summer. Any musician who worked at Disneyland during this period felt blessed to have seen these greats as often as we did. Basie would come for a week, as would Lionel Hampton, Buddy Rich, and many others. I'd play my sets and run over to hear the bands every night on break or after I finished. Jazz clubs in L.A. were often too uncomfortable or dangerous for a young girl on her own, so this opportunity was especially fortunate for me.

One day the word went around that the great drummer Harold Jones, who'd been with Basie and everyone else, was going to sub in the Disneyland Band. I'd never seen this jaded bunch so excited.

At this time, men who worked for Disneyland were required to have short hair, no sideburns, and no facial hair. The only black musicians were "contextual"; that is, they played as a trio in the New Orleans section of the park. The Disneyland Band was a large marching band, dressed in outfits right out of *The Music Man*. The musicians were all white and clean-shaven, with short hair. Harold was black and had longish hair, a full mustache, and long sideburns. It was a wonderful sight to see him march with this white bread band down Main Street playing bass drum, with his small Afro peeking out from beneath his hat and his bandito mustache in all its glory.

The guys always waved when they passed me at Coke Corner. Harold asked who the girl in the dumb outfit was. (I'm sure he didn't use those exact words.)

"She's this kid who plays stride piano."

Harold came by to hear me one day, introduced himself, and after listening for a while asked, "Why are you playing stride piano?"

"Because I love it."

Years later, he told me that this had been an emotional moment for him because he was questioning a lot in his own life and hadn't played music purely for the pleasure of it in years.

"Basie has to hear you," he said to me. "So does his guitarist, Freddie Green. They'll love you."

Harold was delighted to find a young pianist who was focusing on stride, and he brought Basie to hear me during one of his runs at Disneyland. Freddie and many of the other band members came by on their breaks.

"Judy, you don't know how unusual it is for Freddie to talk to someone like he does to you. He thinks you're great."

"Isn't he like this with everyone?"

"Absolutely not. He hardly ever talks to anyone except Basie. When I joined the band, I thought I was hot shit. I was twenty-six and full of myself. I was going to show Basie a thing or two. Ridiculous. Freddie moved his chair *away* from my drums, far away, and didn't speak to me for the first two years I was with the band, except to occasionally tell me what was wrong with my playing. Finally, he moved his chair back to its proper place, closer to the piano and drums, but still didn't talk to me. Finally, one night, he gave me a compliment."

"What did you say?"

"I said, 'I can't believe you've finally said something good about my playing. All you do is tell me what's wrong.' And he said, 'I thought you knew all the good parts.'"

"That's rough."

"Judy, let me ask you something. If you put a band together, what instruments would you have?"

"I don't know, a horn player, probably."

"Wouldn't you start with a rhythm section?"

"What's a rhythm section?"

"I love that you don't know what a rhythm section is."

"I really don't know what I'm doing here."

"Rhythm section: drums ..."

"I hate drums! Drummers are always showboating."

"You do remember I play drums, right? I have to play you some things, Judy. There *are* drummers who support instead of destroy the music."

"I'm not really a jazz fan, Harold."

"You're a jazz pianist, Judy. Have you ever thought about making a record?"

"I don't know. No one plays my style of music anymore."

"I know people who do. You should make a record. I'll tell you the musicians to ask but you have to be the one to ask them."

I had made a ragtime record when I was twenty to sell at the Balboa Pavilion and earn some money. It was all first takes, because I was too nervous to do seconds. It never occurred to me that I would continue to play music professionally or that I should have waited until I was more experienced to record. I only pressed a thousand, and after I'd sold eight hundred I realized I might keep being a musician, so I stopped selling them. That recording, to me, is like early nude shots to an actress or that slasher movie she wishes she declined.

"You should record now; you're ready," said Harold. "I'll play drums. Freddie loves you, so he'll agree to be on it. Use Red Callender on bass. He's a sweetheart and will love your music. Have Marshall Royal on alto sax. He should play with you. You're perfect for his style.

"Ask Freddie first, since you know him, then Red—who'll say yes because he'll know the time will be straight with Freddie and me on the date—and then ask Marshall, who will say yes out of curiosity. We all have huge egos but we'll cancel each other out, since we'd look ridiculous doing an ego thing in front of you."

The big day came and I was scared to death. Once we settled in at our instruments, Freddie took charge and said everyone should wear headphones except me, so I could hear acoustically, since I wasn't used to recording. The guys closed in around me, except for Harold, who had a baffle in front of his drums and was a bit removed from the rest of us. I'd been in a studio once before for my ragtime album, and now here I was, leading a session with four giants.

We played the first song. When we finished, Red blurted out, "I knew my music would come back into style!" That made me slightly less nervous.

I joined the others in the booth to listen to our first track. The engineer got up and gave me his seat, looking at me like I was an alien as he moved to the chair next to me. Almost no one was interested in stride piano in 1980, so most people were shocked to hear me for the first time.

We listened to the playback of the first tune in the booth. I sat in front of the speakers while the guys stood around me. It was thrilling to hear my heroes playing with me on piano instead of Basie or Fats. I never thought I'd do something like this. The guys went back into the studio after we finished listening, but I was frozen to the spot, so emotional I couldn't move. Marshall came back into the booth, took my hand, leaned down, looked me in the eye, and whispered, "We were lucky to get one that good on the first take." He led me back to do the rest of the session.

Afterward, Red Callender stayed around to chat. Right before he left, he turned to me. "You don't realize what a great date this was, Judy. This doesn't usually happen. This was special. You won't appreciate this until, well ..."

He focused his gaze on me and laughed.

"Well, until you're thirty."

I was twenty-six when we recorded *Two-Handed Stride*, and in one of my down moments I said to Harold, "I just don't think I have the experience to continue with a music career. You guys have done so much, got into music much earlier than I and studied music in college. I was a German major. I'm so far behind where I should be with music. I don't know tunes. I'm a terrible sideman. My biggest fear is playing with other people and not knowing tunes."

"You've got time to learn tunes."

"Yeah, but the musicians I know have been playing in bands since their teens or earlier. I started this so late. Just think, when you were twenty-six you went with Basie."

"And when you were twenty-six we all went with you."

"No musicians my age like my music. They all put me down."

"Who are you going to believe—Basie, Freddie, and me, or all those other people? You only need a few of the right people to believe in you, Judy."

The day after we'd made the album, Harold took me to hear the Basie band record a session near where we'd done ours. I was in the booth with Harold, Sarah Vaughan, producer Norman Granz, and a few others. Everyone was dropping by to hear this date.

Freddie waved toward the booth from the studio. I looked around, thinking he was waving at someone else. He pointed at me and waved me in. I walked into the studio past Basie, who gave me the eye and a little smile; continued past the band; then reached Freddie, who set his guitar aside, stood up, gave me a hug, and winked at me. "We'll talk."

A couple of years later, when I debuted at Hanratty's, the *New York Times* critic John S. Wilson became a champion of mine and wrote a number of articles about me, determined to enhance my reputation. *Two-Handed Stride* had finally been released. Shortly after that, John called.

"Judy, I wanted you to know that I nominated *Two-Handed Stride* for a Grammy. You don't have a record label behind you so you won't win, but everyone on the committee will have to listen to this now, so they'll know your music. This will help."

I've never had the support of a big label and have always been a bit of an outlier in the jazz world, but I've had the encouragement of a handful of people who mattered.

Harold called me a few months after the *Two-Handed Stride* session to tell me about an audition for a music series on Black Entertainment Television.

"Judy, you've got to send in a tape. They're doing a series within the series called 'Two-Handed Piano Players.' Don't send a picture or talk to anybody on the phone. Judy Carmichael could be a black woman. If they don't know you're white, I think you'll get the gig."

I did, and showed up for the taping, the only white person in sight, except the guys in the booth and the cameramen. They filmed a few episodes at a time and finally, at the end of the taping, around 6pm, I was the only person left. No one had spoken to me the entire day. I assume they thought I was somebody's girlfriend.

The producer-host focused on me.

"You're not Judy Carmichael, are you?"

"Yes!" I answered cheerily.

"Oh, brother," he rejoined. "OK, come play something and show me what you do."

I played about eight bars and he stopped me.

"OK, OK, stop!" he said, adding, "Quick, start filming," as if my playing might fall apart at any moment.

I played "Handful of Keys." Afterward I had a little on-camera exchange with the host.

"Cut!"

The director, producer, and cameramen stared at me.

"Is something wrong? Shall I do it again?"

"No, no. That's fine. I just don't know what to say. I don't know how *you* happened."

The director, a handsome, theatrical sort, jumped in enthusiastically with, "I know what happened! Fats Waller decided to reincarnate and said, 'This time around, I'll come back white and *fine!*'"

A few years later, I was sitting in a hall, waiting for the stage to be set up for a sound check for Basie and Sarah Vaughan. By then I'd spent a fair amount of time with both of them, and often went to sound checks and rehearsals even if I was going to the concert. I wanted to hear as much of these two as possible. Basie, who loved nicknames, called me Stride.

The three of us were the only ones in the audience in this large, historic theater. We were sitting on the aisle with Basie in front of me, Sarah behind—both leaning toward me as we chatted, waiting for the stage to be set. Suddenly a photographer ran over, snapped a picture of the three of us, then turned and scampered away.

Basie grinned. "Well, Stride, you know who the most important person in that picture is, don't you?"

I glanced at Sarah and turned to Basie.

"I don't know. Who?"

"Well, *you*, of course."

He pointed at Sarah.

"Everyone knows who she is, and everyone knows who I am, so they'll all be asking, 'Who's the girl in the middle?'"

6

Blue Hawaii

Shortly after I had met drummer Harold Jones at Disneyland, he joined Sarah Vaughan's trio. Sarah was one of the greatest jazz singers and vocal improvisers, an acknowledged giant. Harold, ever my champion, repeatedly introduced me to Sarah, who barely looked at me and never used my name.

A few weeks after we'd recorded *Two-Handed Stride*, Harold surprised me with a call from the road.

"Judy, it's Harold. I've got something great to tell you."

"Where are you?"

"I don't know—Nebraska, I think. Someplace flat. Listen: We were on the band bus and I was playing my tapes of Sarah's show to get the new arrangements in my head. In the middle of it she said, 'I'm sick of hearing myself. Don't you have anything else to play?'

"I told her, 'All I have is you and this session I just did with Judy Carmichael.'

"'Play Judy,' she said.

"You should have seen it. She got up and started dancing around the bus to your music. The guys dug it."

Harold was a great friend and mentor throughout my twenties. His perspective on and appreciation of my playing are responsible in large part for my continuing as a jazz musician. I often told him I wasn't knowledgeable enough to maintain a jazz career, and he always countered with something encouraging.

"You don't know the depth of your gift for rhythm and time. Your time is so great, you make a metronome sound wrong."

He'd have me play with a metronome to prove his point.

"I don't read music very well," was another of my complaints.

"Lots of guys can read. You have a special sound. You'll have a career built around *your* music, not working in other people's bands. You can make the other guys read."

A few weeks later, Harold was back in town and called. "Tomorrow you're playing golf with Freddie, Sarah, and me."

"Are you out of your mind? You know I've only played a few times. I'll make a fool of myself."

"Are you going to pass up the chance to spend four hours with Sarah Vaughan, Freddie Green, and me?"

"Oh, God! Where and when? I see serious humiliation in my future."

Sarah and Freddie had played golf together in the 1940s and had been friends forever. Freddie had a twelve handicap, Harold a three, and Sarah hadn't played in years. This would be the first time I'd seen her since the phone call about her dancing to my music on her band bus.

I arrived early and went to the clubhouse to buy a new glove, hoping it would give me luck. As I was looking around, one of the pros made his way over to me.

"I'm Phil, the head pro here. Are you meeting someone?"

"I'm playing with Harold Jones. I need a new glove for the big game."

"Ah, with Sarah Vaughan and Freddie Green," he said as he offered me some glove options. "I've met Freddie before but never Sarah. I'm looking forward to it. I'm a huge fan."

"Aren't we all? I'm nervous, though. I'm new to the golf. I think this black glove is perfect. Makes me look serious."

I looked outside and spotted Freddie first, who gave me an amused grin. I found Harold, who was putting the clubs in our cart. Freddie paired with Sarah, and Harold signaled for me to jump in with him. As predicted, I played like a beginner, although from the minute I picked up a club I had a good swing, so while my score was high, my form was excellent. At least I looked good. Few people were playing the course that day. It was sunny and warm, with a cool breeze blowing in from the Pacific.

Freddie and Harold played well, but Sarah got frustrated after seven holes, claimed a sore back and quit. She rode the rest of the way in Freddie's cart, watching the three of us finish the round. I hacked away to an impressive 140 or some score I've blocked out and said very little the entire four hours. Sarah was impressed that I silently persevered and was much friendlier to me after this outing, calling me by name from then on.

Sarah's first big job, back in 1943, was playing second piano in the Earl Hines big band. Hines was a great, innovative pianist and one of my influences, which Sarah heard in my playing; it's one of the things she told me she dug about my work.

I once asked Freddie why I'd gotten such strong support from older black jazz musicians and so little from white ones.

"I can't speak for the white guys," he said. "I *can* tell you that everyone romanticizes the jazz life, especially the early years, but for young black men back then, there were very few options. We could be criminals or jazz musicians—often both. We look at you as someone with choices. You can do anything you want. You could marry a rich guy or go into business. Hell, you could make toothpaste commercials! You can do anything you want and you chose to be a jazz musician playing stride, a tiny part of a non-commercial music. Of course, we support you."

I went to many of Sarah's concerts, but an especially thrilling moment for me was a show she did at the Dorothy Chandler Pavilion in Los Angeles. She'd decided at the last minute to add some Brazilian musicians who happened to be in town and augment the instrumentation with a new kind of electric piano that sounded more like an acoustic. She thought she could play the Steinway grand if the mood struck and move her pianist to the electric piano; both he and she could play along with the band while she sang from the piano. This is the only time I saw her do this.

Well into the concert, Sarah went to the Steinway and started in on a standard, taking it at a medium tempo and veering into a relaxed stride. She slyly turned to the audience, and said, with her sexiest delivery, "Eat your heart out, Judy."

Years later, I met a fan of Sarah's who was at that concert and had surreptitiously recorded it.

"I was there, too," I told him. "Great concert."

"The one with the Brazilians at the Dorothy Chandler? You were there?"

"Yes."

"It was an amazing evening. I've listened to the tape I made of it repeatedly."

"It was a big night for me because Sarah did a shout out when she was playing some stride and said, 'Eat your heart out, Judy.'"

"You're *that* Judy?"

After one of Sarah's New York concerts, a rich fan invited us to his Park Avenue apartment for a celebratory party. There was an odd, uncomfortable assortment of people, and I couldn't imagine why Sarah would want to hang out with these folks. I grabbed a glass of champagne and wandered to the living room, scanning the incredible collection of art that covered every inch of wall space. There was a stark elegance to the place, making it seem more like a museum than a home.

I went to the overstuffed white sofa and rearranged some pillows for a spot to sit, pondering how long I'd need to stay before I could make a polite escape. The host, a rotund fellow with a shiny pate and hooded, suspicious eyes, came in, smiled, checked me out, popped a tape in the VCR, adjusted the volume, and left.

Porn? Really? This guy has Sarah Vaughan in his apartment and he plays porn?

Sarah plopped down beside me with a sigh, glanced toward the TV, and laughed.

"What do you think of that?" she asked, pointing at the screen and the man and woman on it, working hard at sex.

"Are *you* into this?" I responded.

"Not really my thing," she replied.

"This reminds me of the time backstage in that stuffy, crowded dressing room at the Dorothy Chandler when the guys were getting high, right before you all went on. I was taking in the scene and Harold could see my wheels turning, thinking of my future in music. Through the coughing and smoke, he looked at me and said, 'It doesn't get bigger than this, Judy.'"

"I bet that made you want to stay in the business."

"Right. Sarah, this scene seems extremely strange to me. You and I are the only ones in the living room and this guy puts on porn. I mean, I love you, but—"

"You're too much. I'll be back. I can't sit here with that playing. I need a drink."

A few more people gathered, glancing at the TV and forming little conversational groups. They ignored me, by far the youngest person in the room.

"You look a bit down, young lady. Here, this should help."

I was handed a serving platter with a mound of cocaine on it. I sat and stared, staggered by the Fellini-esque aspect of sitting among the most impressive collection of modernist art I'd ever seen and watching porn with a mountain of coke in my lap, surrounded by a crazy assortment of Sarah's acolytes.

Freddie wandered over. "Hogging that for yourself?"

"Thank God you're here. Take this. And don't say 'It doesn't get bigger than this.'"

"Would you like to leave? You don't look like you're having much fun."

"Please. Get me out of here."

After a long period of touring, Sarah decided she needed a break from the road. She told her travel agent to find her an isolated part of the world to take a little vacation. She offered to bring along her band, her golf pro, Richard, and me.

After much research, the travel agent found us a large, airy house on a spectacular beach at the end of a long dirt road in a remote part of the island of Kauai. It took a while to negotiate our way through the jungle to find the place. When we finally did, we spied three gorgeous gals in bikini tops and sarongs sauntering down the gravel drive to greet us. One had curly red hair, another a long mahogany mane, and the third a blond boy-cut, although she looked anything but boyish.

"Who's that?" the guys asked enthusiastically.

"I think it's our staff, although something tells me they're not regular maids," I said perceptively. "They look like Charlie's Angels."

These three women were in their mid-twenties, like me—much younger than the rest of Sarah's posse—and became good buddies of mine, especially the mahogany-maned one, Lorraine, a surfer chick from Pismo Beach, California whose strong Russian features as well as her dark, cascading hair were a surprising contrast to the usual beach-bunny look.

As I'd guessed, these gals were not "maids" but rather a jazz trio that played around Kauai between various other jobs they did to survive. A realtor friend of Lorraine's had mentioned to them that he'd rented a house to Sarah Vaughan, so they volunteered to be our maids and cooks as a way to meet her.

The house had a great record collection that Sarah used to test my ears and educate me. She put on a duet of "Baby, It's Cold Outside" during one of our sessions and I commented on its lack of hipness.

"Keep listening."

"Wait, is that Sammy Davis, Jr. and *Carmen McRae?* She sounds so ..."

"White?"

"Well, I didn't want to be like everyone who says I sound black."

"Judy, I made plenty of those records too. They *told* us to sound white."

 ～ ～

Going to a faraway place had seemed like a good idea when Sarah was road-weary, but now that we were here, she was growing bored and getting antsy. I was the only one of the group who knew how to swim. I was having a ball bodysurfing all day and lying on the beach, something I had to play down since everyone else was miserable.

I did the cooking for a while until everyone complained about my portion control. Sarah took over and presented more manly meals. I gained seven pounds in three days.

She and I took the helicopter tour with a honeymooning couple who couldn't believe the only other passengers were a famous singer and an unfamous pianist. We explored the island and played golf between rainstorms. I waterskied on a hidden river that meandered through a tropical rain forest, deep in an inland canyon. It was a treacherous exercise, speeding along on one beat-up ski and ducking low-hanging branches that jutted out over the river, while Sarah and the guys watched and smoked some nuclear-level weed.

After a few days of this, she insisted we go out and explore the nightlife, whatever that might be.

"I can't stand it," she complained to Charlie's Angels after they'd finished tidying up. "We've got to find a place for some action. Is there music anywhere on the island?"

Lorraine suggested a little bar they occasionally played in and said they had a good jazz pianist in residence, a friend named Danny. The next evening, we dressed up for the big night out and set off into the dense overgrowth and tangled vegetation that surrounded our beach house.

"Have you noticed how gigantic the plants are here?" I said, leading the party like a cheerful Girl Scout. "Listen! You can hear them grow!

Just think," I added, "they're the main energy of Hawaii, just like the buildings are the main energy of Manhattan. Here plants rule! It's dark and mysterious and the plants are in charge. If we stand still, they'd grow over us."

"Judy, you're creeping me out," Harold called over his shoulder as he tripped on a vine.

"The bugs are eating me alive!" Sarah moaned, swatting away in the dark. "Did anyone bring bug spray?"

We finally saw some lights and made our way out of our tropical entanglement. We came to a—well, to call it a shack is probably a little grand. The place was charming, in a so-this-is-what-the-end-of-the-earth-looks-like kind of way. We walked in, looking around and at one another. The smell of mold oozed from the smoke-darkened paneling, and the lights were low and flickered occasionally. The place probably seated about forty people, if they were friendly and willing to be friendlier. Sarah glanced at me and rolled her eyes. I knew she was wishing she had some of that island smoke to get her through this.

Lorraine jumped into action, introducing us to her piano-playing friend, who couldn't believe he was in the presence of *Sarah Vaughan* and would soon have to play for her. I hung back as I always did, enjoying my anonymity. It was interesting to see how people responded to Sarah and she to them. It was usually fraught and frequently comical.

"This is *Sarah Vaughan*!" Lorraine told Danny with a flourish.

"I can't tell you what an honor it is to meet you, Miss Vaughan," Danny replied. "I've been a fan for years."

"And this is *Harold Jones*!"

"Mr. Jones, those records you did with Basie in the sixties are my favorites. No one ever made the Basie band swing harder. God, 'Magic Flea' blew my mind."

"This is Sarah's golf pro, Richard."

"Hi, Richard. I'm a golfer. I'd love to take you to some of the other courses you might not know around the island. There are some wonderful spots where only the locals play."

"And this is Judy," Lorraine said, casually pointing toward me as an afterthought, as she turned and walked us to our table.

"Wait! You're not Judy *Carmichael*, the stride pianist, are you?" Danny gulped in awe.

"Yes, I am," I said, somewhat stunned by the recognition. *Two-Handed Stride* hadn't even been released yet.

"Oh, my God. *I love you!*" he gushed, grabbing both my hands in his. "I can't believe this. This is the greatest moment of my life! I, uh, ah, damn! I'm stuttering. I'm so sorry. I can't believe I'm meeting you. You're my hero! I'm a stride *freak*! I have your ragtime album. A friend of mine got it in Newport Beach, when you were working that club on the Peninsula. Would it be weird if I hugged you? Wow! Lorraine, thank you *so much* for this introduction! Judy, can I have my picture taken with you?"

I turned to Sarah and sighed. She raised her eyebrows, smiled slightly and murmured, "Well, ain't you shit."

Later she asked me about the ragtime album.

"Trust me, you don't want to know. It's before I knew any better."

7

Gidget Goes to Harlem

It's common today for independent artists to produce their own recordings, but in 1980, when I recorded *Two-Handed Stride,* this was unusual. Most hoped to get a label to record them and produce the record, but I had spent my own money to make *Two-Handed Stride* and needed a company to press the record and distribute it. In another then-unusual move, I retained ownership of the master tapes, which I've done with all but one of my recordings. It has allowed me to keep everything I've done available and make more money than I would have selling the master.

Harold had known the Columbia Records producer John Hammond during his years with the Basie band, and had great respect for his taste and ears. John had made a tremendous impact on the record industry by discovering and supporting many great musicians, from Billie Holiday, Count Basie, and Benny Goodman to Bob Dylan. Harold suggested I send John three tracks from *Two-Handed Stride.* He advised me not to list the personnel, aside from him and me. He thought this would pique

John's curiosity and make him even more interested in my playing, since he would easily recognize the other musicians but not the pianist.

Marshall Royal had worked with Basie and had a distinctive, easily recognizable style, as did Freddie Green and Red Callender, musicians Hammond had known for years. I sent the recording with a note from Harold, who said he was on drums and that I was a pianist he wanted Hammond to hear.

I'll never know exactly why Hammond didn't recognize the players, but he didn't. He wrote back to Harold saying I showed little promise, was "certainly no Mary Lou Williams," and that he was mildly curious about the saxophonist, whom he assumed was a man. Harold was stunned.

Undeterred, I sent the entire recording to Hammond, named the musicians, and said I hoped he'd listen to it, even though I knew he wasn't interested in taking it for Columbia. I asked if he might suggest another company. He wrote back within a week, thanked me for persisting, said he loved the recording, thought I was a great player and asked when I could come to New York to meet him and discuss my future. He told me to call.

This was thrilling news, of course. I phoned him at once and we had a nice chat. He went on and on about my playing and ideas for my future and said he wanted to represent me and have Columbia release *Two-Handed Stride*. It was obvious I was his next big discovery, and this meeting would set the course for my future in the music business.

I borrowed the money for the trip and a new dress and left the next week for Manhattan, ready for my breakout career move. I walked to 10 Columbus Circle, across from Central Park, where John's office was at the time.

"Hi, Judy Carmichael for John Hammond."

"Mr. Hammond is expecting you. Right this way."

Hammond's secretary opened his door and I saw a vibrant, ruggedly handsome man who looked like a fit fifty-five-year old. He was actually seventy-one. I'd been reading about this influential producer for years and was thrown off by how different he looked from my preconception of him.

My appearance was obviously a surprise to him as well. He reached over his desk to shake my hand but became awkward and wouldn't look me in the eye. Then he started nervously moving papers around on his desk. I sat down, a bit unsettled by his attitude.

"So, Judy. I made some calls, and it seems no one knows who you are. What bands have you played with? What musicians?"

"People play with me. I'm not really a sideman. I don't work for other people. They work for me."

"That's not how it's done, as a rule. Musicians are usually sidemen for years before they lead their own bands."

"I know, but that's how I've done it."

Silence.

"I think more people need to know who you are. You should come back to me when you've played with more people and have a bigger reputation."

I was astonished. Our phone conversation had made it clear he planned to sign me to Columbia. Instead, he thanked me for coming and essentially tossed me out. If this were me today, I would have asked about his change of heart, but I was young, inexperienced, and confused. I thought I'd be signing a contract at this point, not being thrown out on my ear.

I went back to the hotel thinking about the money I'd wasted on this trip. I was now facing two days in Manhattan without a plan. I had no friends there. This had been a huge investment financially and psychologically. I was angry and frustrated. I sat on the bed with my face in my hands and cried. I tried to figure out what had gone wrong. Finally, I pulled myself together and called Freddie Green.

"Freddie, it's Judy."

"What's wrong? Are you OK? You don't sound right."

"The meeting with John Hammond didn't go well at all."

"What happened?"

"He got up from his desk to come shake my hand, but when he focused on me, he seemed surprised and stopped making eye contact. He said nobody had heard of me and that I should get more experience. Mainly, he seemed embarrassed and awkward."

Freddie sighed. "Judy, I was afraid of this. He thought you were black. He has a thing for black musicians. I'm sure he assumed you were an older black woman he'd somehow missed, instead of a young white woman who's new on the scene. Everyone on the recording is black, you swing, have time, he assumed you were black too, and when you weren't, he didn't know what to do with you."

This happened repeatedly during my twenties and thirties and still happens occasionally if I meet someone who knows my music but not my looks. Once my records were out and on the radio, most people assumed I was old and black. Many a photographer opened his studio door for a photo shoot, took one look at me, and said, "I need to change the lighting."

Freddie's encouragement after my aborted meeting with John Hammond made me more determined than ever to maximize my time in New York. I picked up the newspaper to see who was playing in town. I thought that since no one, allegedly, knew who I was, I'd meet as many musicians as possible. I was angry and focused. My first stop was a famous midtown club called Eddie Condon's, where I found the great trumpeter Roy Eldridge sitting at the bar, on break from his gig next door at another jazz room, Jimmy Ryan's.

"Mr. Eldridge? Hi, my name is Judy Carmichael, and I'm a big fan of your playing."

"That's nice," he replied, giving me the once over. "What do you do?"

"I play stride piano."

"Really?" He laughed. "You think you can play *stride piano*? Right. Show me. Go up there and play 'Handful of Keys.'" He pointed to the stage.

"Handful of Keys" is the Fats Waller tune that everyone had to learn to prove their technique, time, and feel for stride. Basie learned it,

Ellington learned it, and I learned it. It was one of the first tunes I studied when I took up stride, and always the piece people wanted to hear to see if I was the real thing. I'm sure Roy didn't believe that this young, tan, golden-haired twenty-six-year-old girl in the red spaghetti-strap dress with huge, white hibiscus flowers all over it knew how to play stride, let alone the signature song of the repertoire.

"Hey, guys!" Roy yelled to the onstage band. "Take a break. This chick thinks she can play stride piano. I want to hear her."

The musicians glared at me as they vacated the stage, but everyone respected Roy; so although this was an odd request, they went along with it.

The place was packed, smoke-filled, and noisy, exactly how I pictured a New York club. I was scared to death, since the last thing I'd expected was to have Roy Eldridge ask me to play for him.

People often assume that musicians ask other musicians if they can sit in. That's not usually the case. You have to be invited to play; and if you're an unknown, as I was, it's rare to get this chance. This was a huge opportunity to show what I could do, but to play solo in front of all these musicians was intimidating. The last few years I'd mainly performed in a silly Disney costume for a bunch of people who had ignored me. Eddie Condon's was packed with sophisticated jazz fans and musicians who were now focusing on me. You could hear a pin drop.

I climbed onto the stage, settled in at the piano, and launched into "Handful of Keys." The place went wild. When I finished, the audience jumped to its feet, applauding and shouting with delight.

"PLAY MORE! PLAY MORE!"

Roy grabbed my hand, pulled me off the stage, and shouted back to the crowd as he waved them away from me. "Leave her alone! She made her point!"

The band gathered back on stage, applauding me as they passed. Roy and I settled in at the bar.

"OK, you have my attention. Why are you here? First, let me get you a drink. You're old enough to drink, right?"

Roy flagged down the waiter and ordered our drinks.

"OK," he said. "What's going on? Why are you in town?"

"I live in Los Angeles. I just did a record with Marshall Royal, Freddie Green, Harold Jones, and Red Callender. I came to New York to meet with John Hammond about it."

"How did that go?"

"He was great when I talked to him on the phone. He said he wanted to represent me and release the album, although, when I met him today he got strange and awkward and tossed me out."

"Had he seen your picture?"

"No."

"He expected you to be black. He has a thing about black musicians."

"Yeah, that's what Freddie said. John also said no one's heard of me."

"You're not exactly my image of a jazz musician, either. Listen, I have an idea. Go uptown to a place called Hanratty's and play 'Handful of Keys' for Dick Wellstood. He's the regular pianist there. He also plays stride. Tell him I sent you. Then go downtown to Bradley's. Tommy Flanagan's there this week. Introduce yourself. Tell him I sent you and do 'Handful of Keys,' nothing else. Make sure you play 'Handful of Keys.'"

"OK. And I'd really like you to hear my recording with Freddie and the guys. I'm looking for a label. Would you like to meet here at the gig or during the day somewhere?"

"At the gig. You don't look that bad, and I'm not that old. Safer to meet at the gig."

Hanratty's was at 91ˢᵗ Street and Second Avenue, and Dick Wellstood played there a few months a year. The rest of the time the piano duties were covered with one-to-two week runs by some of the greatest soloists in the world. In those days most jazz pianists preferred playing with a bassist, so other rooms had duos; but Hanratty's had soloists who played "two-handed piano" and sounded great with or without bass.

The night I went to see Dick Wellstood, only four people were there, quite a contrast to my Eddie Condon's blowout. A couple were smooching in the corner. Dick was taking a break, talking to the owner at a table near the piano.

"Excuse me, I'm Judy Carmichael. Are you Dick Wellstood?"

"Yes."

"Roy Eldridge sent me by to play for you."

"I bet you're one of Roy's students. You're going to play one of his tunes, right?"

"No, actually he wanted me to play 'Handful of Keys.'"

"You're kidding." Dick looked at the owner, sitting across from him. They chuckled.

"May I play it for you?"

"By all means," he said, pointing to the piano.

I did the deed. The crowd of four applauded enthusiastically. I went back to Dick's table where he was burying his head in his hands in mock despair.

"She cuts me on my own gig!" he wailed.

The owner, and my future boss, jumped in. "What are you doing next week? Want to play here?"

"So now you're offering her my gig?" Wellstood asked in dismay.

"In *addition* to you, Dick. Don't cry. You're too old to cry." They were having fun with me, but the offer was serious.

The next night I went to see Tommy Flanagan at Bradley's, a downtown club on University Place that featured piano-bass duos of the highest order. Bradley's, like Hanratty's, had a long bar in front and tables and chairs in the back, all around the piano. It was warm and cozy, with low lighting and lots of dark wood. Unlike Hanratty's, with its uptown chic, Bradley's was downtown all the way. Every night was an event. I felt sick to my stomach just walking into the place, which was packed with Tommy's fans, serious jazz listeners, and jazz snobs. Eddie Condon's had been a party, Hanratty's was empty, and this place was something else altogether, the epicenter of jazz cool. I turned to escape. I was stopped by a friendly man with a big grin. Tommy Flanagan.

"You're Judy Carmichael, aren't you? The word on the street is so hot I not only know what you look like, I know what tune you're going to play.

Let me do my set. I'll call you up at the break. Sit here so I don't lose you." He sensed that I was about to bolt.

Tommy went on to play one of the most breathtaking sets I'll ever hear, finishing with "Lush Life" or something equally melancholy and emotionally devastating.

Great. I'm going to follow that with "Handful of Keys," a romping, stomping bunch of rhythmic acrobatics. I'll look like an idiot and sound like a cartoon.

Tommy then made a move so hip, so magnanimous and beautiful, that it's one of those moments I play over like a little video in my mind when I need to feel some love.

He followed his poetic ballad with a brief, fun little ditty. There's no other way to describe it. It was the precise aural sorbet needed to get everyone's ears ready for "Handful of Keys." These guys knew music but they also knew impact, and made sure I was shown to advantage. By having me play at Hanratty's and Bradley's, Roy had given both the traditional music world *and* the bebop world a chance to get to know me. And by telling Tommy what I was going to play, he'd ensured that Tommy would introduce me properly and that the audience would be as surprised—and delighted—as the one at Eddie Condon's.

Tommy became another source of support for me, and I often went to hear him for inspiration. One of my most memorable nights with him occurred early in our friendship.

"Judy! I'm glad you're here. I was hoping you'd come tonight. I want you to meet another piano player." He turned to a man nearby.

"Bill, this is Judy Carmichael, a friend of mine and a pal of Roy Eldridge. Believe it or not, she's a stride pianist."

"That's impressive. Nice to meet you, Judy."

"Judy," said Tommy, "meet Bill Evans."

Years later, after Roy had suffered a stroke and wasn't playing anymore, he'd have his nephew drive him into town when I was doing a run at Hanratty's. The nephew would wait for me to finish the tune, then he'd wave at me and mouth, "Roy's in the car." I'd tell the audience I'd be right back, then I'd dash outside and hop in the back of Roy's car, which was parked in front of the club. Our exchanges always went something like this:

"Roy! How are you?"

"I'm OK. How ya feelin', Judy?"

"I'm great. Happy to see you!"

Then we'd talk music.

One night he said, "Here, take this cassette." He handed it to me over his shoulder. "There's no one alive who can play this anymore. It's up to you. Learn this."

Roy and his generation cared deeply about carrying on the jazz tradition. I often got comments like this from older musicians I admired.

I had been too nervous to accept that first offer to work at Hanratty's, so on my next few visits I sat in. Every chance I had, I went to hear Tommy, Roy, and other musicians I admired, to get used to being in New York and to feel a part of the music scene. I had a lucky break when someone who had been booked for Hanratty's cancelled two days before I was set to arrive in Manhattan. It was October 1982. I got the offer to take the week, and said yes before I had time to think about it and waste time worrying. I still got tremendously anxious at the thought of playing there. I was accustomed to playing at Disneyland or other places where I was background music. Hanratty's was a famous room where people sat quietly and listened to celebrated pianists. I was thirty years younger than the youngest pianist on their roster; what's more, I was the only woman, and the only Hanratty's artist who wasn't famous.

On the Tuesday I opened, John S. Wilson, the jazz critic for the *New York Times*, came in to review me for the next day's paper and to write a longer feature for the Friday arts section. Well after midnight, when I got off work, my friend Todd Robbins and I rushed to a newsstand to await the arrival of the Wednesday *Times*. The evening was cool and a light rain was falling. The city lights reflected on the damp sidewalk and deserted streets. The newsstand operator was bundled in a heavy coat, as were we. We stood shivering and sipping hot cocoa, waiting for the newspaper delivery, filled with anticipation of reading my first review in the *Times*—my first review, period. This was big. Todd is an actor and musician, so he knew how important this was, and he was almost as excited as I was. The second it hit the stand, we lunged for the paper and madly flipped through the pages to the arts section. In unison we read the headline:

JUDY CARMICHAEL, SAXOPHONIST

"*Saxophonist?*" I moaned. "What are the chances that there's a saxophonist named Judy Carmichael? I can't believe it."

Todd was already reading ahead and saw the first line of the review that had inspired that mistaken headline: "When saxophonist Benny Carter first heard Judy Carmichael ..."

The headline was corrected for the next edition. But the review thrilled me. "Judy Carmichael's stride has a joyous, jumping drive," wrote the *Times*'s dean of jazz in an all-out rave. Two days later, the front page of the arts section was divided in half. The top part highlighted three singers. The bottom was devoted to me. The headline at the top of the page said, "New York: Where Three Women Are Singing"; the one above my feature read, "And Where One Is Playing Piano." That weekend the line of people wound around the block, waiting to get in. Whitney Balliett from the *New Yorker* dropped by to write his own review. In those pre-internet days, coverage like this was extraordinary. This was the start of my becoming known to a wider audience.

I'm frequently asked why there aren't more women in jazz, although there are more now than when I started. It was a tough scene when I came up. In interviews I tried not to focus on my place as a woman in jazz, but the subject was part of every article about me. Many jazz musicians were kind and encouraging; even Alistair Cooke, the host of *Masterpiece Theatre* on PBS at the time, came to Hanratty's and paid me one of my favorite compliments, telling me I had a greater command of dynamics than any stride player he'd ever heard.

But just as many musicians and others undermined me. One well-known stride pianist was friendly or nasty, depending on how much he'd had to drink. He came to hear me one night at Hanratty's, towered over me at the bar on my break, poked me in the chest, and said, "You think I've worked my whole life to have Tinker Bell fly in from Disneyland and get all the attention?" I can't imagine he would have said that to a man. He called various musicians in town and told them not to play with me. Fats Waller's guitarist Al Casey turned me down when I tried to hire him, saying he was busy. Years later he came to hear me at a club in Switzerland. At the end of the night, he introduced himself and told me how sorry he was that he had refused the gig I'd offered. He said that this pianist had made him promise not to work with me. "I was wrong," admitted Al. "It was a stupid thing to do."

I continued to work at Disneyland, which was still my main source of income;

I also started doing festivals in the States and Europe. But every few months I would play a one or two-week run at the elegant Hanratty's. The tables around the black baby grand were covered by white tablecloths and adorned with candles; a little spotlight was pointed at the stage. The sophisticated clientele listened well. A small reception area separated the front bar from the rear piano room. A maître d' stood there at a small podium to greet you.

Its location on the Upper East Side—rare for a jazz room—made Hanratty's the ideal neighborhood dinner and music place for the well-heeled crowd who, in those days, dressed up for a night out to hear jazz. It was the '80s, so everyone I met seemed to be an investment banker. If someone came in who wasn't a tall, handsome, white guy in a well-tailored suit, accompanied by his perfectly manicured wife, he stood out.

One evening, a muscular, bearded man with tattoos galore, sporting leather from head to toe and an impressive braid down his back, came in with two gorgeous gals, scantily clad in spray-on dresses and extremely high heels, even though it was a cool, winter evening. He beckoned me to their table after my first set, motioning to an empty seat between his two companions.

"I'm a big fan of your music," said my biker friend.

"Thanks so much. Are you into stride?"

"No, we're into *you*," purred one of the women, as she leaned closer and lightly touched my knee.

"We're making a movie," the man continued. "There's a part I think would be perfect for you—acting and playing the piano. It would be very tastefully done and show you to advantage in every way."

Others in the room were eying my companions with distaste, wondering how a Hell's Angel had found this lovely Upper East Side boîte.

"We're in the movie too and would be your supporting actresses," chimed in the other woman.

"What exactly is the part?" I asked. I guessed it probably wasn't Shakespeare.

"You'd play piano, naturally, and these two lovelies would be listening, seated next to you."

"What do you mean by 'naturally?' Naturally, I'd be playing the piano, or I'd be playing the piano *naturally*?"

"Well, none of you would be wearing clothing. You have a beautiful body and seeing you play the piano, all that action, your muscles flexing, the girls listening, sitting on the bench next to you, being moved by the music, the room would be warm, you would be working up a sweat ..."

"I get the picture. I don't know that this is exactly where I see my career going at this point."

— —

In my initial runs at Hanratty's—when I was barely confident enough to say more than "This next tune is 'Carolina Shout'"—I'd often look up and see someone famous who'd been sitting through the set without my noticing.

One evening, while I was making a phone call at the maître d's desk during my break, around the corner from the piano room came Joanne Woodward with a lovely smile, followed by her husband, Paul Newman, who ambled toward me making intense eye contact.

"Judy, where are you?" asked my phone pal, whom I was now ignoring as I gawked at Paul.

"*Paul Newman* is here!" I whispered in disbelief. "He's walking toward me and looking *right at me!*"

Everything went to slow motion and black and white. I was Ingrid Bergman in Hitchcock's *Spellbound*, naughtily visiting Gregory Peck's room, feeling a tad guilty and oh-so-sexy. Both of us are wearing elegant sleepwear, looking absolutely fabulous, as everyone does in those 1940s movies.

The orchestra swelled as Paul/Gregory came closer. My head was filled with music. I sighed. Paul/Gregory was in front of me. All I could see were his eyes, his lips.

I know why you came in.

Why?

Because something's happened to us.

It doesn't happen like that. In a day.

It happens in a moment sometimes. I felt it too. It was like lighting striking. It strikes rarely.

"Judy! What's happening?" said the voice on the other end of the phone. "Snap out of it!"

"Shhh! I'm in *Spellbound*. I'm Ingrid Bergman and Paul Newman is Gregory Peck."

Paul's face came to mine. He reached to my face, brushed my hair aside, leaned close and whispered in my ear,

"You're *wonderful*."

Kissing my cheek, he gave me one last meaningful glance and was gone.

"*Judy!* Talk to me! *Is Paul Newman really there?*"

"Don't speak for a minute. He told me I'm wonderful and kissed me."

My saxophonist, Mike Hashim, saw the whole thing unfold. He occasionally mentions it, always when others are around, for maximum effect.

"Judy, remember the time Paul Newman kissed you?"

Richard Gere came in one night and returned the next with Diane Keaton. They sat at the front table a few feet from me and freaked me out a bit, although neither one kissed me.

The great stride pianist, Joe Turner, a contemporary of Basie and Art Tatum, had moved to Paris after World War II, as many blacks did, to escape the racism they had experienced in the States. Black jazz musicians were embraced and celebrated in Europe, and Joe was a star there. He rarely played in the U.S. but was appearing at a place called the Cookery in Greenwich Village in 1982, at the end of my first week at Hanratty's. It was an astonishing bit of luck to have this jazz pioneer in town the week I debuted. Hanratty's was sold out in my first week there, and filled with mostly well-dressed Wall Street types and their wives who lived on the Upper East Side, with the occasional hardcore jazz nut from elsewhere in the city. I can't remember seeing a black audience member in all the years I played Hanratty's, with one exception. On closing night of that first engagement, I left the piano to take a break. I spotted a portly, stylishly dressed Joe Turner, leaning back in his chair enjoying a cigar. He waved me over to his table. "Joe Turner?" I said incredulously. "Yes, Miss Judy Carmichael! Take a seat." He waved with a flourish toward the chair opposite him.

I was thrilled and intimidated. He was complimentary, supportive, and amused. Joe was seventy-five then, but had a youthful, devilish air. He asked me to come by his gig the next night.

I walked into the Cookery on that extremely cold New York evening. I found the one remaining seat in the packed room and ordered a cup of tea, hoping to warm up. Joe's set was in progress and the crowd was into it. He nodded to me and started in on "Carolina Shout" by James P. Johnson. Like "Handful of Keys," "Carolina Shout" was a song all stride pianists had to play to demonstrate their command of the style and their ability to play with ease and swing.

After two measures, Joe stopped. The audience shouted, "Keep going!" Joe looked around the room, leaned back and said, "Actually, I want to hear Judy Carmichael play this." His timing was perfect and set me up beautifully, but this was a difficult challenge for me. My fingers were frozen and I had no chance to warm up. My first instinct was to decline, but I knew I had to jump on this. I plowed my way through it, and the audience responded to the surprise of Joe starting and me finishing this great song. He followed with a lovely tribute, the first in a series of introductions he made for me in New York, Switzerland, and Paris.

Joe's regular Paris gig was at a place called Club Los Calvados, where he played late, starting around eleven p.m. Whenever I was in town, I would drop by to listen and sit in on a tune or two. One evening, two excellent French stride pianists my age were also there, planning to sit in. Joe took me aside and said, "These guys are going to play as fast as possible with as many notes as they can squeeze in. I know them. I'm going to call you up last. Be sure to start with something slow and soulful and finish with 'Handful of Keys.' Two tunes, no more." This seemed odd to me, but I trusted Joe.

The first pianist played, and went on for at least twenty minutes; as Joe had promised, he crammed in every imaginable idea on every tune. The next pianist did the same. I noticed that Joe was going around the room while they were playing, whispering to his regular customers. I found out later that he was telling them to stick around to hear the American girl who was visiting from New York. Finally I got my chance. I played a poetic song by Willie "The Lion" Smith called "Echoes of Spring," followed by "Handful of Keys." The crowd responded well to the French pianists but showed even more enthusiasm toward me.

Back at Hanratty's, I continued to meet many fabled musicians. The great pianist Barry Harris dropped by and brought the Baroness Kathleen Annie Pannonica de Koenigswarter (née Rothschild), who was known as "The Jazz Baroness" for her longtime support of jazz musicians. It had started in the 1940s, when she heard Thelonious Monk and fell in love with bebop. Charlie Parker famously died in her apartment, but she nursed many a jazz musician back to health, financially and otherwise.

I recognized Barry and joined them on my break. He introduced me to Nika, as friends called her.

"It's an honor to meet you both," I said.

"Judy, my brother would love you," Nika said. "He was friends with Teddy Wilson and is a big fan of stride piano. Barry, let's get a couple of albums—one for us and one for Victor."

Not long after this, I got a call from Victor, who was Lord Rothschild and sounded like it.

"This is Victor Rothschild. Is Judy Carmichael there?"

"Yes, this is Judy. Nika said you might call."

We talked for a while, and he told me stories of hanging out with Teddy Wilson and other jazz greats. I set the phone on the piano and played him some tunes. He called from London a number of times and we'd always chat for an hour or more.

Shortly after we'd recorded it, I sent a tape of *Two-Handed Stride* to the great saxophonist and composer Benny Carter. I included a note that named the musicians—I'd learned my lesson with John Hammond—and asked if he could suggest a label that might be interested in distributing it. Benny listened to the tape but misplaced my note, so while he recognized the other musicians, he had no idea who the piano player was. He carried the tape with him and played it for musicians he saw on the road, asking if they recognized the pianist. No one did, so it became a bit of a game, with everyone listening and guessing. A year later, I went to a concert of Benny's in Los Angeles and managed to sneak backstage.

"Mr. Carter, I'm a huge fan. Thank you for the wonderful concert."

"Well, thank you. Are you a musician?"

"Yes. My name is Judy Carmichael. I play stride piano. In fact, I sent you a cassette about a year ago of a session I did with Marshall Royal, Harold Jones, Red Callender, and Freddie Green."

"*Oh, my God! You're* the stride pianist? Don't move." He called across the backstage area to his wife: "Hilma! Hilma! I've found the stride pianist! It's a *girl!*" Turning back to me, he explained, "Sorry, Judy. I lost your note, so we've been playing your cassette for everyone, trying to figure out who was on piano. We certainly didn't expect it to be a young woman. And I have to admit, I thought you were black."

— —

One of the things I appreciated most about New York City was the opportunity I had there to show what I could do, even though I was always regarded with skepticism. Upon meeting me, no one believed I could be a serious jazz musician, but they gave me a chance to prove otherwise. A friend told me I loved New York because New York loved me, which is probably true. In Los Angeles clubs, I never got the chance to sit in and show my stuff. The jobs I got were as much the result of my physical appearance as of my playing. I was constantly told I played like a man. Every jazz festival that booked me featured female vocalists, but no other women instrumentalist.

Two-Handed Stride was still unreleased, but at last I found a company in Atlanta that had agreed to distribute it. The owner and I discussed the deal on the phone. I told him I'd do the cover shoot in Los Angeles, making sure he wouldn't know what I looked like and possibly back out, which is what had happened with two previous labels. I sent the finished photo to him only after he had signed the contract. When he received the picture, he called and asked who the girl was I'd gotten to pose for the cover.

I was given an enthusiastic introduction at my first big festival concert, held just outside Manhattan the summer after my Hanratty's splash. The pianist Dick Hyman was in charge, and he mentioned the articles in the *Times* along with the great reception my debut recording had received. He quoted various testimonials I'd gotten from famous jazz musicians.

The audience cheered as I walked onstage, but the roaring stopped cold when the thousand-plus crowd saw me in my blue-and-white striped halter top and white pants—a tasteful but somewhat revealing ensemble. I was confused by the sudden silence, but soldiered on in spite of it, sat down at the piano and launched into my opener. Sixteen bars in, the crowd exploded with applause.

I didn't mind the initial hesitation, although it had thrown me off a bit. In Los Angeles, how I looked was often more important than how I played. Not in New York. This festival experience taught me a lesson. From that point on I wore nothing that would distract from my music. I was determined to be taken seriously, which is hard for a young woman. I waited twenty years to wear a dress on stage.

After I'd become friends with Sarah Vaughan, she capitalized on the surprise of my playing stride and asked me to play at unexpected moments. Sarah and her band took me to a party given by one of the *Tonight* show musicians. Everyone in the room was a heavy player on the show or a top studio musician. After various people had played, Sarah was asked to sing. She stayed seated and sang with her trio.

"Do another! Do another!"

"No, thanks, but Judy will play."

"Judy who?" someone whispered.

Another challenge and test.

Sarah grabbed me as I made my way to the piano. "Play 'Handful of Keys,'" she said, giggling in her delightful way.

My first jazz festival in California was at the Frank Gehry-designed Concord Pavilion in Concord. Carmen McRae, the great jazz singer, was one of the major stars. Carmen heard me through the speakers in her dressing room during my sound check and asked that someone bring the "stride pianist" to meet her. I worked my way downstairs to the dressing-room area, stood in her doorway, and said hello.

Carmen checked me out, looking fairly friendly; then she seemed to remember she was a star. "What do you want?" she demanded with irritation, turning back to her mirror and continuing to apply her makeup.

"Someone said you wanted to see the stride pianist. I'm the stride pianist."

She looked me up and down, sat back, and laughed. "Honey, you sure don't like you play." From then on, whenever I'd bump into Carmen at a concert or club, she'd make a point of introducing me to everyone and telling them to take me seriously.

The pianist Hank Jones also played that festival. His sound check followed mine. As I left the stage, he sat down at the piano and played a well-known Fats Waller phrase. I turned around and said, "Are you flirting with me?" He smiled and said, "Of course."

— —

In the early '80s I worked at a club in Hollywood with the unlikely name of Nucleus Nuance. Located on Melrose Avenue, it looked like a nightspot from the '30s, complete with palm trees, pictures of old movie stars, tables packed closely together, and everyone dressed to the nines. I played in a duo with John Jorgenson, a guitarist friend from Disneyland. We were mainly sophisticated background music, but we amused ourselves and enjoyed the gig. One evening the maitre d' stopped me excitedly in mid-tune to tell me that Michael Douglas was in the house and wanted to buy an album. This guy loved film stars and the club worked relentlessly to get as many of them in there as possible. Although I was a fan of Michael Douglas, I was irritated by the interruption.

"Tell him I'll talk to him on the break."

"No! He wants to talk to you now."

I turned to John and rolled my eyes. He smiled sympathetically.

"Just give him the album and let me finish the set," I said as I continued playing.

"He wants you to autograph it too," the maître d' said excitedly.

"Oh, for God's sake!" I stopped mid-phrase and walked off the stage. John was left playing on his own and looking up at me in confusion. I shrugged and sighed.

Michael introduced himself and said how much he was enjoying the music as he handed me the album for my signature. I signed it and handed it back, still a bit miffed.

"Here, just take it," I said. "I'm glad you like the music, but I've really got to get back onstage. I abandoned my guitarist."

"Wait, I want to pay for it."

"No, really, it's OK."

"Please let me pay. The irony is, once you're in a position to pay for things, people never let you."

John later told me this scene was simultaneously the weirdest and coolest thing that had ever happened to him on a gig: realizing I'd stopped playing with him, and looking up and seeing me sign an autograph for Michael Douglas.

A month later, Rod Stewart's people called my people, meaning his people called me.

"Hi, I'm calling for Rod Stewart. He has one of your albums and loves your work." I only had one album. "He's having a birthday party and hopes you'll play for it. The entertainment will be you and the *Tonight* show band."

"Is this a joke?"

"Is this Judy Carmichael?"

"Yes, I'm sorry. I'm just trying to imagine myself alternating solo piano with the *Tonight* show band."

"Rod has a plan."

I know nothing about pop music, and knew even less then. I figured I'd better do some reconnaissance with my Disneyland musicians to brush up on Rod's œuvre. They were understandably shocked by my ignorance.

"This gig is wasted on you, Carmichael. You don't know *one* Rod Stewart tune?"

"He's the skinny guy with spiky blond hair, right?"

I showed up at nine as instructed and made my way through the security and screaming fans at the gate. Rod opened the door wearing tight purple velvet pants, a violet silk shirt, and a big smile.

The house had been built in the 1920s and was magnificent. The grounds were vast and beautifully manicured, in the style of an English garden. Rod gave me a tour, showed me his art collection, his Irish setter, her new brood of puppies, his books, full-size ballroom, and the balcony above it with my grand piano for the evening.

Each room had a color scheme with matching bouquets of flowers. I was overwhelmed with sights, smells, and spiky hair. I wasn't a fan when I'd walked through the door, but after this tour I would have moved in with him. Alana, his wife of the moment, came downstairs to fetch him for some task. He apologized for having to leave me.

"The guests should be arriving around midnight, so make yourself at home. I'm sorry I can't spend more time with you."

Me too.

I went off to hang with the Irish setters and eventually with the *Tonight* guys, who showed up around 11:30 p.m.

Guests started arriving at midnight, and it was a fascinating mix. I stood by myself and watched as everyone from Gregory Peck to Billy Wilder to Cher to Tatum O'Neal walked by and said hello. The entertainment started with the *Tonight* show band playing in the ballroom for dancing; that was for the Gregory Peck crowd. There was a disco in another part of the house. Billy Wilder's wife sang, giving the event a *Sunset Boulevard* vibe.

After two hours I was starting to panic, wondering how I was going to fit my rousing version of "Rosetta" into this mix. I finally figured I had to offer myself up for whatever Rod had in mind. "I'm sorry I've been neglecting you, Judy," he said. "Wait until the band is done, then come find me."

The band took a break and everyone went to the disco. Rod led me by the hand to the balcony. He motioned to the piano and pulled a chair up close as I sat down to play.

"What would you like to hear?"

"Whatever you'd like."

I played for the next thirty minutes for Rod and only Rod. He applauded and commented after each piece, asked various questions about why I'd made particular choices. Finally he said that he had to get back to his guests.

"That was beautiful, Judy. I can't thank you enough for agreeing to play for me. You made the party."

"Shall I stay?"

Shall I move in?

"Please enjoy the party and leave whenever you like. My office will follow up with payment. Thank you so much, Judy."

He kissed me on the cheek, smiled, and I stayed for the next two years. (Kidding.)

＊ ＊

About a year after my John Hammond encounter, I had a meeting with a producer name Joe Keys. I was still living in California, but coming to Manhattan frequently. I'd taken to the city's vibe, which was much more to my liking than the laid-back, pseudo-friendly Los Angeles attitude.

We were at a midtown deli. I was talking a mile a minute, describing a concert I wanted to produce with Joe, gesticulating wildly to illustrate my thoughts. Our waitress had just placed our gigantic sandwiches in front of us when a huge cockroach ran across the table. Without missing a beat, I reached over, flicked it off with a snap of my fingers, and kept talking.

"Stop!" Joe interrupted, holding his hand up, palm facing me. "I have to say something here."

"Yes?"

"Judy, that move with the bug. Trust me, you're going to do great in New York."

In 1985, I finally moved full-time to Manhattan. I went from a three-bedroom house in Newport Beach to a one-room studio on West 110th Street between Broadway and Amsterdam. The neighborhood alternated between dangerous and iffy, depending on the block and time of day. I loved Manhattan and my exquisite little space. But it was challenging to live in such a tiny apartment. As an actor friend once said, "I worked my whole life to move to New York and lower my standard of living."

Me too.

8

Into the Wild

Most jazz musicians start out working as sidemen for better-known musicians until they have a big-enough name to lead their own groups. Great sidemen have large repertoires, play well in a variety of styles, and enjoy the challenge of doing so. I tried to be a sideman after I recorded *Two-Handed Stride*, but I neither did it particularly well nor enjoyed it. I was passionate about the music I loved, but not about what others told me to play. I knew I had to create a career that would let me do my own thing.

I've always been good at spinning a yarn and making people laugh. Friends from elementary school tell me they remember my getting us all in trouble by making everyone laugh with some goofball story when we should have been studying. I realized that if I developed these skills, I could frame the songs I played with humorous anecdotes that would engage an audience beyond jazz fans. It also got me out of playing tunes I didn't like. To this day I've never played "Feelings" or "Happy Birthday."

I was fortunate to always have a regular club gig in Manhattan when I was in town, first Hanratty's and then a few other clubs, notably

Knickerbocker Bar & Grill at 9th Street and University Place. I also started producing my own concerts, starting at Carnegie Recital Hall, a 268-seat concert space attached to Carnegie Hall.

There's an old joke about a musician walking down the street in Manhattan who asks, "How do I get to Carnegie Hall?"

The answer: "Practice."

In my case: "Rent it."

In those days, renting the hall for one night cost around seven hundred dollars, but carrying the mic onstage, which due to union rules had to be done by Carnegie staff, cost a hundred dollars, and carrying it off was another hundred. Also, Carnegie did nothing to promote the concert; I paid for posters and advertising, as well as the musicians. Phil Schaap, the jazz historian and radio personality and the first person to interview me in New York, said I should hire big names for this first important concert; I got Freddie Green and Red Callender then added Howard Alden, my guitarist from my California days. I knew he'd be thrilled to play with Freddie. Ironically, the ad in the *New York Times* neglected to include the guys' names. The concert sold out anyway on my name alone, a lesson I took with me when producing future concerts.

John S. Wilson had remained a great supporter of mine, so before booking the hall I would ask him when he'd be free to attend, so he could review my concert. I did this a few times. I couldn't predict what he'd write but I knew he'd be there.

I was getting more good press for *Two-Handed Stride* and booking important gigs; but even though I spent a lot of time in New York, I had held onto my job at Disneyland, which paid me too good a salary to give up; additionally I had five weeks' paid vacation, five sick days, and full health insurance.

Rod Miller, the daytime pianist, agreed to cover for me at Disneyland when I needed to work elsewhere. I would book two weeks of jazz gigs in Europe and New York, and Rod would cover both his shifts and mine—Tuesday through Saturday, fourteen hours a day. I'd do the same for him when I came home, giving him two weeks off without a loss of income for either of us. Having done a string of prestigious concerts and high-exposure festivals, I would put on my Disneyland costume, be anonymous, and make some money. This ploy worked until a man walked up to me and said, "Aren't you Judy Carmichael? I have one of your albums. I love it. What are you doing here?"

"Ah, well, um, I, actually, I'm subbing for a friend. I really live in New York and only come out here every now and then." I stuttered on, trying to seem like the Manhattan jazz girl I hoped to one day be.

"We're also from the East," said this vaguely familiar-looking man. He gestured to his wife, who was standing next to him. "I'm in the entertainment business too. We had to move here for work."

I continued pretending I lived full-time in Manhattan when his wife reached over and gently put her hand on my arm.

"It's OK, dear. We don't like to admit we live here, either."

That did it. I had to quit.

Later that week I was watching *Entertainment Tonight*, and there he was, the man I'd met a few days earlier at Disneyland, reviewing a movie. Leonard Maltin, one of TV's most recognized and respected film critics. (I should note that Leonard and his wife, Alice have lived in Los Angeles for years at this point and love it.)

That chance meeting, uncomfortable as it was, had a very happy result, for I wound up on *Entertainment Tonight*, interviewed by Leonard. But it took years and a complicated process to happen. In 1990, a producer from NPR's *Morning Edition* called to get a few quotes from me about the stride pianist Joe Turner for a feature she was doing about his death in July of that year.

"You're the authority on stride," she said, "so I wanted your thoughts on Joe's place in that world."

I laughed. "I'm too young to be the authority on anything. Have you called Dick Hyman or Ralph Sutton?"

"My boss said to call you."

We talked at length, and she was delighted to learn that I'd known Joe personally and had spent a good deal of time with him. She had met Joe years before in Paris and recorded his reminiscences, just for her own interest. Now she finally had a chance to work that recording into a "Morning Edition" segment.

She taped my thoughts on Joe to insert into her piece. A few days later, she called with the news that her executive producer said her feature sounded too much like an obituary and that she should do a feature on me instead, with inserted recorded quotes from Joe. This was the first major radio feature on me, and it gave my career a huge push forward.

After the segment was aired, the executive producer of *Entertainment Tonight* called to say he'd heard the NPR piece and wanted to do a segment on me. These days, features on TV entertainment magazine shows are only a few seconds long and focus on promoting a product or movie, but back then they were occasionally longer, in-depth profiles about the guest. This was what he planned for me. We set a date in January of 1991. Sadly, it coincided with Operation Desert Storm. All news programs turned their attention to the war, not to up-and-coming stride pianists, and my feature was canceled.

A year later, I was still mourning this missed opportunity. I decided to write to Leonard Maltin on the remote chance that my letter would get to him and that he'd remember me from our meeting ten years earlier at Disneyland. I found the address for the studio and sent him a letter. I included the story of my lost chance to do *Entertainment Tonight*. To my shock and delight, he called the day he received the letter.

"Judy, it's Leonard Maltin. Of course I remember you. I'd love to do a feature on you. When are you going to be in L.A.?"

"Great timing, I was planning on being there the day after tomorrow," I lied. I wasn't taking a chance on another war.

Leonard did a five-minute piece. It included shots of me playing, a Fats Waller film clip that emphasized the obvious contrast between him and me, a chat about my interest in stride, and even a four-hand duet between Leonard and me. This spot on *Entertainment Tonight* gave my visibility one more major boost; it even led to two longer features on a series that was very good to jazz musicians, *CBS Sunday Morning*. The first appearance was an eight-minute mini-documentary of my professional life, filmed over six months at various locations—concerts in Manhattan, Sag Harbor, South Carolina, and Florida. The second focused on my simultaneous recording of a CD and a digital player-piano disc, the first time that had been done.

Things were going well. After Hanratty's closed in 1986, I was asked to create a piano room at a midtown Chinese restaurant called Fortune Garden Pavilion, an elegant, upscale room that served spectacular food to a sophisticated clientele. The owner described himself as "a Jewish lawyer who knows nothing about the restaurant business, Chinese food, or jazz."

"My Chinese partner died," he told me, "so I have to take over and try to make a success of this. I was the silent partner. Now I'm not so silent. I've decided to bring in jazz, although I don't know anything about that, either."

"How did you find me?" I asked, fascinated by this man and his unusual situation.

"I wanted a pianist known to other creative people in the arts. I asked a jazz musician, a novelist, and an architect to recommend someone they thought could produce a great jazz series. The only person they all named was you. So I want you to create a jazz room."

I enjoy producing, so this was a great opportunity. I suggested that he lease a Steinway grand so I could entice the best pianists, and that he pay them respectably while not getting extravagant. "You're completely in charge, Judy," he answered. "You play as many weeks as you want during the year and hire the pianists of your choice for the weeks you're out of town. You offer the appropriate fees and I'll back your decisions."

I hired people I wanted to hear, people whom I knew would appreciate playing on a great piano in a convivial environment, respected players who lived in town and would do the gig for an affordable fee. I got Tommy Flanagan, Hank Jones, and other top players. It was a great gig for me and allowed me to create work for others, something I've tried to do throughout my career.

This was a fun and profitable period for me until things got a little too successful. The owner forgot his "you're completely in charge,

Judy" promise and started hiring the Tony Bennetts of the world, ignoring the fact that his venue was an elegant Chinese restaurant in midtown Manhattan, not the Hollywood Bowl. In two months he was bankrupt.

— —

Up to now I had successfully avoided the sideman route in favor of leading my own bands, but there were a few exceptions. One day I got a call from a stranger named Joel Knightly. He explained that he'd gotten my number from Red Callender, and that he was producing a concert in Santa Barbara with Red, Gerald Wiggins, Bill Douglas, and Wild Bill Davison.

"Wow! Red and Bill Douglas, Art Tatum's rhythm section. I wish I could be there."

"Well, that's why I'm calling. Gerald can't do the gig, and Red said he wouldn't do it without him. I suggested a few other pianists, and finally he said he'd only do it if I hired you."

I decided I'd ask my mom to go with me and called her to tell her the big news. She still made me crazy a lot of the time, but I thought she'd enjoy the beautiful drive up the coast to Santa Barbara, to say nothing of hearing me perform with these great musicians. Nonetheless, it was always a major production to go anywhere with my mother, and this particular day was no different.

"Now we'll have to pack sandwiches, water, soft drinks. Judy, get the cooler from the garage."

"Mom, it's only a two-hour drive, and it's just us. We're packing enough for an army."

"We'll need some sweaters if it gets cold, and I really don't think this is enough food. We'll want something for the ride home and ..."

I was already nervous about this concert, and my mother was making me more so. She ran around the kitchen vibrating with nervous energy, bumping into things, gathering food and drink, worrying about every

potential disaster we might encounter, all the time looking fresh, vibrant, and terrific.

I watched her prepare for our drive as if we were readying ourselves
for a trek across the Sahara. Suddenly, everything shifted and I viewed
her objectively. All I saw was her anxiety and fear. Throughout my life
I'd resented her claims of "being tired" and having to take time to "relax
and read." Relax from what, I wondered. She never seemed to work at
anything except getting the rest of us to minister to her needs. Yes, she
sewed some of my clothes and Halloween costumes and yes, she cooked a
lot of meals, but her complaining about it all was constant. Everything
was a big deal to her.

Once, as a child, I had asked her to sew a button on a blouse.

"You lost that button, Judy. It will take me a while to find one that
will match. And then I'll have to sew it on and make it look nice. I think
you'll have to vacuum the living room for me since I won't have time to
do that now."

I also grew up resenting my talented, smart, attractive parents, la-
menting the fact that they could have had artistic careers if only they'd
had the chance. From my youthful perspective, they had everything going for them. I never understood why these two people I loved and admired so much didn't do better for themselves.

But now I saw my mother not as my mom, who didn't mother me, but
as the woman she was, separate from me. I suddenly empathized with
her and knew that she hadn't been avoiding work because she was lazy or
a princess or anything other than a severely anxious, neurotic, fright-
ened woman. It was a painful moment, and I felt profoundly sad that
her father had been a drunk and scared her to death, that he'd beaten
her brothers, that one brother had been killed in the war and the other
had come back filled with shrapnel and demons, that she'd had illnesses
both real and imagined since childhood. How had she survived this and
remained even mildly pasted together? How had she kept her sense of
humor in the midst of such a tragic childhood?

I put my arms around her and held her until she stopped shaking.

"Mom, take a deep breath."

"What's wrong?" she demanded, panicking further.

"Nothing. Breathe. I love you, but you're making me nuts and I need to be relaxed for this concert. This is a big deal for me. You go in the living room and lie down, and I'll get everything together for the trip. I know what to do."

The drive to Santa Barbara was relaxed and scenic, and it brought back great memories of our family road trips. The concert was in a natural history museum, so while the stage was typical, the walls of the place looked anything but.

"Judy," Mom said. "I'm loving those African tribal masks and shields, although the spears make me a little nervous. Are they on the walls for unhappy audience members? Throwing fruit is one thing but ... is that a *crossbow*?"

She found a seat under a war mask while I made my way backstage to find the guys.

"Red! I can't believe you recommended me for this. It's so good to see you, although I barely *can* see you. Why is this place so dark?"

"Romantic lighting, Judy. Come here, gimme a hug. And this is Bill Douglas." He waved toward another welcoming soul.

"Great to meet you, Bill," I said. "I'm thrilled to be here. I'm looking forward to playing with you."

"Me too. Red's told me all about you. Have you met Wild Bill before?"

"No, but I've heard stories. Should I be afraid?"

"We're here for you, Judy."

"I brought my mother too. She's pretty fierce."

Cornetist Wild Bill Davison was famous for great playing and bad behavior. He had a wonderful, long-suffering wife, whom I'd heard stayed busy sending apology notes to various people Bill had mistreated. I was getting more anxious by the minute. Bill came late, so we didn't have time for a sound check or rehearsal. He was friendly and cheerful when he spotted Red, but looked severely unhappy when he saw me.

"Red, who's *that*?"

"Judy Carmichael, our pianist. Wiggins couldn't make it."

"Are you kidding? What is she, *twelve*? I'm not doing this with her."

"Oh, Bill," Red said, moving slightly closer to him. They were both standing, and Red towered over the Wild One.

Mrs. Wild Bill looked worried. I sank into a chair and watched from across the room.

"This is ridiculous. I can't fucking believe this. Whose idea was it to hire her?"

"Mine."

"For God's sake, Red!"

Red let him rant. The room was cold and dreary, like my mood. Bill Douglas looked over at me and winked. He seemed mildly amused.

We've got to talk tunes. I'm not going to know his repertoire. What a disaster. I never should have said yes to this.

"Come on, Red," asked Wild Bill. "Who really recommended her?"

"I did. I made a record with her, Freddie Green, Harold Jones, and Marshall Royal."

"Really? Still, there's no way she can play. Look at her. Well, I guess the way she looks, she doesn't have to play."

Red glared at him. "That's the point. She doesn't *have* to play, but she *does*."

Wild Bill's wife scurried across the room to me.

"It's lovely to meet you, Judy, and we're so looking forward to hearing you play," she said warmly, glancing over her shoulder at her husband with a frown.

"Nice to meet you too, Bill!" I said as I walked to him and offered my hand. "I've been looking forward to this ever since I got the call. Would you like to talk tunes?"

He grumbled, made his way to a table and plopped into a chair. I followed, glancing back at Red, who smiled wryly.

"Want to play 'Sugarfoot Strut?'" I offered as an opening gambit, once we were seated across from each other.

"You mean 'Sugarfoot STOMP?'"

"No, I was thinking 'Sugarfoot Strut.' It isn't heard as much."

"I don't like either of them."

"OK."

"How about 'Let's Fall in Love?'" he countered.

"I love that tune, but I'm afraid I don't play it. How about 'I Got Rhythm?'"

"I'm sick of it. How about 'Buddy Bolden's Blues?'"

"I don't know it. How about 'Keeping Out of Mischief Now?'"

"Do you know how many times I've played that fucking tune?"

"How about 'Rosetta?'" I said, getting more desperate by the minute.

"Just *stop!* This is ridiculous! You don't know *ANYTHING!*"

Incredibly, he'd screamed at me. There was a collective gasp from Red, Bill Douglas, and Wild Bill's wife, but surprisingly, I felt a serenity I'd never experienced before. My worst fear had come true.

I stared down the Wild One.

"You know, Bill, actually, I know quite a few tunes. We've got ten minutes. I'm going to write a list of what we'll play. I'd love your suggestions, but I'm making the list whether you give them to me or not."

Silence.

"Do it," he finally replied. "Let's get on stage."

Red and Bill walked over and patted me on the back as we made our way to the wings. We were announced and followed Wild Bill to our instruments. The place erupted in applause upon seeing this stellar group appear, trailed by an unknown female. I looked for my mom and spotted her smiling at me. She pointed to the war mask hanging above her and gave me a fist pump. I laughed.

Mom, you're nuts, but you're one of a kind.

I surveyed the room.

This has got to be one of the weirdest places I've ever played. Interesting to look out at smiling faces and mounted weapons.

Wild Bill sat down first, bumping the music stand in front of him and knocking it off the stage and into the audience when he turned around to call the first tune.

A couple of college students dodged the flying music stand and a third caught it and handed it back to Bill, who ignored the havoc he was wreaking.

"*SUGAR*! Piano intro, eight bars!"

Thank God I know it. I wonder what tempo he wants? Hmm . . . shouldn't he tell me? And the key?

I guessed on both and dove in. I couldn't believe I was playing with Art Tatum's rhythm section. All we needed was Tiny Grimes on guitar. Who cared about Wild Bill? We were swinging and I was happy. A few measures in, though, I noticed that Wild Bill seemed to be playing a different tune from the rest of us. Bill Douglas and Red looked at me. I shrugged and kept playing. Wild Bill forged ahead but also turned and looked at me. He stopped playing and pointed at me.

"Listen to that girl! Can you *believe* that?"

He resumed playing but kept turning and looking at me.

"Honey, that's *great!*" he called back to me.

Glad he approves, but we still sound off. Is he playing a different tune, or do I have the wrong changes?

Red leaned toward me and whispered, "Which 'Sugar' are you playing?"

I emphasized the melody so he could hear it.

"Yeah, that's the one I'm playing too. What's Wild Bill playing?"

"I can't tell," I whispered back, as my hands continued flying over the keys.

I made a command decision and shouted to the rhythm section.

"*STOP PLAYING!*"

I listened to Wild Bill, who continued on his own.

Solo trumpet. Lovely.

"I got it!" I shouted over Bill's solo and we all jumped back in. "He's playing 'Squeeze Me!' He's going into the bridge!"

Wild Bill noticed none of this, or if he did he wasn't letting on.

"That was an old favorite called 'Sugar,'" he announced at the end of the tune. "Let me introduce you to my band."

"On bass, *RED CALLENDER!*"

The crowd burst into applause.

"And on drums, *BILL DOUGLAS!*"

More loud clapping.

"And on piano ... uh ... ahh ... Isn't she great? Sweetheart, stand up. Let them see you."

More applause.

Red turned to me.

"He isn't being sexist, Judy. I think he's forgotten your name."

In the summer of 1984, I was hired for the Nice Jazz Festival in France, my first major international festival. The biggest stars in jazz played it every year; that year's roster included Dizzy Gillespie and Lionel Hampton.

I was hired to play a concert on every one of my seven nights in Nice, in a Roman amphitheater on a hill that overlooked that beautiful city on the French Riviera. Because of sound restrictions, larger bands had to finish by eleven p.m. I would follow with a solo piano set. It was challenging to follow screaming extravaganzas like Lionel Hampton's Big Band with an hour of solo piano. Fortunately, the crowd always stayed around to see who would have the guts to do this. All the musicians came to see me because I was the only female instrumentalist and the new kid on the scene.

When I had arrived and received my schedule, I noticed that instead of the seven concerts I was contracted for, I was scheduled for fifteen, with a variety of bands. This wasn't happy news. Not only was it more work than my contract stated (for no additional money), but I'd be back as a sideman, an idea I didn't relish after my experience with Wild Bill.

Before leaving for New York I had discussed my schedule with Marie St. Louis, an associate of George Wein, president of Festival Productions. George was the legendary producer of the Newport Jazz Festival and other prominent ones, including Nice. Marie had called me a couple of weeks before the festival.

"We're happy you're going to be with us, Judy. Let me ask you something. I'm putting the program together. What do you think about playing a set with Linda Hopkins?"

Linda Hopkins was a big-voiced, big-energy, rockin', stompin' black blues and gospel singer discovered when she was eleven by Mahalia Jackson. Linda expressed the pain and joy of her race in every note she sang. She was a Tony-winning Broadway star who grabbed the audience by the throat and owned the stage the second she walked on. I was a thirty-two-year-old white girl who invited the audience into her world with swinging music and witty anecdotes. I had planned on telling funny stories in French and presenting my music for the first time in a major European arena, not accompanying a blues singer whose music I had no experience with nor feeling for. I love the blues, but I'm not a blues player.

"Wow. I love her, but that's not really my style of music. I don't think we're a great fit."

"It's OK, Judy," said Marie with a sigh. "I told George this was a dumb idea. All you and Linda have in common is that you're both women. Don't worry about it. I'll fix this. Thanks for being honest."

"I should probably just play solo or maybe some piano duets."

"That's how you'll be scheduled."

Now in Nice, I was looking at a schedule that had me playing with many different bands, duets, and solo sets—much more than I'd agreed to—in settings completely inappropriate to my skills. I'd fended off Linda Hopkins but now there were other situations for which I was equally unsuited.

The next day I was plotting how to get out of this when a distinguished-looking man stopped me backstage.

"You're Judy Carmichael, aren't you? I'm looking forward to our duet set. I'm John Lewis."

John Lewis was the pianist and arranger for the Modern Jazz Quartet, one of the most successful jazz groups in history. There aren't many jazz musicians who appeal to non-jazz fans, but the Modern Jazz Quartet did. John was a major figure and a lovely, encouraging person.

"Oh, Mr. Lewis! This is such an honor! I'm a huge fan!"

"Please, call me John."

"Thank you. Wow, I didn't know we were playing together."

"Yes, they just added it to the schedule."

"They keep adding concerts they didn't tell me about. I'm a bit frustrated, to be honest, though I'm thrilled I'll be playing with you. George has me in bands that have nothing to do with my musical style. I want to be the pianist musicians *want* to play with, not the one who ruins the set."

"Let's look at your schedule and see if I can help."

We sat behind various tents and refreshment tables with musicians and technicians bustling around us.

"This is very kind of you, John. The set I'm most dreading is with Sweets Edison and Lockjaw Davis. I'm not in any way appropriate for this band. They'll be extremely unhappy and probably throw me off the stage. Any ideas?"

Harry "Sweets" Edison was a renowned trumpeter and his frequent musical partner, Eddie "Lockjaw" Davis, was an equally esteemed saxophonist. Neither man was known for his patience with newcomers, especially someone like me who wouldn't know their repertoire.

John looked amused and leaned in conspiratorially.

"Here's what you do. Find George and tell him you've been dying to hear *him* on piano and wondered if he'd play your set with Sweets and Lockjaw. And I hope this won't offend you. If you can bat those big green eyes of yours, it would help your cause."

"No, I'm not offended. I'm result-oriented. You think this'll work?"

"Yes. George is over there. Go for it and report back."

It worked, of course. John knew his man.

I also got to play with the great bassist George Duvivier, a close friend and musical collaborator of Benny Carter. Benny had heard that Duvivier and I would be in Nice together, and had told George to find me once he got to the festival. Like John Lewis, George was encouraging and supportive and made a point of telling me to play a solo at one point during our set—"so the audience can really see what you do."

Joe Bushkin was a wonderful swing pianist who had co-written a major hit of the big-band era, "Oh! Look at Me Now." Joe had been off the scene for a while, having married well and shifted his attention to his racehorses and his daughters, not necessarily in that order.

He and I were scheduled for a duo set. For some reason he didn't want to use two pianos, as I'd done with everyone else; he preferred to play four hands on one piano, something I don't enjoy. Joe was a great player, and I wanted both of us to have our own keyboards.

Everyone dressed casually for this festival and never wore jackets, since the temperature usually hovered around ninety degrees. I always dressed up a bit more than the guys because I was the youngest in the festival and the lone woman. For my set with Joe, I chose a lightweight white linen jacket with matching cropped pants, a little blue tank and some sexy strappy heels, elegant and understated. Or so I thought. Joe wore a tux. I was stunned.

He played a few solo tunes before our duet; in between he told jokes to the primarily French-speaking crowd, who had no idea what he was saying.

He must be roasting in that tux. It's like he's stepped out of a 1940s movie. Oh, man, now he's talking about his time in Vegas with Frank.

Joe played great, but it was as if he'd been in a time capsule and didn't know that things had changed while he was with those racehorses in Santa Barbara. He finished his set and stepped off to bring me back onstage for our duets.

"*Wait!* You can't wear *that!*" he gasped, eyeing me with horror.

"What are you talking about? We're about to go on. This is what I'm wearing."

"But I'm wearing a tux! Why didn't you dress appropriately?"

"Are you kidding? It's a hundred degrees. None of the guys are even wearing jackets."

"Joe and Judy! It's time to walk out. *Now!*"

"I'm not going out there with you looking like this. I even brought flowers to give you! See? Here they are. I can't give flowers to you dressed like that!"

I grabbed the flowers from him and pushed him onstage.

"I'll give *you* the flowers!" I called to him as he stumbled toward the piano.

He turned to the audience and awkwardly smiled. I followed, waving at the crowd and greeting everyone in French. I turned to Joe and gave him the bouquet.

"Ya got balls, sister," he hissed, as we sat side by side at the Steinway.

"Yes, and I'm told I 'play like a man.' Let's see."

Fortunately, I'd had some experience in navigating the temperaments of difficult men. One of them was cornetist Warren Vaché, another musician famous for great playing and questionable behavior. When I had first started gigging in New York, my original trio consisted of Warren and guitarist Howard Alden. I'd known Howard since our teens, when he used to sit in with me at the Tale of the Whale at the Balboa Pavilion in Newport Beach.

Howard had moved to Manhattan shortly before I did. One night he brought Warren to Hanratty's to hear me and sit in. We played well together, so I immediately asked Warren to join us on a record that Howard and I were recording the next week with Red Callender.

Warren was good to me in the beginning, even warning me not to hire him too much. "Judy, you're the only person left in the business that I haven't offended. Just hire me for special gigs now and then, and we'll see if we can keep it that way."

I followed his advice. He then surprised me by calling me for one of his concerts.

"Warren, you don't want me as a sideman. I'm a terrible sideman."

"Ah, come on. You'll be fine."

"I don't know your tunes. You should get someone else. Seriously, I'm not being humble. I'm bad at this."

"Make a list of your tunes and we'll play those. I like everything you play."

"Are you sure?"

"Yes. Come on. It'll be fun. I want you on this gig."

It was an outdoor concert in New Jersey with Howard on guitar along with a friendly bass player. We walked onstage and I handed Warren my song list, which he perused intently.

"Yup, I love all these tunes," he said. He then crumpled my list and threw it aside, adding, "We're not going to play any of those."

He called the first tune and we were off. I was lost. I turned to Howard.

"Howard! Tell me the changes."

"Nah, you can do it."

I stumbled along in a panic.

Why did I say yes to this gig?

Eventually the audience started calling out songs I was known for.

"Judy! Play 'Honeysuckle Rose!' Play 'Carolina Shout!'"

That saved me for a minute, but it was Warren's gig. I wasn't there to steal the show.

It was a disaster. Humiliating. The bass player, seeing my agony, turned to me between songs and said, "You know what we're going to do? We're going to play for an hour, then go home."

He's right. It's only an hour, not the end of the world. But wait! I want every hour to be good. Why am I trying to be a sideman? I hate being a sideman.

Dave Frishberg wrote a delightful tune called "I Want to Be a Sideman."

In my case, not so much.

9

You're Smart, You're Talented, You're Pretty

The months that followed my Hanratty's debut and the release of *Two-Handed Stride* were heady. The album had received glowing reviews from *Downbeat*, the most important jazz magazine of the time; and from many other periodicals, including *People*. In the midst of all this, my father died.

I had fought a profound sadness and sense of isolation most of my life by focusing on accomplishing things. My drive and energy enabled me to keep up an almost nonstop work schedule, which left me little time to contemplate how lacking I was in emotional support and how inconsistent, sad, and irrational my family life had always been. My father had been drifting away for years into alcoholism and depression. The realization of that was horrible in itself, but his death was something else altogether. He was the one who was demonstrably sick, but also the best of the bunch, kind, generous, empathetic, and loving. I could no longer deny how alone and hopeless I felt. My career was soaring, yet nothing had meaning for me.

I soldiered on with gigs for the next two years, surviving by force of will. A therapist I'd seen in my early twenties had retired, so the time between Dad's death and my move to New York two years later, at which time I finally found another therapist, was emotionally fraught. Most people bought the cheerful mien I presented; I tried to believe it myself. Yet long crying jags would come on at unexpected times. I even considered suicide. My new analyst, George, asked me why.

"I don't know, George. Doesn't everybody think about suicide?"

"No."

"I do remember telling Mom it was a viable option."

"What did she say?"

"She said, 'Viable means: surviving or living successfully.' She always made sure I used language well."

"Rather than dealing with what you were actually saying?"

"Yes."

"How did you respond?"

"I said I *had* chosen my words well. That suicide was a viable option for someone who believed in reincarnation. I think I was being passive-aggressive because I was so angry about it all, that everyone knew Dad was an alcoholic except me, and that I perceived her as abandoning him after he'd stuck with her through her various illnesses."

"You said you came close to killing yourself. Tell me what happened."

"I was in Manhattan on New Year's Eve. I'd just watched a wonderful concert of the New York Philharmonic on *Live from Lincoln Center*. I'd fixed a steak, had a good bottle of wine. It felt great to listen to someone else's music and not be working on New Year's Eve for once. The violinist Shlomo Mintz was featured, with segments of conversation interspersed with his performance. He talked about music, inspiration, and beauty. I was tremendously moved and felt peaceful and sad.

"I was staying in a friend's apartment in the city I love, with the career I wanted. I realized I had everything I desired, except the ability to surround myself with good people. I knew it was something lacking in me that caused this. Most of the people I knew were self-centered and uncaring. I had everything, but it meant nothing if these were the people who would be in my life.

"I felt I had to pretend to be happy all the time, take care of everybody. I couldn't imagine how to change that. I was certain no one would miss me. It was sad thinking about killing myself but it was mostly just a relief to imagine having it over. I was tired of performing, never being honest. My father had died shortly before this and nothing seemed to have meaning."

"Why didn't you do it?"

"I was sitting in the middle of the floor after listening to Shlomo Mintz. I was meditating, doing deep breathing exercises with my eyes closed, planning how I'd get some sleeping pills and where I could kill myself so no one who knew me personally would find me. I was trying hard to think if anyone would miss me because I didn't want to hurt anyone. I couldn't think of one person who would.

"I went deep into the meditation, with tears running down my face. Suddenly I heard a voice say: 'You're smart, you're talented, you're pretty. You've been given everything. You don't get to kill yourself.'

"It wasn't until much later that I realized it was the phrase Dad had said to me my entire young life: 'You're smart, you're talented, you're pretty.' It saved my life. It was a struggle but I had to fight my way back.

George broke in. "You've mentioned your vocal cords hemorrhaging when you were a teenager. Tell me about that."

"I had tonsillitis most of my childhood off and on, which got particularly bad in high school. By the end of every school year I was sick as a dog. I was never healthy enough to get them out, because I was too busy with school activities, or caring for my mother, to get enough sleep and take care of myself. By my senior year, I had two beauty titles with lots of events I had to attend, plus clubs I was running. It was ridiculous.

"I'd always had voice trouble, and finally it gave out completely when I was seventeen. I couldn't make a sound for three days. I had to be severely sick before Mom would take me to the doctor and no sound coming out of my mouth got her attention."

"Mrs. Hohenstein, this child is seriously ill. Her tonsils are infected, she has a fever, and her vo-cal cords have hemorrhaged. You said she hasn't been able to speak for three days. Why haven't you brought her in sooner?"

"I don't know, doctor. She didn't seem that sick. And please call me Jeanne."

Mom smiled coquettishly. Flirting with my doctor, Mom? Really?

"I'm sorry this has happened to you, Judy. Try not to speak for a couple of weeks. I'm going to give you some medicine and my phone number. Call me directly if you don't start feeling better in the next few days. And I want to see you next week. Please stay here a minute, Judy. Jeanne, I'd like to speak to you in my office."

"Judy?"

"Sorry, George, I was thinking back to when I found out about my vocal cords. Where were we?"

"Your mother was so focused on her own needs that she ignored yours. How about your father?"

"My father was always lovable, although he became progressively forgetful and distant after I was in elementary school. Every time I said something about this to Mom or Bob they said it was my imagination. I thought I was going crazy.

"Dad was getting fat; his eyes were often red and watery, although I never saw him drink. I was so intent on winning things, getting good grades and keeping the house going, it took up all my time and focus. I didn't know what an alcoholic looked like; I just knew Dad looked worse."

"Did you mention anything to your dad about your being sick?"

"Periodically. Mainly, I was so angry with my mother that I tried to talk to him about her, not me. He'd say, 'There are things you don't understand,' which made me furious. No one was honest with me. I felt that Mom, Dad, and Bob knew things they kept from me. I was right.

"One evening, during my senior year in high school—I could barely talk because of my vocal cords—everything seemed to overwhelm me. I'd finished serving dinner, done the dishes and retreated to my room. I wanted to sob and let go for once.

"I was surprised to find my dad sitting on the edge of my bed with his head down when I walked in. I was filled with love and relief that he was there, thinking that he would hold me and let me cry—that someone would take care of *me*.

'Dad?'

"He looked up and had tears running down his face and the strange forced smile he used to have when he'd spank me as a child. Whenever my mother would get angry with Bob or me when we were kids, she'd send us to our rooms and say Dad was going to spank us when he got home from work. We'd sit there anticipating this punishment for hours. It was horrible. Dad would come home in a good mood and the first thing my mother would say was, 'You have to spank the children.' He would walk in, take off his belt, and start in. He always had a strained look that I interpreted as a smile, which made it all the more confusing. Looking at him now, sitting on my bed, I realized he'd been holding back tears all those times he'd hit me as a child. I sat down next to him and held him as he cried.

"He finally spoke. 'I just want you to be happy. I'm a failure, your brother parties and gets lousy grades, and your mother's a hopeless neurotic. Everything depends on you, Judy. I want you to be happy.' It was a plea.

"I felt something die inside. I decided I'd never cry again. I'd never let anyone know what I was thinking or feeling. I'd decided I'd always pretend to be happy no matter what. I told Dad everything would be fine, that I was happy and always would be happy.

"I thought I could keep it up, and did for a while. In my sophomore year of college, however, I started to lose it. I'd taken a full load my freshman year and went right into the hospital for a tonsillectomy the following summer, which was major surgery at seventeen. I was in the hospital for three days. I got out and immediately started six weeks of summer school, followed by another hospital stay for my first vocal cord surgery. I got through the first semester of my sophomore year, then, during my second, I started losing track of where I was. One day I answered a question in German in my French class and didn't notice I was in the wrong language. Later, I did the same thing with my German professor—spoke French, instead of German.

"I'd suddenly start crying for no apparent reason or find myself somewhere and not know how I'd gotten there. I remember one day, when I was sitting under a tree, in the beautiful common area, I got a lovely, floating feeling. I stopped trying to make sense of things. I knew I was losing my mind. In a strange way, it felt wonderful. It was a relief to stop trying to think clearly."

"What kept you from giving in to that completely?"

"Somehow I knew that if I did, I might not be able to come back.

"One day I came home and Mom, Dad and Bob were in the living room, waiting for me. They'd obviously been talking about me. They told me I should drop out of school because I wasn't well, which devastated me. At this late date they were focusing on me, which angered me. Why now? I couldn't imagine quitting. I was distraught. I was the person who won things, got straight A's. I'm not a quitter."

"Who finally convinced you to do it?"

"Bob said, 'Who gets to drop out of college with straight A's?' That appealed to my ego, I guess. I felt tremendous pressure from all fronts and was falling apart physically as well. I dropped one class at a time, which was more expensive, but I just couldn't imagine quitting anything, so I couldn't do it all at once. It was profoundly painful. I felt like a failure."

"I thought you went back to school."

"Yes, but that was later."

"Is there another time you can remember making a conscious decision that no one would protect or take care of you?"

"Yes. We used to visit the grandparents in Illinois and one of us would stay with Dad at his parents and one with Mom at hers. Mom's folks had a much nicer house—bright and sunny, with air conditioning, which Bob and I especially appreciated, since the Illinois humidity in August bothered us; we were used to dry L.A. weather. It was particularly difficult for me since I had severe, allergy-induced headaches, which were like a mini-migraine. I needed that AC.

"Bob would always dib to stay at Mom's, while I would feel sorry for my dad and volunteer to stay with him, even though I knew I'd get the headaches. I was also afraid of my paternal grandfather. Once, when I was around ten, he asked me to sit on his lap. My skirt bunched up when I sat down. When I smoothed it back in place, he quickly pulled it back up my leg and put his hand on my thigh, rubbing it and said, 'I'm your grandfather! If I want to feel your leg, I will!' It was creepy and frightening. I didn't tell anyone about it but I did tell my dad from then on that I never wanted to be there alone."

"Did your dad honor that request?"

"No. After I played 'Maple Leaf Rag' for my grandfather—he'd said he'd give fifty dollars to the first of his grandkids to learn it—he begrudgingly gave me the money, but it was obvious that he wasn't happy about it and told me not to bother learning 'Cannonball Rag', another song he said he'd pay me to learn. He took me to get a soda and told me to tell his friend behind the counter what he'd done for me. It was about his largesse not my accomplishment.

"I said, 'Grandpa said he'd give fifty dollars to the first of his grandchildren to learn 'Maple Leaf Rag' and I was the one who learned it. He offered a hundred dollars for 'Cannonball Rag,' but after he heard me play 'Maple Leaf,' he told me not to bother learning it because he won't give me the hundred dollars, even if I do.'

"Grandpa was furious. He threw money on the counter, pulled me off the stool, and dragged me out the door. We drove home in silence. Once there, he locked me in the bedroom, cornered my grandmother and told her I was never to be allowed in the house again. I was scared and confused. I cried myself to sleep, praying to God to let me die. I was angry Dad had left me there alone and felt abandoned by everyone. He had promised he'd be there when Grandpa and I returned from getting a soda but wasn't. I assume he was out drinking. I woke in the morning to find Dad next to me, passed out."

"How did you get through the time after your dad's death? You said you had concerts to play."

"Yes, a week at a club and a TV show. I knew everyone expected me to be cheerful, so I told the three friends I saw during that time that my dad had died and I couldn't talk about it further. I knew they'd know something was up but also knew if I talked about it I wouldn't make it through my gigs.

"After I left college, dad's drinking was more in the open. I was twenty-two the first time he and I discussed it. I asked him directly how long he'd been an alcoholic and without hesitation he said twenty-four years. He'd been an alcoholic my entire life.

"It got worse through my twenties. My career was taking off, and Dad would show up at gigs looking like the homeless person he was becoming. I loved him so much that I couldn't see him clearly. I'm touched that none of the clubs I worked for threw him out.

"One time, he came to Disneyland and brought me a case of Good 'n Plenty candies. I'd loved them as a kid, so in his addled state he thought it appropriate to bring a case of them to me at work. I was in the middle of a set, surrounded by people when he presented them to me. It was bizarre and embarrassing. He wanted to let me know that he remembered something special about me.

"He came another time and I lost track of him until one of my friends came to the piano and said, 'Judy, your dad is asleep in Frontierland.' He'd passed out and I had to go find him.

"The last time I saw him, I went to his apartment and he was delusional, talking about all the money he was going to invest and make. This person I'd looked up to, whom I'd seen command an audience, be funny and bright—was going on about investing and getting rich when he hadn't shaved or bathed in days and was living in a small, dark, unkempt apartment."

—– —–

I was staying with my friend Sharon, who lived around the corner from Hanratty's and would sublet her apartment to me when I was in town. It was three months after my New York debut at the club. I was back in town for another appearance there and had just come home. Sharon had waited up since it was my last night and we were going to celebrate.

"Sharon, I'm feeling like I should call my mom."

"It's after eleven-thirty p.m. in California. Will she still be up?"

"I just have a feeling I should call."

"Hello?" said a voice I didn't recognize.

"Hi, it's Judy Carmichael. Do I have the right number?"

"Oh, Judy. It's your mom's friend Alice."

"What are you doing there so late? Is Mom OK?"

"Judy, it's your dad. Let me put your mom on."

Mom was sobbing.

"Judy ... your father is dead."

I dropped the phone. Sharon grabbed it and turned to me. "What's wrong?"

"My father died. Oh, God!"

"Oh, honey. I'm so sorry. Here, take the phone."

"Mom. *Mom*! Stop blubbering. What happened?"

"*He shot himself.*"

I couldn't breathe and started gasping for air as I sank to the floor with the phone in my hand. But my mother's hysterics sobered me.

"Mom, *stop it*! You left him two years ago. He's my father! For once let this be about someone besides you! Tell me what happened."

I could hear her breathing more slowly.

"The police found him this morning. He'd shot himself through the head. I don't know where he got the gun. He'd lost his apartment and was homeless, so he got a motel room, I guess."

Dad is dead.

I returned to my mother. "I can't believe you waited this long and didn't call me. When were you going to tell me? And for God's sake, why didn't you tell me he was homeless?"

"We thought it might be better not to. You're so busy, and your career is going so well. You hardly ever come to California anymore so we didn't want to bother you. Finally, Bob said we had to tell you."

I didn't cry for a long time after that. I got home and no one talked about it. No funeral, nothing. I didn't want to hear anything out of my mother, and I think Bob felt so guilty, he didn't say much either. I went to see my then-boyfriend, a guitarist who was gearing up for a trip to Japan. We talked while he packed.

"John, something terrible has happened," I started in, speaking to his back as he shoved clothes into his suitcase.

He didn't turn around. "What did you say?" he said over his shoulder.

"My dad died."

"Oh, I'm sorry."

He continued looking around for what he might need for the trip, obviously distracted. I started crying.

"It's worse that just dying. He killed himself."

He turned around, a bit irritated and focused on me.

"Judy, I'm getting ready for a big tour. I can't deal with this now."

Don't tell anyone. People want you to be happy.

A few days later I saw my vocal cord therapist. I talked about my gigs, told her I'd split up with my boyfriend, and said my voice was doing well.

"Actually, your voice sounds a little rough. Anything else?"

"While I was in New York my father killed himself."

"What?"

"I'm OK. We don't need to talk about it. I'm fine."

"Judy, listen to me. We're going to talk about this."

"Really. I'm OK."

"I don't buy it. I feel like you have in your calendar: Monday: practice. Tuesday: concert. Wednesday: grieve for my father. This isn't how it works. We need to talk about it. Now, tell me about your father."

"You know what bothers me the most? Between my parents, he was the good one."

10

Your Family Is So Much Fun

A recurring thought haunted me throughout my childhood: *I'm not the kind of person people take care of*—as if there were something inherently wrong with me that precluded nurturing from others. I used this as an excuse to explain my sense of isolation. As I got older, this belief bolstered me as I soldiered on, thinking: I don't *need* anyone to take care of me.

I remember swimming with my brother in a motel pool on vacation when I was about three. My folks were watching us while they sunbathed. I got tired and just didn't care to try and stay afloat. I let myself sink, even though I knew no one would save me. Perhaps I hoped someone would, but I don't remember thinking that.

Everyone was lounging around the pool, drinking their cocktails, and chatting. Bob and I were the only kids swimming. My brother tried to help when he saw me sinking, but Dad jumped in and grabbed me, pushing Bob aside. I remember being surprised that someone would save me.

After I had graduated from high school, Mom's many physical and mental issues, and my being the main caretaker and homemaker whenever she was in the hospital, were taking a toll. I had been sick with tonsillitis throughout my school years, but had never been healthy enough to have them taken out. I pushed on because I was busy and because the main focus was always on my mother. My father was progressively less emotionally accessible, and less the talented, engaged, interesting father I'd loved in elementary school. I never saw him drink but his eyes were usually red and watery and his focus wavered.

"Dad, you don't seem to be listening," I'd say with frustration.

"Of course, I'm listening!" he'd respond angrily. This was the man who had previously never raised his voice to me.

I repeatedly asked Mom and Bob if they'd noticed a change in Dad. They both said it was my imagination.

After high-school graduation I got a summer job at the telephone company. I hated it. I felt guilty complaining though, because it was a sought after position that paid well and my father had gotten me the position. I'd witnessed his recent bitterness over his working there and didn't want to fan the fire. I once asked him why he didn't quit and he responded, "And admit I've been wrong for thirty years?" My mother whined constantly but my father's complaining was something new. It started when I was in my early teens, and it was terribly sad and confusing.

Near the end of my three months in this position, I pulled out of the parking lot at the end of the day in my VW Bug, heading home. Into a left turn, I was broadsided by a speeding truck. I saw it coming, knew I was going to die, and didn't care. I rolled slowly across two lanes of traffic, trying to see around a much larger truck, which was blocking my view. The driver in the larger truck waved me into the turn as the truck behind him made an end run around him, accelerating and smashing into me. I saw the truck barreling toward me, heard a scream and instinctively turned away, crossing my arms over my face as it slammed into the driver's side of my Bug. I wasn't wearing my seatbelt, so the impact threw me over to the passenger side door. The entire driver's side collapsed. If I'd worn my seatbelt, I would have been crushed. When I came to, I realized the scream was mine and that I wasn't dead.

— —

I've worked hard over the years to change my belief that no one would take care of me. In my early twenties, while my father was seriously deteriorating, I got to know my father's older brother Ed and his family, who lived in Springfield, Illinois. They were loving and kind and didn't pretend everything was perfect, like my family did. It was a revelation.

In my family, no one admitted my father drank. I was twenty-two when it finally sank in, and I confronted him about it. He looked terrible and sometimes smelled of alcohol, so his condition could no longer be denied.

This same year, my parents planned a visit to Springfield to see their parents. I decided to surprise them by also making the trip. Mom left a few days before Dad. Bob and I drove Dad to the airport, and I suggested that I walk to the gate with him while Bob waited in the car. I accompanied Dad onto the plane, which you could do back then. When he said I should leave since they'd be taking off soon, I surprised him by buckling up and telling him I was going with him.

One afternoon during our visit, my Uncle Ed took Dad and me out for a round of golf at a local public course. I played well for a beginner but wasn't great, and my dad grew impatient with my game, which grew worse the more irritated he became. I grew up with a father who was endlessly kind and encouraging. It was painful to experience this new behavior. At one point Ed pulled me aside and whispered, "Is your play going downhill because your father seems frustrated with you?"

"Yes," I answered, surprised at his directness.

"Fuck him."

I was stunned.

"I can say that because I'm his big brother. Listen, I'd like you to visit us without your parents some time. Call me and I'll send you the money for the flight. In a month, in a year, whenever you like."

Ed and his wife Kathy talked frankly about their joys and problems. They were the opposite of my family, who let their troubles boil away underneath a perfect facade. Ed and Kathy's kids told me they always wondered why Bob and I seemed like "little robots" when we visited as children. "We didn't want to play with you and get you dirty," remarked my cousin, Kathy Jo.

My first visit to Ed was difficult, but cathartic. I often felt physically uncomfortable, constricted in some way like I was suffocating. I cried a lot after I went to bed and had terrible nightmares. I owe a lot to my uncle, who set me on a much healthier path by talking directly about my father, his depression, and their shared past with a cruel father.

When I was in elementary school, I had two dreams that epitomized how starved I was emotionally. In the first, which was in black and white, I was sitting alone in a huge school cafeteria at a long, stainless steel table with no food on it and no one else in the room. I woke up sobbing. I was probably eight at the time. In the other, I was running from some sort of danger and finally made it home. I rushed into my parents' room, yelling for them to save me, and saw them in bed with the covers over them like corpses. I threw back the blankets and saw, to my horror, that both of them were robots. I awoke from that one screaming.

The painter Carol Anthony, whom I met shortly after my father's death in 1983, was an important source of strength and inspiration. I hadn't yet bought my condo near Columbia University and moved to Manhattan full-time. I still had my house in Costa Mesa, CA and a small sublet on East 92nd Street and split my time between the two. Carol often invited me to stay with her for a few days after I'd finished a run in New York. She had a beautiful old farmhouse in Connecticut that was warm and inviting, the opposite of how I viewed my life in California.

On one of my visits, I pointed out a drawing of hers that I loved, called "The New Tie." It showed an eccentric-looking man in a brightly colored tie. The next morning I came down for breakfast to find a miniature of it propped up on her kitchen table. She had painted it for me after I'd gone to bed the night before. It was flanked by flowers and accompanied by a note saying that she'd gone for a walk, but would be back soon to make breakfast. I was touched by this gift, but at the same time felt a familiar feeling of suffocation.

Carol came back from her walk, hugged me, and started making breakfast. I sat at the table staring at the painting and listening to the Mozart concerto she'd put on. I thanked her for my gift but couldn't say much else. I was tremendously sad when I should have been happy. Nurturing overwhelmed me.

When Carol set a steaming mug of cocoa in front of me, I started crying and gasping for air. Between sobs, I managed to choke out, "I can't have you be this nice to me."

She turned from her cooking and looked at me.

"Well, then, I guess we can't be friends," she replied casually, "because a huge part of who I am is about mothering people." She turned back to the stove and continued making breakfast.

I realize now that she had made the perfect move by not participating in my neurotic behavior. I stopped crying and pulled myself together. I told her I loved being mothered. We never discussed the episode again.

— ~

Shortly after this conversation with Carol, I played golf with an analyst friend of hers named Jonathan. Carol was always introducing me to interesting characters, since I knew so few people in New York. Jonathan and I had only met about a month before, so it surprised me when, in the middle of our game, he said, "Judy, I think you made a decision when you were very young, possibly as early as six months old, that no one would ever take care of you." Even coming from a professional, this was an extraordinary comment. I knew he was right, though, so I decided to call my mother and see if she would enlighten me. She got defensive easily, so I was careful.

"Hi, Mom."

"Are you still in New York?" she asked.

"Yes. How are things in sunny California?"

"Sunny, smoggy," Mom responded with a laugh. "You know."

"Mom, I watched one of those Andy Hardy movies the other night. I can't believe how much you look like Ann Rutherford."

"She looked like *me*, honey. People told me that all the time. Ann Rutherford and Maureen O'Sullivan."

"Maureen O'Sullivan was Jane in the Tarzan movies, right?"

"Yes. I like to think I'm a combo of the two."

"I like to think I'm a combination of Ursula Andress and Christie Brinkley."

"Of course you are, dear."

"I love how you lie to me, Mom."

"I think appropriate delusion can be useful. I tell people I'm older than I am so they can tell me how young I look."

"I like it. Listen, I want to ask you something. Did anything interesting happen to me or the family when I was just a few months old? I have a vague memory of someone in the family saying something happened when I was a baby."

"Not that I can think of, unless you mean my going to the sanitarium when you were six months old."

"You left when I was six months old?"

"That was one of the times."

"How long were you gone?"

"Three or four months."

"Three or four *months*?"

"Now Judy, you're always so melodramatic."

"Mom, I was a baby! Who took care of me while you were gone?"

"You know, I can't remember. Wait. I do remember that when I was in the hospital with cervical cancer—you were two then—we sent you to Bob's preschool, so that's where you were during the day. Your dad took care of you at night. We didn't know many people in California yet. We hadn't lived there long. Aunt Pat and Aunt Alice both worked, so they were busy during the day."

Pat and Alice were mom's best friends. She'd met them years earlier in group therapy when she and Dad had first moved to California in their early twenties. Pat and Alice were a few years older than my folks. Bob and I referred to them as our aunts.

"So you were gone for a while when I was two as well?"

"Yes, when I had cancer. And then I went back to the sanitarium for the shock treatments. I really can't remember it all. I'm still pretty angry about those shock treatments."

A few days later, I called Aunt Pat.

"Judy? This is a wonderful surprise! It's so good to hear your voice. It's been ages."

"I have to tell you, I still smile thinking about the few times Mom let me spend the night with you and you'd let me walk Tiger. Tiger the Weiner Dog, Bob and I called him. Those excursions were big to me."

"I wish your mom would have let you come over more often. I loved your visits."

"Pat, I want to ask you something. Can you tell me about Mom going into the sanitarium when I was six months old?"

"I can't believe you remember that."

"I don't. I'm hoping you can fill me in a bit."

"I still feel bad about that time. I don't think Alice and I--or anyone for that matter-- protected you and Bob enough from your mother. We talked about it with your dad. We finally had her committed because her rage was so intense."

"I didn't know that."

"She was hitting Bob, who was only two at the time. We were afraid if she hit you, she'd kill you. We didn't think it was safe to leave a baby with her. I feel guilty about this whole period. Alice can't even talk about it."

"I guess it's hard to intrude on someone else's family. And Dad was so passive."

"Yes. But it's no excuse. We didn't realize how bad it was. I regret it all. We should have intervened sooner and we didn't."

During the golf game with Jonathan, he commented that my father's recent death was bothering me more than I'd realized, and asked if I'd be open to therapy. I had been in therapy with an excellent psychologist in California. I hadn't found anyone I liked in New York, but I jumped at Jonathan's suggestion of someone he knew, which is how I started in with George. I was in terrible shape when we first met. My sobbing would bring sessions to a halt until he calmly told me I had to stop or we couldn't continue. I stopped sobbing and gently cried instead, through most of my sessions for the first year I was with him.

— ⁓

Two years later, I was still seeing George. One day during a session he asked, "What's going on, Judy?" He sensed my distraction.

"I feel a little odd. Louie's in town and wants to have lunch. It's bringing up all kinds of feelings."

"Who's Louie?"

"The guy who lived with us my senior year in high school."

George looked at me with surprise. "You've never mentioned him in all the time I've seen you. Do you have an extra brother or sister I don't know about? A husband?"

I sighed. "I think so many things happened during my senior year that only through our sessions together have I remembered a lot of them. I realize now that a lot of the things I thought happened over the three years I was in high school actually happened in the nine months of my senior year. It wasn't a good time."

"Tell me about Louie."

— ⁓

Louie and I were seniors together. I can't remember exactly how we got to know each other, but like so many of my friends, he became smitten with my family—my handsome, dashing brother; my pretty, listen-to-everyone's-problems-mother; my amusing, talented father. Louie was tall, dark, and good-looking but a bit shy. My family brought him out. "Your family seems so much more normal than everyone else's," Louie said with admiration.

People said this to me constantly, making me feel even more isolated than I already felt. I often came home from school to find an ex-boyfriend sitting in deep conversation with my mother while she stared intently into his eyes, nodding sympathetically.

"Mom, I split up with Dwight over a year ago," I'd say after the boy left. "I don't want to see him again. Please don't ask him over."

"But he's so sweet, Judy, and still likes you. I can't just turn him out when he asks to come over."

"Why not?"

I looked at my mom sitting in her red potato-chip chair, her feet resting on the multi-colored shag carpet. I always wanted cozy, overstuffed furniture and neutral colors, anything to make me feel warm and comforted; but Mom was a hipster, with her Eames-inspired ideas about design.

"Why not throw him out? I break up with somebody, and the next thing I know, they're in my living room with my mother. It's weird, Mom."

When I was in elementary school my mother often asked, "Aren't you proud that your mother is prettier than all the other mothers?" I hadn't noticed, but I had observed that she was less mothering than the others.

Louie and I had gone out on a few dates; the next thing I knew, my mother had asked him to move in, and he did.

"Your family is so interesting and funny, Judy. You're so lucky."

"Everything isn't exactly as it seems, Louie. My mom has some issues and I think my dad's depressed."

"Yeah, well, my mom used to be a prostitute and my father's in jail."

That brought me up short. I thought I had it bad, but Louie's situation was so beyond my comprehension I was speechless. There were Mexican gang members at our school, but if Louie came from that, he certainly hid it well. I'd met his mom, and she was attractive and always well-dressed; in fact she looked like a Hispanic version of my mother, so

I'm still not sure if he was telling the truth or just looking for an excuse to move in with my family. His mom was happy with the idea, too, and shared Louie's high opinion of us. I suspected we were being played. There were no demonstrably dangerous neighborhoods in Pico Rivera when I lived there, even though there were dangerous people, but Louie didn't look like one of them, nor did his mother.

Louie bought a Corvette like my brother's, started wearing beautifully tailored suits, called my parents Mom and Dad, and wanted to marry me. Our house was small, so having another person around was unwelcome to everyone except my mother, who was thrilled to have someone nearby whose family was even more troubled than ours.

My brother remained in touch with Louie after high school; they socialized often with their wives, Louie's looking creepily similar to my brother's. I hadn't heard from Louie in years when, out of the blue, he called. He said he'd be in New York, and wanted to get together.

We met for lunch at the Plaza. Louie and I sat at a corner table as a string quartet played softly nearby. I looked across at him, sharp in a bespoke suit as he ordered an expensive bottle of wine.

"You look great," Louie said. "I like your hair curly. Is that natural? I don't remember it being like that in high school."

"I used to comb out the curl. You look good too. Even more handsome, I must say. How are you, Louie?"

"I still haven't recovered from your dad's death, to be honest. I can't believe no one called to tell me. We haven't stayed in touch, so I understand your not calling, but no one from California called to tell me, not even Bob."

"They weren't going to tell me either. I just happened to get a sense something was wrong, so I called my mom late after I'd finished the last night of a weeklong gig here. Alice was over and answered the phone. I knew something wasn't right because it was almost midnight out west and Mom wouldn't have had anyone over that late. Alice put Mom on the phone, and she told me Dad had died and that they weren't going to tell me."

"That's incredible. What did you say?"

"Well, between sobs, I choked out, 'Don't you think I would have noticed he was *gone*?' Mom just wailed on. It was all about her and it made me furious. I couldn't come home for a week because of work commitments, which was a blessing because I was afraid of what I'd do to her. It took a while to get the truth out of her, but she finally admitted he'd shot himself."

"I've started to look at your mom more realistically now," Louie said. "She is a little crazy, but you and she were always so funny together. I loved how you tossed puns back and forth and finished each other's sentences."

"She's my best audience, you're right. I always seem to be funnier around her. She's so clever and bright, and I think I'm great at understanding different types of people because I grew up interpreting her to myself and everyone else. And as odd as it sounds, I've grown to appreciate her looking pulled together and cheerful when she wasn't angry and screaming. Remember those times in the hospital? Somehow she managed to look great and upbeat.

"It was only in later years, when I'd introduce her to someone, that I realized how irrational she was. One friend actually said, 'Your mom is great but she's a teeny bit insane, right?'

"A few years ago I was having a conversation with her and suddenly saw her differently. I told her, 'You know, you were a great mother, except for your narcissism, neuroses, and irrational behavior.' She laughed and said, 'Yeah, I think you're right.' I mean, that's a special person who can take a statement like that. And yet, when I was twenty-one, had my own place, and all the pain was hitting me, I wrote her a long, harsh letter about everything as I saw it, how angry I was, how she'd failed me. When I talked to her after she'd read it, she cheerfully thanked me for writing and went on to something else. I was stunned. If she'd been hurt, furious, defensive, I would have understood, because those were all legitimate reactions. Instead, she was cheerful and thanked me for writing. I was devastated, realizing how seriously emotionally detached she was."

"Judy, I loved your dad so much, and still love your mom."

"You know," I continued, "one of the hardest moments for me was a year after Dad died. I ran into one of his distant cousins who lived in California and he asked how Mom and Dad were. I had to tell him Dad was dead. It was awful. I couldn't believe Mom hadn't called him. He was devastated, of course. And interestingly, when I said, 'Well, you know Dad was an alcoholic, right?' Dad's cousin said, 'Actually, no, I didn't. I always figured your mother for an alcoholic.'"

"Seriously?"

"Louie, we obviously missed a lot."

11

Don't Tell Mom . . .

As I write this, I'm looking out at Pitcairn Island in the South Pacific, where the descendants of the Bounty mutineers still live—a place I never thought I'd see, even though I've always been an optimist and figured I'd eventually get to every place I wanted to visit. It only took me until 2014 to do it. I saw both film versions of *Mutiny on the Bounty* as a kid and discussed them at length with my father, so if he were alive he'd be especially pleased to know I'm here.

He was an idea man and stimulated my interest in everything. He was a flyer and navigator in the Navy, stationed in the Aleutians during the war when he was nineteen. As a child, I wanted to hear about the battles he'd been through but he said the main danger was landing a plane with huge snow-covered mountains on three sides, the ocean on the other, and fog everywhere. I didn't find out there was fighting in the Aleutians until I visited as an adult.

Dad taught me the names of the constellations and once I had become a jazz musician, enduring long drives home after my gigs, I'd call and wake him to point out something interesting in the two a.m. sky. I once asked if he'd ever seen the man on the moon angled on his side, which I'd glimpsed a number of times after a late gig. He didn't think he had. One night, while driving along the ocean from Newport Beach to where I lived in San Pedro, I saw it and called him.

"Hi, Dad."

"Hi, honey," he said, sounding a bit groggy.

"Wake up and look out the window."

"Is that the ocean I hear?"

"Yes. I'm using a phone near the Huntington Beach pier."

I could hear his footsteps heading to the window.

"I'll be damned."

"I knew you'd want to see this. Goodnight."

"Drive safely. I love you."

Dad also told me about Easter Island, where I'll be in a couple of days. I keep thinking how pleased he'd be to know I'm living so many of his fantasies. Mom could talk ideas, but much of the time her fears brought her focus inward and made her behavior bizarre, frightening, or irritating, so she was less fun to be around. She was also impatient with children.

When I was a child I asked her if she liked children.

"I hate kids. But I like *my* kids."

"Why did you have us, then?"

"So there would be someone to take care of me in my old age. That's why everyone has children."

— ⁓

Dad's focus didn't start fading away until I was around eleven, and even then he'd come back for lovely moments, like our conversation about the moon. Still, I missed the more engaged connection we'd had when I was a kid.

"Dad, your eyes are bloodshot. Do you feel OK?"

"I'm fine, sweetie, just tired."

"Are you paying attention? You don't seem engaged."

"Sure, sure … what were we talking about?"

On some level I knew I was losing my dad bit by bit every day, but I didn't know why. It never occurred to me that it was alcohol because I had never seen him drink; he didn't have bizarre mood swings, just a steady, sad fading away. What bothered me more consciously was that he never stood up to my mother. The only time he made a decision was when he and I would go off somewhere together without Bob or Mom. "Let's take a drive and see if we can find some weather," he often suggested. He was as bored with Southern California weather as I was.

They say siblings grow up with different parents; that was certainly the case with Bob and me. Bob talks about Dad's beautiful clothes and how strict he was. I remember his sense of humor and stage presence. A few years ago, I mentioned this to Bob's wife, Jan.

"Of course you remember your dad's sense of humor," she said. "You're funny. Let's face it. Bob isn't funny."

"I think he's funny."

"I know, but you're the only one who does."

"He says Dad was strict."

"I think Bob wants to remember your Dad that way. I remember your Dad as a pussycat."

"Me too."

Interestingly, Bob and I both remember taking care of our mother but don't remember the other one doing it. Bob's a psychologist now, so mom was probably his first patient. I think she complained about her emotions to him and I did the grunt work—cleaning, cooking, and running the house when she was either in the hospital with periodic arthritis surgeries or "too tired" to do anything.

It was easier when she was in the hospital because I could perform my chores without the burden of pretending she was participating or trying to make her madness seem sane, which was the most enervating task of all.

Mom's arthritis surgeries were barbaric. She once had surgery on her knee, and a year later, when it wouldn't bend past a certain point because scarring had formed, they put her in the hospital for a couple of days, knocked her out, and forced the knee to bend in order to tear the scarred tissue. She woke in massive pain but with a knee that could bend properly.

Still, she loved going to the hospital. When I was a little kid, I snuck our dog in once to cheer her, but she didn't need it; there she was entertaining everyone, surrounded by nurses. She relished being the center of attention. She told her hospital stories like someone else would talk about winning the Nobel Prize. When I became ill myself later in life, I was hyper-aware that I didn't want to gain any currency from it. I saw how my mom and her friends reinforced, even enjoyed, the drama of their ailments. Mom loved the shocked response to her tales of woe, the sympathy both real and imagined.

— —

When we were little, Bob used to inflict the typical big-brother tortures, teasing me and indulging in other nonsense; it could be intense because of his own rage about our deteriorating family situation. I was the one he could abuse; it was his one small area of power, since he was two and a half years older.

His line after every ruckus was, "Don't tell Mom. You'll spoil her evening." It worked, because the minute my parents returned home from a night out, I'd start in on whatever pain I'd endured and my mother would throw her forearm across her brow and wail, "I can't even have *one* evening out without it being spoiled by you kids!" She'd leave the room in a huff. My dad would glower at Bob, but somehow it was always my fault. If I were lucky, Bob would recite the "Don't tell Mom" line, then find the Good Humor man and buy me with off with an ice cream cone. He still tortured me, but at least I didn't have to listen to my mother.

The denouement of this particular brother/sister dance happened when Bob and I decided to play "chicken" with me on my bike and Bob standing in the middle of our street. The idea was, I would ride as fast as I could and we'd see who'd move first—Bob jumping out of the way or me turning before we collided. Neither of us was chicken, so Bob grabbed my handlebars and threw the bike and me to the ground. My elbow went into the asphalt, tearing a huge gash and causing blood to spurt everywhere.

I went into shock and felt nothing, but from the look on Bob's face and the amount of blood spattered all over me I knew it was bad. Bob carried me out of the street and lay me on our lawn, ran to the garage, grabbed a rag, and pressed it to my arm. I was feeling faint.

"Don't tell Mom . . ." he started weakly.

"Bob, we have to tell Mom."

He sadly nodded and helped me up. We both knew that bad things were about to happen.

It must have been some holiday because there were other people over at our house, and it was a bit dramatic when we came in covered in blood, dripping even more on the carpet. My dad immediately turned to Bob and yelled, *"WHAT DID YOU DO TO HER?"*

I'd never seen my father so angry. All I could think of was protecting Bob.

"He didn't do anything to me. I tripped." My dad knew I was lying but this at least delayed punishment.

"I can't have *one* afternoon without something upsetting me!" my mother wailed resentfully, dragging me to the bathroom to clean me up. Bob hovered in the corner in fear.

❦

On one of my visits to California in the late '80s, when I was already living in New York, Bob and I decided to visit our old street. When we lived in Pico Rivera, there were knife fights after most sporting events and places you wouldn't visit after dark; but when Bob and I went back to visit, the old neighborhood looked even less inviting and more threatening, so we didn't stay long. Billboards were now in Spanish, something new since we'd lived there. Buildings were run down and vacant lots overgrown.

We stood together looking out at our old street—my handsome brother and his little sis. Our mom had died the year before, our father a little over three years before that. Our home had been razed; our beloved avocado trees, the tree houses, the farm, and the haunted barn were gone. I started to cry; Bob put his arm around me as we silently looked ahead. In the distance I heard the mariachi music of an ice cream truck. Bob quietly laughed.

"Don't tell Mom or you'll spoil her evening."

"I won't."

"Want an ice cream?"

"Yes, please."

12

Bye, Bye, Blues

Children of alcoholics are often assiduous observers, interpreting the deeper meaning of behavior because their parents' is so seldom straightforward. Inexplicable adult conduct leaves young souls confused and untrusting of their own understanding of events.

Mom and Dad can't be crazy. If they're crazy, who will take care of me? I must be the one who's crazy.

Just over three years after my father died, my brother Bob decided to visit me in New York, something he'd never done before.

"Bob, you realize the dates you'll be here include Mom's birthday. She'll never tolerate us both being away on her big day. She'll get sick or pull something to keep you home. Can't you come another time?"

"This is my window."

"We'll see, but something tells me this isn't going to happen."

A few weeks later there was a phone message from Bob asking me to call. I reached his wife, Jan.

"It's Mom, right?"

"They've found a spot on her right lung and think it's cancer."

"When will they know?"

"In a few days. It's very small. Even if it's cancer, it's not serious. They're optimistic."

I hung up and looked at Bill. He and I had met shortly after my father died and moved in together a few years later. He was a great source of support throughout that period.

"It's my mom. They've found possible cancer on her lung. They don't think it's serious, which I don't believe. I think she'll die, and soon."

"You should go to California."

I went a few days later and as usual, my mom was her chipper, optimistic self. Part of it was her natural perkiness and reality-avoidance; but in fairness, when she'd had cervical cancer in her twenties, they told her she'd die and she didn't.

Alice was visiting, and I had prepared lunch and was about to serve it when my brother called with the results of Mom's tests.

"I'll get it, Mom," I said. "You and Alice sit down."

Mom ignored my suggestion and followed me as I picked up the phone. "Hello."

"It's Bob. Sit down."

"Hi, Bob. I'm here with Mom and Alice."

"Is Mom looking at you? Don't react."

I know the news is bad. Just tell me.

"The cancer is everywhere, even her brain. She could die in two months or any minute with a stroke from the brain tumors."

"Great, Bob. Thanks for calling with that."

"Judy, you've got to get her to the hospital immediately to start the radiation on her brain. The growth of the tumors is profound and the pain could be severe as they grow. The radiation won't cure her, but it'll retard the growth and keep the pain at bay. Don't tell her. We'll let the doctor do that."

Don't react. Be cheerful.

"Well, Bob, Alice is here and I've just fixed something to eat. I don't think skipping lunch will make a difference one way or the other, do you? Why don't we eat, and I'll call you when we're done?"

Silence.

"Is she still standing right there staring at you?"

"Yes. So you'll take care of everything, make an appointment, and I'll call you after lunch, right?"

I hung up and looked at my mom with Alice standing next to her.

Alice knows. Don't make eye contact or she'll cry. So strange to be in the old kitchen with Mom standing there.

"Judy?"

"Sorry, Mom. I spaced out for a minute thinking about cooking in this kitchen when I was in high school. Remember the time I put Ripple in the spaghetti sauce because I'd heard people used wine when cooking? I think Bob was out with friends and bought it. I didn't know it was swill. You all loved it and asked me what the secret ingredient was."

"It tasted good! You were always a creative cook. I don't think you let on that you'd used that cheap wine. Guarding your recipe, or some excuse. How's Bob?"

"He's great."

"What did he say?"

"You've got to get more tests. No big deal. Let's have lunch and I'll call him afterwards."

Mom is dying. Soon.

That night I lay in bed listening to Mom play one of her beautiful ballads. I wept, remembering how much I loved hearing her music when I was growing up. I was in my old room experiencing the lovely embrace of her lush chords and sensitive melodies as they floated through my open door, lying in the same bed I'd sat on and held my father while he cried, claimed he was a failure, and told me everything depended on me.

"I just want you to be happy, Judy."

The next day we met Bob at the doctor's office. As usual, Mom was in a great mood as she anticipated a medical visit and a new doctor.

"Hello, Jeanne," he said soberly.

"Hi, doctor!" she answered with enthusiasm.

Bob paced back and forth. I gave him the evil eye, willing him to stand still. I sat off to the side, closer to Mom, and glanced around the sterile room.

Another hospital: stark, cold, and uninviting to everyone but Mom.

The doctor sighed and started talking, occasionally glancing at my mother's chart in his lap.

"Jeanne, I'm afraid I have some bad news. We have your results and the tests show you have cancer. It probably started in your lungs. Unfortunately, it's metastasized throughout your body. My immediate focus is your brain, where you have a number of tumors, which are growing rapidly. These could cause pain as they get larger, so I'd like to start radiation immediately to shrink them."

Mom sat straight-backed in her chair, with her hands folded in her lap, fetching and upbeat in her uniform of white jeans, freshly pressed blouse, and sandals. Sixty-one, looking fifty, acting fifteen.

"Jeanne? Did you hear me?"

"I'm sorry. I was thinking about what you said. Is there any really bad news you have to tell me?"

Bob looked at Mom incredulously, as did the doctor, who stuttered, "Jeanne, it's about as bad as it gets."

I jumped in, always ready to translate.

"Doctor, I think my mom wants to know how to proceed, what she can do to be helpful with her treatment. I think she's in excellent health— except for this issue we're addressing today, of course. She should probably continue to eat well—lots of vegetables, not too many sweets—and exercise as she's been doing. That will give good support for any treatment you deem appropriate."

Give her something to do, doctor.

Silence.

"Doctor?"

"Yes, yes. I see what you mean. Of course, Jeanne, your health— other than this—is excellent. Eat reasonably and exercise as you've been doing."

"You and Bob can discuss how we proceed."

I've got this, Bob. Mom doesn't want to fall apart in front of us, not here.

The doctor was pale and silent as I took Mom's arm and led her out of the office.

We walked out into the warm Southern California day. I put my arm in hers, hugging her close as we made our way to the car. The air was unusually clear, which made the flowers surrounding the medical center look especially beautiful, as did the ancient oaks and eucalyptus trees that shaded the parking lot. I inhaled deeply, enjoying the delicious fragrance, and felt Mom do the same.

My mother's line when she took us to the doctor when we were kids was, "If you're well-behaved, we'll go for ice cream."

"You were well-behaved, Mom. Want to go for ice cream?"

She laughed as we got into the car. But she stopped me as I started to put the key in the ignition.

"Let's sit for a minute."

Follow her lead.

"This is a cool ride, Mom. I love that new car smell. It's about time you upgraded."

"It's nice, isn't it?"

"Very. I'm envious."

"Judy ..."

"Yes?"

"I'm not going to die."

"Of course you're not going to die. But only you and I know that. We have to go through these motions on the off chance we're wrong. You know Bob will feel better if we do all this. He's the doctor in the family. Let's make him feel in charge."

"He's a doctor of *psychology*."

"Yeah, but let him play doctor, Mom. We're just musicians. What do we know?"

She sighed and tears filled her eyes. She seldom cried, so even with the cancer news, this was a surprise. She started sobbing, something I'd never seen.

"It's my fault your father killed himself, Judy."

I was stunned. After all those years of my blaming her for abandoning my father in his time of need, I was now hearing her admit her part in his sadness. For once, she was sincere. I knew she wasn't fishing.

"It wasn't your fault, Mom. Dad couldn't go on like that. He had to end his pain."

"His pain was because of me. I never let him know that being a good person was enough. I constantly made him feel like a failure, that he wasn't successful enough, that he was a disappointment to me. What made him special was that he was a good person, a kind, generous man. I should have told him."

I reached for her hand and held it as she continued to cry. I looked out the window at the California landscape—warm, golden, and inviting to so many, but stark, brittle, and withholding to me. We sat quietly for a while, thinking about my father.

The next day I took Mom to see her new oncologist to deal with her brain tumors. She was her usual radiant self. I was a wreck. I hadn't slept the night before, kept awake by thoughts of the short time we had left together and the rekindled sadness over my father. The doctor came out to greet us in the reception area. He looked at me—a worn-out thirty-three-year-old—and at my youthful, energetic mother. He turned to me, confused.

"I know, I'm the one who looks sick, but I'm not your patient, she is," I said, pointing at my mother. "I'm Judy, and this is my mother, Jeanne."

"Nice to meet you both," he said, laughing. Focusing on my mother, he continued, "Jeanne, I have to say you do look wonderful."

I sighed. "She's always been the better-looking one."

"Come with me and we'll discuss your treatment."

I spent the next six weeks traveling to California to care for my mother between trips abroad for concerts. Bob and I developed a pattern in how we handled her treatment. She and I would go to the doctor when I was in town. She'd be cheerful, positive, do what was required, and never specifically discuss the cancer. The doctor would then call Bob and report the progress of the disease. Bob would call me with the news and I would present whatever was necessary to my mother. She and I maintained the illusion that we were doing it all for my brother, complicit in the fantasy that she'd recover and that everyone else was wrong about where this was going.

My parents had been raised Catholic but had left the church by the time they married. Mom used to joke that the only good Catholic in her wedding party was the flower girl, her little sister, Jodi. I always felt they had baptized Bob and me, just in case.

"Mom, we know you're not going to die, but we need to get a will together, on the off chance we're wrong."

"OK. We can do that this afternoon. By the way, I want a funeral."

"What?"

This was yet another conversation in the car after a trip to the doctor. Each time was like a meeting with Watergate's Deep Throat. I'd receive shocking information in some parking lot that changed my view of everything.

"You and Dad always told us you hated funerals. You said you didn't believe in them."

She ignored this relevant point, a common move.

"I want a place people can visit me. I don't want my ashes scattered."

"But you're not going to die."

She looked at me like I was an idiot.

I can't believe I'm still surprised when she's suddenly rational.

"I'm on it, chief," I said. "A funeral. I don't know anything about funerals, though. They're for dead people, right?"

"You kill me, Judy."

"I'm not killing you, Mommy. It's the Big C."

She sighed. "You do make me laugh. I wonder why Bob isn't funny?"

"I think he's funny."

"I think you're the only one."

"Well, you make me laugh too, when you're not irritating me."

"Judy, do you remember when you were in your early teens, telling me you wanted to be the first woman comic who didn't put herself down, but rather one who could be smart and feel good about herself?"

"I do. I hated women comics talking about being fat, unsexy, single, all of it. There were sexy, smart women in the comedies in your day but somehow they often wound up being strong at the start of the film and cooking eggs for their man in the last reel. And when I was a kid it was all about, 'I'm fat, bitter, and can't get a husband,' although there were a few exceptions."

"You've reached your goal, Judy. You're smart, empowered, and funny."

"You're my model."

"Thank you. And something else I've been thinking about. I want the last thing heard at my funeral to be 'Bye, Bye Blues.' I'll record it. Get a decent sound system so it sounds good. That will be a nice touch."

Later that day, Bob called to ask how it had gone with Mom.

"Fine. You know how great she is with doctors. This one's fallen in love with her, as they always do. For a minute, he thought I was the patient instead of her."

"You don't look that bad."

"Thanks loads."

"Judy, I have to ask you something. Have you noticed how great Mom's being about all this? Not histrionic, self-indulgent, or melodramatic?"

"You mean, like she's been our whole lives?"

"Exactly."

"Now that you mention it, I've never seen her so appropriate. She's even rational a good part of the time."

"It's like she's been rehearsing this scenario her whole life and now that she really is sick, she's calm and dignified. It's amazing."

"I know. Also, she's stopped being competitive with me. It's weird. She seems to be getting less crazy. So, now that you're feeling good about everything, Bob, brace yourself. She wants a funeral."

"*What?*"

"She wants a place for people to visit her. We've got to get that together too. No scattering ashes or any of that."

"We're not having a funeral! No way. She told me she wants to be cremated."

"Sorry. She's changed her mind on that too. She insists on a funeral, so we've got to pull it together."

— —

Mom continued along in her surprising new role of concerned, practical parent.

"Judy, you can't sit around waiting for me to die. This concert in Italy is big for you, right?"

"Yes. It's a small recital for some fancy people in a palazzo in Milan, the home of Gianni Agnelli, owner of Fiat and everything else. He's been known as an international playboy, a style icon, and an all-around impressive dude. Married to a famous beauty. Remember how I met him at that intimate, insane dinner party at Pamela Harriman's in D.C.?"

"I can't believe the people you get to meet. I do remember that party. Pamela was married to Churchill's son, right?"

"That's the one."

"And then Averell Harriman? Wasn't he Governor of New York? And she married some others I can't remember."

"Good job, Mom. Your brain's still working."

"And Yoko Ono served you pigs in a blanket."

"Now you're messing with me. You know that was a different party."

"You're right. I'm teasing. But that was crazy. Did she really serve you pigs in a blanket?"

"Yes. It was a little recital at her son's apartment downtown with Joshua Bell and Richard Joo. Richard invited me. And yes, it was a bit of an out-of-body experience having Yoko Ono serve me hors d'oeuvres."

"Judy, you have to do this Agnelli recital. Go to Italy and come here afterwards with stories for me."

August 26, Mom's birthday, was shortly before the Agnelli concert. She was still at home, looked good, and seldom broke down despite her decline. All her friends were there; somehow I knew that this was probably the last time I would see her. Bob and I stood away from the others and watched her entertain everyone. Our old living room, looked exactly the way it had when we were young, with the worn beanbag chairs, faux wood paneling, shag carpet, and family photographs.

I leaned my head on Bob's shoulder and whispered to him as we viewed our mom in all her glory. "I told you she'd get sick if you told her we'd both be away for her birthday. Her dying is a bit more over the top than I anticipated, but I did call it."

"You were always good at predicting the future, Judy."

"Can you believe how great she looks? I've never seen her happier. She's going out in style."

I joined Mom in regaling the crowd with stories of family adventures. Then I gathered my things to leave and walked over to hug and say goodbye to her. She was seated like a queen in the middle of her subjects.

Lorraine, whom I'd remained friends with since our meeting in Hawaii during the Sarah Vaughan vacation, was now living in California and had come to pick me up and take me to the airport. I turned and looked back for a final farewell and saw my gorgeous Mom surrounded by friends, a baseball cap on her head and a party horn to her lips. She blew to squeaky effect, rolling out the multicolored paper toward me like a long, skinny tongue in answer to my goodbye, a reveler to the last.

Lorraine put her arm around me as we walked into the damp night air to her car. We sat quietly for a few minutes until she finally started the engine.

"You never mentioned that you were so close to your mother," she said.

"What do you mean?"

"You've always talked about your father. The connection with your mother is obvious, though. You finish each other's sentences. It's remarkable."

"Funny, I don't think about that."

"And I've been thinking about her cancer. Your mother is very powerful."

"How so?"

"She decided to die, and now, a few weeks later, she's going to. Didn't you tell me once that she never wanted to grow old, that she'd said that to you?"

"Yes, but I didn't take that seriously. Now that you mention it though, she is extremely vain, and it does seem like she's leaving us exactly when she wants to, when she still looks great, and on her birthday, no less."

— ◡ —

"Judy, wake up."

"What? Is it time to get ready for the concert?"

Bill sat on the edge of the bed, took my hand, and I knew. "She died during our flight over, didn't she?"

"I'm afraid so. Do you want to cancel the recital?"

"No. I can do it," I said groggily. "She'd want me to go through with it. I wish it were a bigger crowd, though. It's only for about twenty of the Agnellis' friends, right?

"Yes."

"That will be hard."

— ◡ —

Soon I was back in California, looking around at a small chapel filled with flowers, friends, and soft light. We'd found one of the few churches in Southern California that didn't look hard-edged and angular. I sat with Bill holding my hand, at my first funeral, my mother's, someone who didn't even believe in funerals.

Doug Simmons, an old family friend and an elder in the Mormon Church, officiated. Somehow, with my complicated past, it seemed fitting that a Mormon elder was in charge of a funeral service for an ex-Catholic who didn't believe in funerals.

It was a small gathering and a loving one. I was fascinated to hear people speak of my mother as the most interesting, intelligent, talented, amusing person in their lives. None of those attending, except for Bob and me, had been subject to her darker traits, and to hear others tell such admiring stories about her was a revelation. I realized I had been just a small part of her life. Her friends were the larger part. They saw the best of her.

Listening to those who loved her and knew only the amusing, entertaining bits of her made me happy. She had had relief from her pain and enjoyed the company of many who adored and appreciated her. Hearing story after story of her talent and wit made me think back on how she was a favorite among my friends, as was my father.

It's a tremendous gift to have parents who have great imaginations and humor and stimulate your own; who are gifted and bright and encourage you to develop ideas outside yourself. My parents led fairly small lives, but they thought beyond those boundaries and encouraged us to do the same.

Doug finished the service by inviting us to sit quietly and think of my mother as we listened to her recording of "Bye, Bye Blues," her final, creative, beautiful goodbye.

13

A Perfect Day

"I love playing tennis on grass," I called across the net to my opponent. "Don't you love how soft and cushy it feels under your
feet? Listen, you can hear the ocean."

I raised my face to soak in the warm rays, inhaling the fragrance of
freshly cut grass and slightly salty air.

I was treating one of my friends to a tennis match at the Meadow
Club in Southampton, a posh hideaway of endless manicured lawns;
courts with flawlessly drawn lines; perfectly measured nets; and beautiful, fit members in pristine white who frolic about, pounding shots
that only a hundred thousand dollars in lessons can buy. I'm a poor jazz
musician with neither the social standing nor the pocketbook for mem-
bership. I have decent strokes and connections, though, so I visit this
luscious place often.

My town, Sag Harbor, is a historic little village in the Hamptons that
was less well known before various factors, including the TV series *Royal
Pains*, made the Hamptons one of the hotter places on the planet. When

I started living here part-time in the late '80s, shops closed at 6pm and the area was deserted after Labor Day. Not now.

I moved here full-time in 1992 to get a bit of a life beyond my career and to become the athletic girl I'd always wanted to be. This area gave me colorful falls, peaceful winters, sparkling springs, spectacular summers, small-town ambience, and the opportunity to play sports in impossibly beautiful settings. In the late '80s, when I was first introduced to Sag Harbor, I started a weekly summer softball game in our local park, an idyll so quaint and serene it looks like a scene from an Andy Hardy movie.

In the Southern California of my youth, a beach day started with a hot run across scorching sand through side-by-side sunbathers, in search of an empty spot to call your own before your toes turned to toast. You hoped to find space without a blaring radio nearby, screaming children, or a beach ball game in progress that could knock your head off with an errant shot.

My first visit to the beaches of Sagaponack, a bucolic ten-minute drive from Sag Harbor, reminded me of my early California years, especially when I saw the expanse of farmland, weathered barns, and colorful produce and flower stands along the way.

The reveal of these two oceans, though, is much different. The Pacific appears as a dramatic crescendo from the elevated vantage point of the tectonically raised landscape in California. The Hamptons' Atlantic sneaks up on you. You ride through storybook-perfect fields, reminiscent of Iowa or Illinois, and suddenly the farmland ends, the sand begins, and the stunning surprise of the ocean comes into view.

The summer I moved to Sag Harbor was memorable for many reasons, but mostly for the fact that I had some time off with a well-paid fall tour already booked. Everyone thinks musicians spend all their time making music. In fact, most of our energy goes toward hustling gigs, traveling, and practicing. Performing is the smallest part of what we do. This particular summer, a good deal of money was in my immediate future so I could stop hustling for a minute. This was a rare opportunity to forget about work, embrace my new environs, and have some fun.

Along with sports, my other passion is eating. When I moved to Sag Harbor, my best friend was my golfing buddy, Jim, who grew up in Sag Harbor and is an excellent eater, so we were destined to be pals. He was a waiter for years at my favorite local hangout, the American Hotel, a beautiful historic inn and fabulous restaurant. Jim knows fine cuisine and believes in making his friends gastronomically happy in an almost Zen-like way. This man orders food better than anyone I know.

"No, Judy! Don't order *that*. You'll like the sautéed crab legs better. Start with the arugula, grilled portobello mushroom, and blueberry salad with the walnut-infused champagne vinaigrette. Let's order the Montrachet. It'll complement everything perfectly."

After three months on the road, an exchange like this can make me weep.

Our summer plan was to meet once a week for golf and dinner, with Jim taking me to various spots he'd loved as a kid to help me get acquainted with my new home. This particular day started as our other golfing days did, with Jim picking me up and describing the course to me on the drive over.

I should add here that we're both a bit competitive. But we're friendly.

We played a beautiful course on the North Fork of Long Island, which overlooks the Long Island Sound. Afterward we decided on a little restaurant Jim knew on Shelter Island "with the best oysters you'll ever eat."

After the dark chocolate mousse and crème fraiche raspberry parfait, we pondered our next move over espresso and a rare grappa served only at this particular haunt.

"You know, I used to play pool at a place near here. It's got a cowboy vibe and plays great country-western music. I wonder if it's still open."

"I love pool!" I didn't tell Jim about the Bob and Judy Hustle.

"Cool. Let's find the place."

Later, after I'd had my way with Jim at the cowboy pool hall and won a few bucks, I asked, "Now what? I wish there were another sport we could do."

"There's always the Whale's Tale Mini-Golf," he said. "The course is lit, so they're open late."

Jim is taller, stronger and younger than I am, and well, a man, but other than that our competition is fairly balanced. Still, mini-golf is the great equalizer. This is a game that depends on finesse, control, and the ability to hold back a giggle when aiming at a clown's mouth. I was born for this.

I won't take you through a blow-by-blow description. In short, it was harrowing. Jim pulled ahead, then I pulled ahead, and so it went. It became a bit awkward, as the place was mainly populated with children and teenagers who couldn't understand why two adults were betting on every hole and taking their time as they aimed.

We were holding things up a bit, and a few parents were starting to comment. But this was nothing compared to our finishing in a tie and Jim insisting on a sudden-death playoff.

"We can't keep going, Jim. People are getting pissed off."

"We'll keep playing until one of us wins. I'll have you in two. Let's talk to the owner and tell him what we're doing. I'm sure he'll appreciate our commitment."

"Jim, this is *mini*-golf."

"So?"

We were now on the ninth hole. We continued playing despite the increasingly irritated families around us. "Excuse us," announced Jim. "Could we play through? We're in sudden death. We just need to play one more hole." All this, as though any of those kids understood "sudden death" or cared about anything other than our rudely butting in front of them.

"Jim, we really should stop. This is embarrassing."

"Are you kidding? Where's your competitive spirit?"

I perform for a living and happily compete under pressure, but infuriated moms with golf clubs in their hands made me nervous.

Finally I faced the tenth, a dogleg left with a windmill straight ahead. With the fog rolling in, the fake grass was damp, so I planned on a slow roll. I was confident. If I could tap the ball through the windmill on the right and bounce left, I might get a hole in one and end this.

A small voice piped up. "Mommy, what's wrong with those two people? I saw them already play once and now they're playing again."

That was it. I flubbed the shot. I've never really forgiven myself. I'm usually cool, but now I realize that an angry mother with a weapon and a whining child is my limit.

Time passed. After years away, Jim returned to Sag Harbor for a visit and took me to the American Hotel for a reunion dinner.

"You know Jim," I said, "someone asked me the other day to describe my fantasy of a perfect day. I told them I'd already lived my fantasy perfect day."

"Funny you should say that. I was just telling my wife about a perfect day, years ago. Do you remember the time we played golf on the North Fork, had those amazing oysters on Shelter Island, then shot pool at some cowboy dive and finally had that killer competition at the Whale's Tale Mini-Golf?"

14

The Sun Is Red, and Mao's Thought Is Clear

ay Street Café was a cozy little spot that housed a variety of restaurants over the years. It was a hangout for me when I first moved to Sag Harbor in the early '90s. The Café was built in the 1800s as a residence, and subsequent owners have left it mostly intact. The room is small and comfy, with painted wood floors, a high ceiling, a few small tables nestled together, and a perfectly proportioned bar. Windows behind it overlook the harbor, giving a spectacular view to those who sit there sipping their drinks.

Bay Street's owners were a fun-loving gay couple: Rob, a caring, empathetic mensch; and Jerry, a charming, naughty wild man. One evening, in between ministering to his customers, Rob joined my table, sitting next to me to catch me up on local gossip. Our waiter, Christian, placed a plate of calamari on the table which my friends dove in on. He turned to me and interrupted my tête-à-tête with Rob. "Judy, that guy wants your autograph," he said, surreptitiously nodding toward the man in question. "That guy in the corner. He keeps waving and smiling at you and acting like he's writing on his hand. Haven't you noticed?"

"It's great having a celebrity in the restaurant," Rob chimed in, to which I answered: "I love that my friends pretend I'm famous. It helps balance all the people who ignore me."

"I just saw him look right at us, pointing at you," said Rob. "He did the writing thing in his hand."

"Oh, honestly. OK, I'll go over."

I pushed back my chair and reached for my bag to grab a pen. I looked up to see my "fan" making his way to our table, looking a bit miffed. He walked up to Rob with obvious irritation.

"I've been sitting here for fifteen minutes and kept waving at you to ask for my check and all you did was ignore me and talk to this blonde. What kind of restaurant are you running?"

— ‿ —

Jazz musicians experience these kinds of things all the time. Usually, no one knows who I am—sadly, even people I hope will hire me. But at unexpected times, I'm recognized. Last week a young woman rushed up to me with absolute glee.

"I can't *believe* I'm meeting Judy Carmichael! This is the most exciting moment in my life!"

I looked around to see if someone was pulling a prank and filming this.

"Well, thank you. That's very sweet of you."

"No, you don't understand. This is huge! I'm from Saskatoon, which is in the middle of nowhere."

"I've never been there but hear it's beautiful," I said encouragingly.

"Yeah, yeah, it's fine, but it's seriously out there. I went to a Catholic high school, and on the wall in the band room, behind where the teacher stands, are three things—the Cross, the Canadian flag, and a picture of *you*! I stared at your picture for four years and never thought I'd get to meet you."

I'm still not sure how I wound up on that wall.

A few years ago a woman cornered me at Bloomingdale's.

"I know I recognize you! Don't tell me, don't tell me, let me guess who you are. I've seen you on TV. I *know* it!"

"Yes, possibly," I admitted.

"This is so exciting. It's killing me that I can't think of your name. What were you on recently?"

"*CBS Sunday Morning.*"

"No, it wasn't that. OK, tell me."

"I'm Judy Carmichael."

"Judy Carmichael? I don't know that name. What are you on?"

"I'm not on anything regularly. I'm a jazz pianist."

"A *jazz pianist*? She turned away with obvious disappointment. "Shoot, I thought you were an actress."

A few years later, in Lafayette, Louisiana, I was hanging out with my friend Jamie with time to kill before my sound check for a concert that night. Jamie worked for me for years until (as I've often told her) she selfishly decided to get a life of her own, got married, had three kids and moved to New Orleans. In spite of this, we've remained close.

When Jamie's kids reached five, seven, and eleven, she started working for me again as my publicist. She occasionally enlists Carter (seven) and Emily (eleven) to help out with our projects and is trying to interest Molly (five) in joining them.

Emily designed the posters for my last concert in Mandeville, and Carter sold my CDs. Carter is a cutie pie with big brown eyes that he used to great effect as he walked through the crowd at the intermission, holding the albums over his head and shouting, "JUDY'S CDs RIGHT HERE! THERE ARE ONLY TWO LEFT. THIS IS YOUR LAST CHANCE!"

Carter managed to sell those "last two" to fifty people.

Back in Lafayette, Jamie suggested a pedicure. We found a sorry-looking strip mall where Jamie said a heavenly pedi awaited. "Perfect Pedicures and More," said the sign over a quaint little shop with a Rite Aid on one side and a pet supply store on the other.

"Hi, I'm Reese, the receptionist. Do you have an appointment?" Reese fluffed her tastefully highlighted tresses as she scanned the book.

"Yes, it's under Judy Carmichael."

"Gosh, you look like an actress. Are you?" chimed in another Southern belle, who walked up to join Reese at the counter.

"Wait!" said a third equally appealing co-worker, scurrying up to join the conversation. "She's not an actress," she continued, looking at her friend with distain. "You're Judy Carmichael the jazz pianist, right?"

— ~

Fame is helpful in getting gigs. But while I'd like a bit more of it to help with booking, I prefer the connection I have with people who know my music and enjoy it because of the music, not because they think I'm famous.

I once had a presenter tell me he didn't have room to write much about me in an ad for my concert but needed something exciting to say. "Judy, you're not that famous. Give me just a couple of catchy lines that will entice people to come to your concert. Tell me something spectacular about you. I don't care what you say, just give me something flashy that will bring a crowd."

I thought for a minute. "OK. Say, 'Judy Carmichael, Grammy-nominated pianist and stripper.'"

"We can't say that."

"Why not? I'm not really going to strip. You wanted something to get people's attention so they'd come to the concert."

"We still can't say that. Too many words."

"Then take out 'Grammy-nominated pianist.'"

I'd always gotten thoughtful comments about my playing and respectful, interesting fan mail early in my career. Then I got a long, positive review in *People*, with a picture of me above the article. Suddenly, those intelligent, appropriate notes from fans were replaced by five-page letters from men in prison telling me I was beautiful, that they only have thirty years to go, they hoped I'd wait for them, and in the meantime, could I send a pair of panties?

— ~

Steinway periodically commissions a limited-edition piano by a famous designer and plans an event around the unveiling. In 2000, the furniture designer Dakota Jackson created the TriCentennial Piano. Herbie Hancock and I were hired for a bicoastal blowout, he doing the Los Angeles recital, I the one in Manhattan. I decided to attend the one in L.A. to hear Herbie and get a sense of what to expect for my event.

Steinway's vice president at the time, Peter Goodrich, is a good friend and was my date for the evening, which was held at the Pacific Design Center in West Hollywood, a Cesar Pelli extravaganza of modern architecture. The setting was slick and the crowd, Central Casting beautiful. Champagne and hors d'œuvres were served on silver trays by unemployed actors. Everything was glass, steel, and hard surfaces, so Peter and I were practically shouting to be heard above the din.

"The piano looks great in the middle of the room! Fits right in with this incredible setting! I feel so Hollywood, Peter!"

"Come closer, Judy, so we don't have to yell at each other. It's right out of a movie, isn't it? I like your little white dress, by the way, instead of a little black one. Calvin Klein, right? Are those Manolos? Love the zebra print. You've got a Sarah Jessica Parker thing going on."

"Impressive call on the Calvin Klein, Peter. Thank you. Do you think these folks will shut up when Herbie starts playing?"

"Good question. I hope so."

The crowd hushed when Peter introduced Herbie. Peter returned to my side as the great man made his way to the piano. Four bars in, everyone started chattering. I was horrified.

"I can't believe this," I whispered to Peter, who looked stricken.

"Sadly, I can."

Herbie finished the first song to tepid applause. Incredibly, the conversation got louder.

I leaned toward Peter and moaned, "This is happening to Herbie Hancock! Don't these people know who he is?"

Right then, a tall redhead playing the part of a server dropped her tray of freshly filled champagne flutes. The sound of breaking glass and splashing bubbly silenced the crowd but only for a minute. Herbie soldiered on for another twenty, finished, bowed and left.

"Maybe you'll be luckier in New York," Peter said hopefully.

Serious musicians struggle with these contrasts—respect/no respect, famous/not famous, great gigs/horrible gigs—except for the rare few who break through to broader popularity. Often they've made artistic compromises that haunt them in other ways.

One misguided notion that irritates professional musicians is that we play music because we love it, not for money. This is inferred from the fact that we make so little money we must do it for love. The truth is, full-time musicians do it for money. We happen to love making music, but we also expect to be paid.

Another line we hate (in case you're thinking of using it) is, "You should do this performance. I can't pay you anything, but it will be great exposure."

Free gigs lead to other free gigs. Or as a friend once said, "The Donner Party *died* of exposure."

I recently did a concert at a spectacular estate in Cornwall, England, for a sophisticated group of people who'd come from far and wide to this private, black-tie dinner and recital. I was housed well, fed well, paid well, and provided a Steinway grand, so I was a happy girl. This gig paid four times what the famous jazz club in London had offered and had a better piano.

I finished my recital and was enjoying a glass of champagne when a handsome couple approached me.

"Thank you for the lovely concert. Do you mind a question?"

"Of course not."

"We were wondering throughout the performance why a world-class American jazz pianist would come all the way to the wilds of Cornwall to play a concert?"

It's fascinating how they never think it's for the money.

People often say to musicians, after hearing a price quote for a two-hour concert, "You want *that much*? You're only going to play for two hours!"

At this point I like to quote designer Charles Eames who, when asked if an idea came to him "in a flash," answered, "Yes. A thirty-year flash."

— ~

Cut to the fall of 1991.

"Judy, it's Susan Brown from the State Department. We met when you were serving on a National Endowment for the Arts panel last year here in D.C."

"Hi, Susan. Great to hear from you."

"I've got interesting news I want to discuss with you. I need some advice."

"I've always wanted to be a spy," I replied. "Is that why you're calling? Is this finally my James Bond moment?"

"Very funny. No. I've got something much tamer. Well, now that I think of it, maybe not.

Things are settling a bit in China since Tiananmen Square. We think it's time to send some American culture and get a friendly exchange going again."

"Wow! I'd love to go. Thanks for thinking of me!"

"Oh. Well, actually, I was calling to get recommendations from you. It never occurred to us that you would want to go."

"Why not? I've done lots of State Department tours. I love these things."

"Well, frankly, we thought you were too famous."

"Too famous? That's hilarious. Trust me, I'm not a household name in China. Ask me. I'd love to go."

"Well, this puts an entirely different spin on things. We love you here at State. You'd be perfect for this. It's going to be sensitive on all levels, and you've done the political thing with us so know what's necessary. It's going to be a long process, though, with a complicated application, a blind panel judging the music, the whole bit."

"It's like the NEA grants, where you'll have a group of musicians listening to the music submitted, not knowing who the artist is? The panel will rate the ensemble, and the highest number gets the gig?"

"Essentially, yes."

"OK. Obviously, I can't be on the panel. Let me tell everyone I think appropriate for this and tell them to apply. I'll send my music as well, and we'll see who's chosen. When do you want to do the tour?"

"May 1992."

Months passed before I heard back from Susan.

"Do you know anything about the tour?" I asked.

"Interesting that you had everyone in your band apply with their own CDs, as well as those other bands. We also had a huge response from other quarters. We were thrilled to get so many submissions."

"I didn't get it, did I?"

"Wait, listen. We couldn't get any jazz musicians to be on the judging panel so the panel was made up of classical musicians. They hated everyone but you."

"Even my musicians' CDs?"

"Yes. It was odd. They liked your musicians when they played with you but not on their own CDs without you. The panel genuinely didn't like anyone but you, so it was a simple decision to give you the tour. For final approval, we had to send your CD to the Public Affairs Officer, our top man in Beijing. We thought it was a cinch. He hated it."

"He hated my CD? You're killing me. So the panel liked my music and the big dog hated it. So now what?"

"That's the interesting thing. Do you remember Heather Rollins? You worked with her in India. Well, she's in D.C. now and working on this China project. When she found out that our man in China didn't like your CD, she sent him a different one of yours she'd bought for herself some time ago, when she was back in the States. That one he liked. So, yes, you're going to China.

"And listen. This is important. You'll be the first jazz musician sponsored by the U.S. government to tour China, and this will be the first tour of any kind sent by us since Tiananmen Square. They'll be tons of State meetings, press, dinners. This will be the largest grant we've ever given for a tour like this. We see it as a launch in getting a better relationship going between our governments. Every concert will be for an audience of a thousand or more. You'll teach in some universities and play at the ambassador's residence and various consulates around the country. You'll be there for a month. And I should warn you: We've already gotten feedback that jazz is too controversial because of the improvisational component. So we've told them you're a folk singer."

"You know I don't sing, right?"

"And you don't play folk music. Yes, we know."

"What happens when they hear me and discover I'm not Joni Mitchell?"

"There needs to be a Communist official who likes you and will sponsor you. We're confident that will happen after you play your first concert. We just need to get you there. If no one steps forward with their seal of approval, you'll be sent home, but we'll still pay you for the tour."

Most great jazz musicians are interesting characters, but saxophonist Mike Hashim and guitarist Chris Flory, my partners in this adventure, are particularly fascinating—well read, stylish, insightful.

Chris is dark and handsome with soulful eyes, which I'm told prompted the nickname early in his career of Dondi from the comic strip character. Chris is slight of build and said he finally felt at home being surrounded by Chinese men because of their similar body type. Both Mike and I thought this a ridiculous notion, seeing no similarity between the Chinese and Chris, until one morning when I saw Chris at breakfast, came up behind him, leaned over, and kissed him on the cheek. The Chinese man I'd just smooched turned around, horrified. We saw few other non-Asians while we were there so our presence was a shock to most people we met on the street, especially if I spoke the few words of Chinese I'd learned. So you can imagine what an unexpected kiss from a tall blonde did to this man. Mike has his mother's Lebanese appearance; wears small, round, wire-rim glasses; and always sports a stylish vintage hat. In heels, I'm taller than both these men, so we're an interesting-looking trio.

— —

We were introduced for our concerts with Chinese translations of our names. Chris's and mine were unpronounceable, but Hashim became the extremely appealing Hashimoo, which I still call Mike to this day.

Most of our performances were for huge, enthusiastic crowds. We had noticed that Mike was getting particular attention from young women in the audience, who would rush the stage when we finished, waving programs for Mike to autograph. The audience often laughed when I introduced him, and we were all a bit confused by this peculiar response. One night when the crowd got especially rowdy, Chris called out, "*Hashimoo, they think you're Brad Pitt! You're stealing the show!*"

We all laughed and continued. I was happy the audience was into our performance but the tittering when I introduced Mike was getting distracting.

One night I finally motioned to Mike after his chorus, cuing the audience to applaud. They started chanting, "*Benny Hill, Benny Hill, Benny Hill!*"

"Brad Pitt my ass," he muttered under his breath.

A fascinating man, whose father was the last living general of Chiang Kai-shek's army, had seen our first concert and agreed to be our official Communist sponsor, enabling us to continue our tour rather than being thrown on a plane and sent back to the States. He was a fan of America and had built a school for children of working couples that was painted red, white, and blue. All subjects were taught in English. This was 1992, so this guy was seriously ahead of his time. He loved us and we loved him.

Very few of the Chinese for whom we played were familiar with jazz, but some of them had heard it from Americans stationed in China during World War II; they still had a soft spot in their hearts for us because of America's role in helping China fight the Japanese. Our trio's music held deep meaning for these older Chinese, especially since we played jazz from that era. One woman came to me after our concert in Chongqing, took my hand, held it to her face, and cried.

We traveled all over, and because China is huge, the contrasts were great. Our State Department representatives were constantly talking about the change in China, the broader acceptance of a capitalistic view. The air pulsed with energy, possibility, and the early enthusiastic embrace of entrepreneurship. Everyone seemed to be starting a business or selling something. A few times, we spotted an old man or woman selling items on the street from a makeshift stall, items that were obviously from their personal possessions.

"Is this out of need?" I asked my translator.

"No, it's viewed as opportunity. They consider it a small business."

"Selling their old clothes?"

"They wouldn't have been allowed to do this until recently."

China's Great Leap Forward was an unsuccessful attempt by Mao Zedong from 1958 to 1960 to hasten the process of industrialization and improve agricultural production by reorganizing the population into large rural collectives and adopting labor-intensive industrial methods. Cultural artifacts were destroyed and artists were discriminated against. This attitude intensified in 1966–76 during the Cultural Revolution; the political upheaval then was designed to bring about a return to revolutionary Maoist beliefs. Many intellectuals and artists were thrown in prison, and any dissent was discouraged.

We witnessed the effects of China's difficult history many times when an "ancient" landmark was pointed out; we could tell at a glance from the materials used that it was actually new, because the original had been destroyed. Sometimes someone would hand me a resume that listed early music training followed by twenty years in prison, then a resumption of music study and a performance career. It was heartbreaking.

We had a State Department translator with us at all times and a local counterpart whose English was elementary and often confused. In the beginning, the State Department insisted that I have a hostess of sorts on stage with me to translate what I said during the concert. This was always a tall, beautiful woman wearing a sequined, floor-length gown. Very Vegas. The translations were four times as long as my commentary and getting longer as we went along. I could never pronounce the translators' names, so the guys and I took to calling each of them (amongst ourselves) "The Babe."

I insisted to our various handlers that I didn't need this helper, as I was learning more Chinese daily and the Chinese audiences were extremely quick at understanding a jazz presentation and knowing when to clap. This was remarkable since, as I explained, most or them had never heard jazz.

We usually started with a swinging tune called "I Found a New Baby" and played it at a fast clip, very upbeat. I would introduce it by saying, "We're now going to play a classic tune jazz musicians enjoy, called 'I Found a New Baby.'"

The translation for this sentence grew each night to a final tally of around fifteen minutes. I was also noticing a few audience members dabbing their eyes during this recitation.

"You've got to get rid of the translator," I pleaded to Tracy, my State Department rep. "Please, I can do this on my own."

"Chinese audiences are used to this," she replied.

"Each one tells the audience when to applaud and when to *stop*! This is ridiculous. Talk about controlling behavior. Last night we played the concert, built the audience up to the finale, they stood for an ovation, and as we returned for an encore, the Babe told them to *stop applauding* and leave! I can't take this anymore. Seriously, it's ruining the experience."

"Let's see what happens tonight," Tracy replied like the bureaucrat she was, wondering if this problem should go to committee.

"Have you noticed the audiences have started to cry during the 'I Found a New Baby' translation?"

"I haven't noticed anyone crying, Judy. I think you're exaggerating."

I sighed. "Watch tonight. You'll see."

Out we came to an audience of two thousand-plus. Unfortunately, the piano was a Pearl River upright—a horrible instrument I refer to as "pre-firewood." This hunk of lumber was not adequate for a classroom, let alone a concert hall. I was grumpy, tired, and ready to strangle anyone who got in my way.

I greeted the audience in Chinese, telling them what an honor it was to be there and that we hoped they'd enjoy the concert. Then, continuing in Chinese, I said the line that always got a laugh, pointing to my musicians as I said it: "When I speak Chinese to you, my band can't understand a word! Isn't this fun?"

Everyone would cheer and the Babe would enter stage right, ready to tell the audience the meaning of whatever I had said in English and how to behave in response.

Reverting to English, I said, "We're now going to play a classic tune jazz musicians enjoy, called 'I Found a New Baby.'"

The Babe translated for what seemed like an hour. People started crying, and finally she turned to me, confused. In English, she asked, "What exactly does "I Found a New Baby' mean?"

"What do you mean, what does it mean?" I asked with irritation.

Ms. Vegas was unsettled but determined. "I've been telling a story of a woman who loses her baby from a miscarriage, then walks through the woods and finds an abandoned child. She's happy now because she's found a *new* baby. It's a sad story with a happy ending. Is this what the tune is about?"

The top State Department person, with whom we dealt, was Gene, the Public Affairs Officer. Periodically he would call and check in with me to see how we were doing.

"I hear your Chinese is expanding. Impressive, Judy."

"I test it before I walk onstage every night and the feedback alternates between 'Judy, that's awesome, to 'Judy, I have no idea what you're saying.' But yes, I'm improving."

"Good job. And I have good news for you. We're getting rid of the Babe, as I hear you're calling her."

"Thank goodness. Sorry about the Babe moniker. I can't pronounce what they really call her and you have to admit, the gals they get for this job are stunning."

"It's an honor to have that position and yes, being beautiful is a requirement." He added: "I hear you're playing a Cultural Revolution tune to teach about improvisation. That's an inspired idea."

"Thank you. I thought a tune they knew would illustrate it easier. Everyone seems to like it."

"Which one are you doing?"

"'The Sun Is Red and Mao's Thought is Clear.' A real finger-snapper."

"Probably best not to play it on the anniversary of Tiananmen Square or when you play in Beijing."

"Thanks, Gene. I'd figured that one out on my own."

I liked Gene, but it took him a while to trust my judgment. He was bureaucratic and mildly sexist, slow to accept the fact that a woman was leading the band or fully understand how a jazz ensemble works onstage and on the road. Mike and Chris didn't want to know every detail of the visit nor did we have time to discuss it all. I'd told Gene to talk only to me and I'd give the guys the gist of the conversation. Nevertheless, he called us all, asked the same questions, had long discussions, and got a different opinion from each of us. Everything took three times longer than it should have.

"Gene, jazz isn't a democracy. I'm the leader for a reason. The guys *want* me to be the leader. Please talk only to me. Everything will be faster and more efficient."

He insisted on continuing in his own way until a particularly important press conference.

"Gene, let me do the press conference on my own. Don't invite Mike or Chris. They're tired, would rather rest, and I don't have time to brief them about our grant and the various aspects of the tour, which only I know at this point."

"No, they should be there too."

"These are highly intelligent, opinionated men. Trust me, don't do this."

"I want them there."

"OK. You'll see."

And he did, with the first question.

"Mr. Hashim, do you think the United States funds the arts sufficiently?"

"Absolutely not," Mike answered with conviction.

It went downhill from there, as Mike offered a scathing critique of America's meager support for the arts to China's most important newspaper. And it wasn't a short recitation. Unbeknownst to Mike, the grant I'd received to fund this month-long tour was the largest ever given to an individual by the United States for an arts tour of this kind, although it was a relatively small amount. It's a sad truth, of course, that the U.S. doesn't fund the arts well. When the State Department sent me to tour India in the late '80s as a soloist, the Soviet Union sent the Bolshoi Ballet.

Still, this was a large amount for America to invest in this project. I paid our salaries, hotels, flights, and all expenses from the grant. The dollar amount was large and the details were boring and extensive, so I hadn't burdened the guys with it all. That's why I'm the leader. And that's why it's often more fun to be a sideman.

I smiled at Gene and mouthed, "I told you so."

꘡ ꘡

Since we were the honored guests from America, we often met celebrated Chinese musicians, and if we went to universities, the students would sometimes play for us. The highlight was a string group in Chongqing who played a mournful "Swanee River," a surprising, touching choice, played so beautifully on Chinese instruments—erhu, dizi, yangqin, and sheng—that the three of us couldn't make eye contact lest we break down. To this day, we can't talk about it without tearing up.

We were honored at various dinners, each unique and surprising. We thought the food was spectacular, highly sophisticated, always gorgeously presented, and, not surprisingly, nothing like Chinese food at home.

Two dinners stood out. One was in the home—a large lean-to with a dirt floor, creaky wood table, chairs, and nothing else—of "peasant" farmers in the countryside where we ate in a room that was open to the elements on one side. I was always the only woman at these events, except for our State Department representative.

Our host wore a T-shirt, baggy pants, and no shoes, and was joined by the local Communist boss who had a large, jagged scar that started at the top of his forehead and snaked down his face, throat, and chest, continuing into his pants and ending I know not where, thankfully. He sat shirtless throughout the meal and stared at me as he ate, turning only to spit noisily. Little was said. The only interruption was when the wife served various courses, all presented simply and beautifully. She didn't join us, but stood nearby so she could jump in if needed.

The other dinner I remember vividly was a larger group of fifteen men in Mao suits, seated around a large, oval table with me at the head, and Mike and Chris nearby. A cool breeze flowed through an open window at one end of the gray, starkly furnished room. Large fans turned lazily above us.

I took in this remarkable scene, glancing at Chris, who looked weary and dazed. The setting, and Chris' gaunt, angular good looks, reminiscent of early Frank Sinatra, brought to mind *The Manchurian Candidate*, that fabulous, creepy 1962 film about a Communist plot to assassinate the President with a brainwashed American soldier.

As the most honored person present, I was often presented with a special delicacy. The rarer the item served, the greater the honor. This particular evening, a tiny, exotic-looking bird was placed in front of me on a small, burnished plate of brushed gold. I was the only one served this creature. I turned to Mike and sighed, "I'm afraid it's the end of a species."

Dinners usually started with shots of Maotai, a killer drink distilled from fermented sorghum with an alcohol content of fifty-three percent. As the guest of honor, I was served first and expected to down it quickly so the rest of the group could follow suit. Often, one of the participants would pass out, drop his head to the table, and snore softly as the rest of us carried on.

The seat to my right, at the head of the table, had been empty for the first few minutes of our dinner until a man of importance raced up, settling in next to me with a satisfied sigh. He was completely bald, and in the Mao getup, looked like Number One, the James Bond villain Mike Myers spoofed as "Dr. Evil." I instinctively checked his lap for his Persian cat, but then remembered Hashimoo pointing out what he thought was a pet store a few cities back with a number of caged kitties out front, and our realizing in horror that it was a *grocery store*. Not a lot of loose felines wandering about.

My new dinner companion grinned maniacally, leaning toward me. He was obviously elated to be at this celebration and seated next to me. He almost quivered with excitement.

"Miss Nevada was here last week!" he said, enthusiastically. "I was out of town on business and missed meeting her, so I was determined not to miss *you!*"

Chris jumped in. "This is your lucky day! Judy was Miss California!"

Dr. Evil moved his seat closer and smiled slyly. "Want to be my Miss Hollywood?"

Great.

— —

When we were in China, the airports were crowded, disorganized, and confusing. People pushed their way through lines and charged like cattle to get on the plane, shoving anyone in their path, trampling the fallen. Once on the plane and seated, everyone instantly went into an almost Zen-like state, quiet and still. Mike, Chris, and I found it bizarre and stressful. Finally, in Harbin, a city in the far north near the Russian border, Mike and I decided to change our tack.

At every stop we were met by photographers, dignitaries, the press, and various others who gave us flowers and gifts and interviewed us about our thoughts on China, so I always dressed up a bit. We'd been overdressed in the last couple of cities and roasted in the boiling temperatures. This time we prepared. I wore a skirt and T and thought, for once, I wouldn't be a sweaty mess when photographed getting off a plane.

"Judy, let's sit here while everyone exits," Mike suggested after we'd landed. "We'll be relaxed, leave when we want and not get beat up with all the jostling these folks do."

"Excellent thinking, Hashimoo."

When the plane was empty, we ambled down the aisle to the doorway.

"*Oh, my God!* It's freezing! Mike, watch your hat!" I was shouting over gale-force winds that slapped me in the face. "It's pouring. It must be forty degrees! What were we thinking? This is entirely different weather. Oh, man, is that bus pulling away supposed to take us to the terminal?"

Mike barreled down the ramp, ran to the bus, and tried to climb aboard to tell them to wait. He was pushed back with a hand to his forehead and fell flat on his back onto the tarmac.

I caught up to him and pulled him to his feet. "Are you OK?"

"They must know we're big stars," he said, brushing gravel from his pants as we watched the bus plow through the downpour.

We looked up at the plane, whose door had already been shut, and then back at the departing bus driving away. We stood on the tarmac in pelting, freezing rain, looked at each other and laughed.

"Do I look as drenched as you?" I asked him.

"Well, you have a nice wet T-shirt thing going on Judy, and your hair ... It's probably good you can't see your hair. We should try to avoid photographers."

— ~

We finished the month with a performance at the ambassador's residence in Beijing. Ambassador Stapleton Roy had grown up in China and was a favorite with the people I knew at the State Department. I've done many of these evenings and always enjoy them. Ambassador residences are elegant abodes, and the Roy residence was particularly lovely.

There's a musician's joke that goes like this: A man asks a musician to play a recital at the Harvard Club and asks the musician's price.

"It's three thousand dollars for a quartet."

"Are you *out of your mind*? That's way too much. I can't believe it. And we were going to ask you to stay for dinner."

"In that case, it's seven thousand dollars."

This joke nicely illustrates musicians' attitudes on receptions. Personally, I seldom want to mingle after a concert, although at State Department dinner recitals I do. They're always filled with fascinating people who are interesting and well-traveled. Even so, this night was different. It had been a challenging tour on every level and I was exhausted. I couldn't bring myself to talk to anyone. I wanted to hide and did, in the kitchen. I found a motherly looking sort and almost asked for a hug.

"Hello, I'm Judy, the one who just did the recital."

"Oh, you dear thing. I'm Fran Owen, the chef. You look beat."

"I am. I'm hiding."

"Would you like me to fix you a plate here? I won't let anyone find you. Let me get you a nice glass of wine."

"That sounds wonderful."

Fran set a table, handed me a glass of delicious Merlot, and served me the most soothing soup I've ever had.

"Soup is so comforting. Is that sage I'm tasting? It's perfect in a tomato soup, especially with the crème fraiche."

"Ah, yours is an educated palette. I'm glad I asked you into my kitchen."

Then I heard a man's voice.

"Excuse me, Judy, do you mind if I join you?"

"Ambassador Roy!" I said, standing. "You've caught me."

"I sometimes hide in here myself. Do you mind if I have dinner with you?"

"I'd be honored. Won't you be missed?"

"Not for a while. I'd rather talk to you. Fran, would you set another place? I'll join Judy in a glass of Merlot."

"Well, this is a perfect end to my tour. Thank you for finding me."

"Judy, I've heard wonderful things about you from everyone. Thank you for it all. And I have something you'll enjoy hearing. When you did your opening greeting in Chinese, I turned to Tracy and said, 'You didn't tell me Judy speaks Chinese.'"

"Seriously? That's big from a native speaker. You've made my night."

"Tracy broke it to me that you were faking it, but you fooled me. Great accent."

"I can't believe no one found us," I finally said when we were finished.

"Yes. I hate to do this but I probably should get back. But one more thing. I'm so impressed with what you've done for us here in China. Is there anywhere else in the world you'd like to go? I have a few contacts and could probably make it happen."

I laughed. "A few? I bet. Let me think. Oh, I know! I've been dying to go to Libya."

"Ah, yes, a fascinating area. Not surprised you'd mentioned that. Please don't repeat this, but actually, you don't want to go there."

"No?"

"Interesting things are about to happen in that particular part of the world."

"I see. How about Paris?"

"Perfect."

15

Road Weary

Travel can be fun, or you can find yourself stranded on an island talking to a basketball. I've experienced both.

I've done a lot of tours in which I drove across America, playing towns both large and small. I've tried it solo a few times to save money, but even though my sense of direction and map-reading skills are excellent, it's a strain to drive eight to ten hours, check into a motel, sleep a few hours, then get up the next day for a five-hour drive, a sound check, and a concert. Periodically I'd have a girlfriend come along to share the duties. Unfortunately, most of them thought it was a vacation, and didn't understand why I wouldn't stop at every Dollywood or shooting geyser along the way.

I employed my friend Ellen to be my road manager for a while. She'd call the concert halls to set up my sound checks and share the driving and navigating duties. Sadly, and unbeknownst to me, Ellen has no sense of direction and can't read a map. She did grow up with theater, though, so she knew what was needed for good sound, lighting, and staging. Her impatience with anyone who didn't was inconvenient though, since the majority of soundmen are clueless.

"I can't believe these idiots, Judy. They don't have your dressing room appropriately put together—no tea, no food. And the person I talked to didn't even know you're supposed to have a sound check! The mics aren't there, and the piano hasn't been delivered. I'm already sick of Iowa. Why are you doing a concert here?"

"Ellen, I'm paying you so I don't have to hear any of this. And I like Iowa. You know my thing for pigs. So cute."

"I don't want to hear about your farm fantasies. This is upsetting and stressful."

"Welcome to my world, Ellen."

"You *don't* understand."

"Of course I understand. I'm paying you to deal with this. Relax and take in this lovely, bucolic scenery—corn, cows. Roll down the window and smell those freshly cultivated wheat fields."

"I'm not enjoying this, Midwest Girl."

Ellen is entertaining, so her company made up for her lack of skills as a road manager. One of the duties I gave her was to grab some goodies for me during the after-concert receptions to take back to our room. There would always be an extensive array of yummy treats at these events. I never eat at receptions because as soon as I bite into some gooey chocolate extravaganza someone comes up to say hello.

"I just *loved* the concert, Judy! Thank you so much!"

"Umm, ooh, ahh, excuse me, my mouth is full. Sorry. Thank you."

"Here, let me wipe that whipped cream off your cheek, Judy."

Ellen describes herself as a "big girl" and finally, after our first two weeks out and being sent on one too many dessert-finding missions, she snapped.

"Listen *skinny girl!* You think everyone believes the fat girl when she's stuffing brownies and cookies into her pockets and says, 'Honest, this is for Judy Carmichael?'"

Ellen and I had various coping mechanisms to keep us from killing each other, after having spent hours on the road together. She bought a stuffed animal for her young nephew, one of the creatures from Maurice Sendak's *Where the Wild Things Are*, which became a third member of our traveling party.

Our new pal had blue fur, horns, and a gray beard. We named him Harry. Ellen and I are both film buffs, so Harry and I would do charades and Ellen would try to guess the film while she was driving.

Harry and I were an excellent team and could get Ellen to guess the film in question in a few seconds. A banana on his head and a time step was Fred Astaire in *Flying Down to Rio*. A twist of his beard and he was Tevye in *Fiddler on the Roof*. If it rained, he'd point out the window, put his claw on his horn, lean his head back, and act like he was belting out a tune.

"Lena Horne in *Stormy Weather*!" said Ellen with an appreciative nod.

Harry loved the film *Single White Female*, so he insisted on taking one of my Jimmy Choos and opening the bathroom door when Ellen was taking a shower and leaning over the curtain as if he were going to attack her with it.

"*Single White Female!*" Ellen called out over the running water and steam. "Good one, Harry. I didn't know you'd seen that film."

When Harry started dictating the charades, we knew it was time to go home.

━ ━

When I toured cross-country with my quintet, we opted for two Lincoln town cars instead of a bus and would trail each other in caravan. Our drummer, the only other decent driver besides me, was adamant that we should drive at the same speed, lest we lose each other. To constantly watch each other, though, added to the stress. While I would try to keep the other car in sight, I thought it better to go our separate ways and meet at our destination.

The guys agreed that seven miles over the speed limit was acceptable and thought no cop would give us a ticket if we stayed within that range.

I felt our driving speed should be fluid; that we should go with the traffic flow, and as long as someone was going faster, we could ramp up the speed a bit and the cop would go for the other guy. I felt that my training on Los Angeles freeways gave me an edge over my East Coast musicians.

We were a few miles outside of Chicago when, to my astonishment, I was pulled over. "I *knew* it!" I angrily grumbled to my sax man, Mike Hashim, my only passenger at the moment. The others pulled over behind us to watch the action. "Instead of using my instincts, I was doing the stupid 'seven miles over rule' you guys said would never get us a ticket."

Up walked the officer, who leaned his head down and motioned for me to roll down my window.

"Hello, Miss. Give me your license, please."

"But officer, I was only going seven miles over the speed limit!"

Did I just say that out loud?

"Thank you for that information—that's helpful."

"Sorry, officer. I'm a little preoccupied, I'm afraid. I've got a big concert tonight in Chicago, and I may have been rushing things."

"What kind of concert?"

"I have a jazz quintet—my other musicians are in the car behind us—and we've got a performance tonight. We play swing music."

"You're a jazz musician? I love jazz! I never give tickets to jazz musicians. Here, write down where you're playing and I'll come."

"Wow, thank you. I'd leave tickets for you, but that would be a bribe, right?"

"We won't exchange tickets on this one."

The guys felt that his generosity had more to do with my being female than a jazz musician, but I don't agree.

— —

Another time I was driving some monster four-wheel drive that Avis in Steamboat Springs, Colorado, insisted I take, since the winter weather was severe. It was snowing heavily, and the road was slick, with everything an icy white. I drive well in snow but don't welcome it, since I didn't even see snow until I was nineteen. Unfortunately, here I was, driving a car with two different levels of gears, which I had no idea how to use.

I pulled onto a major four-lane highway to make a left turn across it and couldn't get the damn thing to switch gears. I was creeping along at thirty-five miles per hour, forcing cars to screech to a halt to avoid hitting me, as I inched my way into my turn. I finally made it to the other side and pulled off the road in a panic. I parked and jumped out, hyperventilating and freezing. I stared at my offending vehicle. "You almost killed me, you lousy hunk of metal!"

"*Excuse me!*"

I turned to see a police officer towering over me angrily.

"Do you know you *just ran me off the road*?"

I grabbed his arms and looked up at him with relief.

"*Thank God you're here!*" I shouted up at him, my fingers tightening around his biceps. "I can't control this car!"

Nice muscles. This guy must work out.

When I came to my senses, I realized I was manhandling a cop. I gently released him and sheepishly stepped back, almost falling into a snowdrift.

"Sorry, officer."

He tried not to laugh, but a slight smile came to his lips and recognition in his eyes.

"Wait a minute. You're that piano player from New York, right? You're on the front page of our newspaper today. Aren't you doing a concert tonight?"

"Yes. And I'm obviously out of control and need help. This car is impossible."

"OK, let's see what's going on here."

For him, I left a couple of tickets. Don't tell anyone.

A few months after this, Ellen and I tackled the South. We had a night off and decided to rent a movie at the local video store, a beat up little shack in a 1970s-era strip mall. We thought we'd have a nice dinner and watch the movie afterward.

"This place kinda scares me," Ellen said. "I don't see anything of interest. Why is it so dark in here? It's creeping me out."

"I've got this one, don't worry. Let's find someone who works here." I turned to the gum-cracking teenager behind the counter. "Excuse me, do you have a classics section?"

"What's a classic?" she asked.

"You know, anything with Cary Grant, Katharine Hepburn, Jimmy Stewart."

"Well, I've heard of Jimmy Stewart—he's in that Christmas movie, right, with the angel? But Cary Grant and Katharine Hepburn? Never heard of 'em."

"Judy, let's just leave—this is depressing me," said Ellen, the movie maven who can tell you which shade of pink Ginger Rogers wore in *Swing Time* to get just the right hue for the final black and white print.

"We'll find something, Ellen. Be patient."

"Thanks, Pollyanna."

"That's an old Disney movie, right?" chimed in our Dentine-smacking friend.

"OK, we'll look around ourselves. Tell me, where's the best place in town to get a nice meal, something that would include vegetables and a salad?"

Ellen looked at me dumbfounded.

We'd had trouble finding fresh vegetables on this tour. Upon asking for "a green vegetable" a waitress in Alabama told me, "Well, honey, only vegetable we have is rice."

"Judy," Ellen muttered, "this girl doesn't know Cary Grant. You think she knows fine cuisine?"

"I like Hardees," the kid responded. "They have a great salad bar."

We headed toward the door.

"I always give people the benefit of the doubt, Ellen. And I liked her leopard skirt and boots. A bit much for a job in a video store, especially with the heavy eye-liner, but she had a certain flair."

I've played a lot of major world capitals: Kewanee, Illinois, "The Hog Capital of the World" and Dixon, Illinois, "The Petunia Capital of the World", which also happened to be Ronald Reagan's hometown. I met a childhood sweetheart of his at the post concert reception who told me, "I'm sick of petunias. The whole town looks like it's covered in Pepto-Bismol when the festival is on."

"Why do you always use pink petunias? Petunias come in other colors," I offered, revealing my extensive botanical knowledge. "Do you use pink because Ronnie was gay?"

The man next to her looked stunned.

"Oh, my God! Ronnie was *gay?* We were in the same class! I never knew!"

The Brits say Americans aren't good with irony.

Later, on a solo tour, I found myself in Waycross, Georgia, whose inhabitants proudly call it "The Bird Dog Capital of the World."

"You know, Judy, you're a lot more famous than I thought," said the Waycross concert presenter.

"Why do you say that?"

"Well, the bird dog trials are going on right now. Usually no one comes to the concerts during the trials, but you're sold out!"

I reached Waycross near the end of a five-week tour of the South. My lodging for the night looked like the Bates Motel. As I checked in, the big-haired proprietress lamented the fact that she couldn't attend my show, nodding toward the large poster of me on the wall, which advertised the concert. "I gave my boy here my ticket though and he's been looking forward to it all week. "Her boy" was a lanky, dark-haired creep-o-thon who leaned on the front desk and eyed me like his potential Janet Leigh. I told big mama that I needed to relocate.

"Well, honey, I'm afraid the only other motel in town rents by the hour.

My last concert on the tour, when Ellen was with me, was in Punxsutawney, Pennsylvania, which we knew would be charming and friendly because of the great scenes of it in the movie *Groundhog Day*. In every disappointing place we visited, one of us would say, "But we're finishing in Punxsutawney. We know that'll be great!"

The weather was gray, damp, and dreary. Ellen and I were exhausted. Even Harry had nothing to say. We were moaning about how anxious we were to get home when it hit me.

"Ellen! I can't believe we've been so naïve, especially since we're movie buffs."

"What are you talking about?"

"What if they actually used another location for *Groundhog Day*? They probably found one of those exquisite Illinois or Iowa small towns we loved. What if the real Punxsutawney is a depressed, industrial, seen-better-days Pennsylvania town like the ones we've just passed through?"

We contemplated this unhappy thought.

As we feared, Punxsutawney looked nothing like the idealized small town in *Groundhog Day*, which we later learned was filmed in Woodstock, Illinois. Instead, it is a dreary, lonely place that has probably *never* seen better days.

I had more fun on a subsequent Southern tour with my quintet. We went at a warmer time of year, and I had a better plan for our concerts. I'd been hired to put a band together to celebrate the music of Benny Goodman, so I gathered four of my favorite musicians and set off. I love the South and was excited to have the guys with me.

Mike Hashim was again on sax. After all our fun together in China, I knew we traveled well together. Not only is he a wonderful musical companion, he's one of the best read, most interesting people I know. He's also usually even-tempered—so much so that I once handed him a hundred-dollar bill in the middle of a tour just for being my only low-maintenance sideman.

In the course of many weeks touring, everyone had had a breakdown moment, but not Mike. We were all weary of the "complimentary breakfast" of bad coffee, cold rolls, rubber eggs (if we were lucky), and stale cereal.

I always tried to cheer my men, so I was smiling broadly as I approached the lobby breakfast table one morning with the four of them sitting around it, silent and sullen.

"Good morning, men! How are you?"

Mike stood up, threw his napkin on the table as if he were challenging someone to a duel, looked straight ahead and shouted, *"I WANT A HOT MEAL SERVED BY A PROFESSIONAL!"*

I put my arm around him, eased him back into his chair, and suggested we check out early and find the local Cracker Barrel.

"They have excellent biscuits and killer pancakes," I said with my cheeriest morning voice. "My treat."

I thought I saw a tear in Mike's eye, but it might have been the light.

No one mentioned the "complimentary breakfast" for the rest of the tour, although our trombonist, Joel Helleny, whom we called "Hell" for various reasons, had his own variation on this theme.

One morning as a desk clerk and I were settling the bill, the front-desk phone rang. "For you," the desk man said, handing me the phone. A soothing male voice on the other end said, "Miss Carmichael, this is your complimentary morning phone call. May I say you're looking *especially* beautiful today. The color of your sweater is perfect with your clear, green eyes and is tremendously flattering."

"Thank you, Hell."

"My pleasure."

I never knew when a "complimentary phone call" would come, but it happened fairly often in ensuing years.

Ring, ring, ring, ring . . .

"Hello, ugh, what, hello? Who is this? I'm asleep."

"Sorry to wake you, Miss Carmichael. This is your complimentary phone call. May I say you're looking especially lovely on this fine, winter's day."

"*Hell,* I'm in *Switzerland.* It's three a.m.!"

"Well then, let me say that negligee you're wearing is especially fetching."

16

My Affair with Brad Pitt

Throughout my twenties I would tell my friends, "If this jazz thing doesn't work out, I'll do something else." I didn't know what that would be, but somehow this made me feel better as I soldiered on. With this in mind, my friend Sharon, a native New Yorker who at twenty-eight was already well established in business, said she wanted to take me out for my thirtieth birthday and, as she put it, "talk to me."

I had met Sharon four years earlier when she appeared alongside the piano at Disneyland. She listened for a while then started in chatting with me. She was visiting from Manhattan, and I wasn't surprised that I liked her immediately. Most Disneyland visitors walked by without a glance, but the New Yorkers who spotted me came over, listened to a couple of tunes, then told me I was too good for the place.

"Disneyland is creepy, too clean. Why is everybody so overly happy? It's not natural to smile so much. And look at you, in that dumb costume. You should come to New York where people recognize talent. And you could wear what you want."

This happened a lot. New Yorkers and people from other countries stopped and listened. Somehow, they saw beyond the hotdogs and my silly costume and heard the music.

I told Sharon that I would be debuting at Hanratty's the following month. Coincidentally, she lived a block away. Sharon would become a great friend, my first in New York, and something of a Jewish mother to me. After my opening night at Hanratty's she offered her apartment to me and said she'd stay with her boyfriend. This was extremely generous (and trusting) considering she'd met me once at Disneyland and again my opening night. Sharon taught me loads of Yiddish, how to dress in cold weather, and many other lessons that would serve me well once I moved to New York.

Now that I was entering my thirties, she was adamant about giving me "the talk." We'd had a few birthday drinks when she got serious.

"Judy, you know how you always say if 'this jazz thing doesn't work out' you're going to do something else? Well, you're thirty. If you're going to do something else, now is the time."

This was not a good moment. I realized I didn't want to do anything else. Although I'd gotten lots of attention, support from people who mattered, a half-page feature in the *New York Times* and a Grammy nomination, nothing had gotten easier. I still hustled constantly for gigs and was barely able to pay my bills.

"I can't do anything else, Sharon. Well, I can, but I don't want to. God. This is never going to get any easier, is it?"

"I don't think so. But you should stop saying you're going to do something else and commit."

Max Morath, the ragtime pianist and cultural historian, concurred, telling me, "All musicians think about quitting every five years or so. Accept it. You're not going to quit."

The jazz writer Dan Morgenstein once told me, "You play stride piano, for God's sake. You're lucky *anyone* hires you. You know how incredible it is that you have a career?"

That made me feel better. A little.

I particularly enjoyed a conversation I had on this subject many years later with my friend Kyle Kirkland. Kyle is a handsome investment banker who, with his partner Dana Messina, bought Steinway & Sons along with several other musical instrument companies, when he and Dana were in their early thirties.

Kyle always took me to dinner when I was in L.A. and frequently gave me advice about my career. We usually went to a restaurant in Santa Monica called Ivy at the Shore, a hangout on Ocean Avenue that overlooks the beach. The Ivy is a cheerful explosion of pastel colors and potted palms. Comfy cushioned bamboo chairs surround elegantly set tables, and bright bouquets of flowers are arranged just so throughout the room. This in- spot is frequented by Hollywood movers and shakers and film stars, as well as those who want to look like Hollywood movers and shakers and film stars.

Kyle sensed my subdued state of mind and jumped in.

"What's up, Judy? You seem a little down. Waiter! This woman needs a glass of champagne!"

"Thanks Kyle. Champagne always helps."

"Talk to me."

"I'm sick of the music business being such a struggle. I've been at this a long time. It should get easier at some point."

I took a sip of my champagne.

"I'm sick of the whole business, Kyle."

"Don't you know that everyone in this room wants to be Judy Carmichael?" he said, waving his arm toward the room.

"What are you talking about?"

"Listen, everyone wants to be a great musician or a great athlete. *Everyone.* Think of all the actors who have a pathetic rock band because they want to be a musician, or the fat cat businessman who'd rather be Roger Federer. What we need to do is 'bridge the disconnect' from you to all these people and have them know you and your music.

"And Judy, be honest, you're so life-rich it's ridiculous. You do exactly what you want, in every imaginable, exotic location, and people genuinely love you, not because you're rich or happen to be a celebrity. You have friends everywhere. When you say you're going to Paris, five people offer you their home. When I say I'm going to Paris, five people give me the number for the Ritz."

"You have a point. But all I do is worry about money."

"I'm rich and all I do is worry about money."

꧇

After that birthday lunch with Sharon, I decided if I wasn't going to be rich or even solvent, I needed to have more fun and at least pretend to be rich. I started doing creative exchanges in scenic spots I wanted to visit or gigs with sports involved. I did a little recital in Carmel because a round of golf at Clint Eastwood's Tehama Golf Club was promised; for years I was given a cabin for two weeks and lift tickets in Aspen for concerts there. Twice, I managed two weeks in a villa in Rome for a little palazzo recital at the American Academy in Rome.

One of my more successful creative arrangements was on the gorgeous little Caribbean Island of Anguilla. A tennis pro friend emailed to tell me he'd taken a job at a big deal Anguilla resort called Malliouhana and that I should visit. I reminded him that I was poor. He said Malliouhana's chef had a little shack on the beach, just a few yards from the water, at a cozy spot called Sandy Ground. He would rent it to me for twenty-five dollars a night. He promised it wasn't a dump.

I called Ellen and asked if she wanted to spend a week on the second most expensive island in the Caribbean for twelve dollars and fifty cents a night.

"You're kidding, right?"

"No, it's the house of a friend of a friend."

"And you trust this guy?"

"Of course. He's a tennis pro, a kindred soul. He's like me and knows how to live a good life on a meager income. Tennis pros and jazz musicians have more in common than you'd think."

Ellen and I had first met in 1992, when she interviewed me for an article for the newspaper she worked for at the time. We bonded over a shared love for Fred Astaire and early musicals. That's what we have in common. What we don't, is our upbringing. I grew up in the ugly urban sprawl of Los Angeles with parents of humble means. Ellen spent her childhood in a Gatsbyesque area of Long Island in classic WASP style, with riding lessons, a private beach club, tennis, lots of alcohol, scandals, and annual winter jaunts to the grandparents' place on St. Thomas with servants galore. There are no servants in her life now, and she's only mildly snobbish. She'll even hang out with jazz musicians, something her mother would never have allowed.

What I admire in Ellen is her skill in creating a good time. She possesses a wonderful sense of entitlement I envy and aspire to. I expect disaster. She expects a cocktail.

I travel constantly, of course, so I seldom have the time or desire to do much research before a trip. Ellen is the opposite. She not only learned everything there was to know about Anguilla, but had become a celebrity on the island's Chamber of Commerce website chat board thanks to her witty, entertaining posts. Her opinions were now sought for the best eateries, beaches, and hotels—and she'd never even been to the place. Her reputation inspired a number of restaurants to offer us dinner, hoping she'd write something favorable about them.

Ellen had discovered that another Judy Carmichael lived on the island, and she decided to send her a quick email.

"I'm coming to visit your beautiful part of world for a few days with my friend Judy Carmichael. I know Anguilla's a small island, so I wondered: Is there room for two Judy Carmichaels?"

To her surprise, the other one wrote back immediately.

"Is that *the* Judy Carmichael, the pianist? Everyone's always asking if I'm *the* Judy Carmichael!"

So now Ellen had two Judy Carmichaels in her life. Somehow she charmed the second into inviting us to her husband's birthday party, which was conveniently occurring during our visit there. My namesake decided to combine it with a "Judy Meets Judy" event, complete with two cakes, one of them a chocolate, grand-piano-shaped yum-fest.

We arrived on my birthday. The customs people, unlike many around the world, looked closely at my passport, wished me a happy birthday, and asked if I knew there was another Judy Carmichael on the island.

Our little home for the week was a baby-blue shack with hot-pink shutters. The house was surrounded by trees and nestled in a little cove a few yards from the water. The interior was butter-yellow with dark-blue floors and windowsills. A gentle breeze wafted through, so the mosquito netting swayed gently over the bed, which was spread with well-worn white linen.

It was all terribly charming and cozy, and I immediately went native. I threw off my clothes, jumped in the ocean, and splashed around like a crazed dolphin. From there I had a lovely hang with our Rasta neighbor, singing duets with him under the palms while I dried off and got a contact high from his "cig."

Meanwhile, Ellen looked for the non-existent AC.

"There's no hot water!" she moaned. "How can we shower?"

"We'll bathe in the ocean, not worry about our hair, wear hats the whole time, and pretend we're at camp!" I answered, like the endearing (some say irritating) Pollyanna that I am.

"Are you out of your mind?"

I didn't care that the roosters woke us at four a.m., that the water was lukewarm, or that there was no AC, especially for only $25 a day. But Ellen was less enchanted. She said, "Next time: Cuisinart," which I thought was a vegetable chopper but she knew to be a five-star resort.

While we never made it to Cuisinart, our next visit to the island was more upscale, since Ellen had taken over. We'd both fallen for Anguilla, so we agreed she'd be in charge of figuring out how we could get back without spending a fortune, while still ensuring that we had AC and could get a full night's sleep. She decided that I would perform to pay for these luxuries. Ellen began posting about my music and trolling for gigs to get us another trip.

"You should teach at the school and do a fundraiser to get a piano for them."

"How do you know they want a piano?"

"I've gotten to know the people there, and they want you to do this. I got the idea and contact; now you have to figure out how we do it."

"Let's ask three different resorts to give us a room for a couple of nights each and a few different restaurants to feed us every day. That way everyone contributes to the school's piano and we have free room and board. It's about a $15,000 vacation in exchange for a concert."

Anguilla became a home-away-from-home for both of us. I'd done TV and radio there and had a number of interesting encounters. But no one seemed to know about Anguilla until Brad took Jen there to tell her he was dumping her for Angelina. (I'm sure he put it differently.)

My church gig took place shortly after that event, so the Jen-Brad breakup was the talk of the town. I appeared on a local TV show to publicize my concert. The interviewer, a young lad, was so nervous he could barely blurt out the questions. It was live TV, so I decided I had to help him move things along with a distracting interjection. He stuttered, "Tell, tell, tell, me, me if it's true . . ."

"I'm sorry; I really can't talk about my affair with Brad Pitt. It's a sensitive subject, so please let's talk about anything but that. I will say this: I'm not the reason he left Jen."

(Note: As of this writing, Angelina has just left Brad. I'm not responsible for that either.)

Ellen has now been to the island many times with a group of fellow Anguilla-lovers she's met through her online postings; I occasionally join them between gigs for a few days of fun. This is an eclectic group of world travelers and any encounter with them is amusing.

One dinner with this bunch stands out. It was at a restaurant called Oliver's, which has great food and a wonderful view of the ocean. Like so many island eateries, Oliver's sides are open, so the sound of the sea roars in the background.

I'd joined the group well into their stay, so I was meeting everyone at this dinner for the first time. I was a bit confused as to which ones were coupled and what exactly anyone was saying, since the place was packed and noisy, with the sound of waves crashing and people chattering.

A particularly soft-spoken woman named Ginger was recounting her short-lived stage career as the Baby Jesus. The combination of her restrained delivery and the ambient noise allowed me to hear only every other word of her story, even though she was sitting right next to me. I was enjoying a particularly delicious flounder and a lovely Pinot Grigio, while trying to chew and sip as quietly as possible to catch what she was saying.

I gathered she felt the most extraordinary aspect of this particular thespian outing was the unusual casting of her, a woman, in the role of Jesus. I thought of Mary Martin and Cathy Rigby as Peter Pan, thinking Ginger's *size*, not her sex, might have been the main concern. I know there's been controversy over the years about the exact *look* of Jesus, but everyone pretty much agrees that the Baby Jesus, was, well, a baby.

Confused, I glanced across the table at Ellen as she mouthed, "That must have been one gigantic crèche!"

To Ellen's right sat a lovely couple—I somehow learned they were a couple—named Ellie and Wylie, to whom Ginger's tale was directed. Ellie, also concerned about the size issue, asked, or rather shouted, "*You played this role a YEAR ago?*"

"No! I was *one year old!*"

"But Ginger, you describe this like you remember it. You were *one!*"

"Of course I remember this. It was a painful experience." I thought she meant painful in some Method Acting sense. Maybe she'd had trouble "being" a boy, or channeling the right religious spirit.

"In what way was it painful, Ginger?" I queried.

"I had to wear a halo and they *stapled* it to the back of my neck!"

Straining to keep up, someone from the other end of the table asked: "Did someone say something about some stables? Are there horses on Anguilla? I'd love get in some riding."

"*No! I had to wear a halo and they STAPLED IT TO THE BACK OF MY NECK!*" Ginger shouted, obviously frustrated with all of us.

"You know, Harrison Ford did the same thing with his hat in the Indiana Jones movies to keep it from falling off during his stunts," Ellen contributed, always ready with a bit of movie trivia.

I've imagined that being born is pretty painful too, squeezing out of the womb, the bad lighting, the slap on the rump, the creepy strangers in gowns all smiling while you're screaming. I wondered if Ginger remembered that too. She obviously had an impressive memory. I never got to ask her, though, since we all got distracted by the Harrison Ford comment and shifted to a discussion of his enduring hotness.

Trying to focus, I turned to Ginger to bring up the birthing question. She turned away, angry, no doubt, that we didn't take her seriously and weren't appropriately sympathetic. That's when I noticed the tiny, horizontal puncture scars on the back of her neck.

17

No One Can Love You Like You

O occasionally play concerts on high-end cruise ships, the smaller ones that carry two hundred to four hundred passengers. These floating parties attract well-traveled sophisticates who appreciate and can afford the posh surroundings, great service, and gourmet meals.

I was hosting a dinner on one of these trips when the man next to me made a comment I hear a lot.

"You must have lovers all over the world."

I was trying mightily to keep up my hostess duties and carry on a conversation with this guy, an American named Alfred, who was in his mid-seventies, six feet tall, with a rugged jaw, thick salt-and-pepper hair, and a vague Ronald Reagan vibe. He was one of those men whose entire identity was attached to his job, and now that he didn't have one had nothing to say. He was in that confused state that extremely self-centered, attractive, wealthy career men reach when they no longer have a position that forces people to be nice to them.

I'd tried every imaginable subject and finally went to my fallback.

"What's the most interesting thing you've done since joining the ship? You embarked in Hawaii and now we're in New Zealand. You've seen some amazing places."

He thought for a while.

"I've read some books," he said, with a yawn.

"Which books?"

"Marge!" he yelled across the table, attacking his filet mignon as if he were skinning an elk. "What books have I read?"

"You read that lawyer guy from the South."

"John Grisham?" I jumped in, happy to find a connection.

"Yes, that's the guy."

I'm going to need more wine.

"I've read a lot of Grisham," I added. "He's fun."

"I guess."

"What else?"

"Marge, what else have I read?"

This went on for a while until I finally gave up and focused on others at the table, simultaneously carrying on four conversations that included politics with a former ambassador, art with a critic for the *New Yorker*, religion with a newly ordained priest, and astrophysics with, well, an astrophysicist. It was a fascinating group. Nevertheless, Alfred was bored.

After fifteen minutes of watching me juggle the various exchanges around the table, he leaned over and whispered in my ear, "You must have lovers all over the world."

"Well, not *everywhere*, just in my favorite places."

I find it interesting that while the musicians I know have a good idea what non-musical jobs entail, most people are confused by the life of an artist. Everyone comments that my worldwide travels must be exhausting, but they're clueless about the rest of it. Since most stories about touring musicians are the ones we hear from rock stars, it is often inferred that my career must be similar, albeit with less income and drug use.

In general, most married women with husbands and kids to care for, jobs to perform, and never enough time for any of it, tend to:

ENVY my travel and my lack of kids and a husband.
HOPE I have a hot, young guy in every port.
WISH I'd tell them about it.

Married men with corporate jobs and loads of money tend to:

ENVY my career and wish they'd stayed in that college band and become a jazz musician, claiming they'd "give it all up" if they could do what I do.
HOPE I'll invite them to sit in with my band.
WISH they could be a jazz musician while continuing to earn the money they do at their current job.

The rare young women who aspire to be jazz musicians tend to:

ENVY my career and think I've gotten a "break."
HOPE I'll tell them my secret to getting that break.
WISH I'd tell them where I get my vigor, which they infer is from lots of sex but is really from good nutrition and tennis.

Single men want to be me. I've been told this by men of all ages because they:

ENVY what they perceive as my unlimited international opportunities for sex.
HOPE I'll tell them what it's like to be the female Mick Jagger. (Mick and I are similarly lean but I like to think I'm prettier.)
WISH they could have my shagging opportunities without foregoing the money they make at their current job.

Gay women also think I lead a wild life and:

> **ENVY** my hair.
> **HOPE** I'm really gay.
> **WISH** I'd stop talking about my boyfriend.

Gay men love the jet-setting aspect of my life and:

> **ENVY** my hair.
> **HOPE** that the handsome man talking to me after the gig isn't really interested in me, but is gay.
> **WISH** I'd finally reveal whether Tom Cruise told me he's gay when we met a few years ago in Manhattan.

Male musicians frequently tell me they got into music as a way to meet women. I have yet to meet a female musician with this particular motivation. I went into it for the money, as we established earlier, so the guys obviously had a more realistic plan.

I do meet nice guys on gigs, but they're usually with their nice wives or girlfriends. And in the early days, when I played more bars, if a guy came in every night, I didn't assume it was my music that attracted him but rather that he had a drinking problem—a thought that was reinforced when I once asked the bartender if she thought a guy I liked sat at the bar for the entire evening because he was into me.

"Oh, yeah, he thinks you're great," she responded, "but he's here every night whether you are or not."

Also, as a pianist, I tend to miss a lot because I look down at the keys, whereas other instrumentalists face the audience and can surreptitiously scan the room for fetching folk to chat up on the break. More than once a band mate has asked, "Didn't you notice that guy hitting on you?"

"Not really. I was busy thinking about your weird modulation to B."

That said, Chris Noth, the tall dreamboat who played Mr. Big on *Sex and the City* during my years at Knickerbocker Bar and Grill in Greenwich Village, used to come in to hear me, and him I noticed.

And things sneak up on me. Once in Brazil, the country where everyone is sexy, knows they're sexy, embraces being sexy, and at some point *gets* sexy, I had the first of many sexy encounters.

This was one of my first trips to Brazil, and I was returning home from Rio's Antonio Carlos Jobim Airport. You have to love a city that names its airport after a musician rather than a politician.

I checked in with the alluring, perfectly tanned attendant at American Airlines. My green eyes met his smoky brown ones as he ran his hand through his thick black hair. I leaned my head back slightly and tossed my golden curls. He looked at me intently and drew a breath. I glanced back and sighed.

All this before I'd even given him my passport.

I eventually finished checking in and enjoyed the afterglow while I waited for my flight under a huge exotic plant that would have been happier outside but was thriving remarkably indoors.

While Rio suggests images of warm breezes, brilliant sunshine, and azure skies, the airport delivers none of this seductive experience to the weary traveler. Cranky attendants, pushy duty-free salespeople, and ineffective security are the norm, so while I should have noticed that only I and a potted palm were left in the waiting area, I'd drifted off with thoughts of Samba Man and hadn't noticed that each of my fellow passengers had left the immediate area because, unlike me, they spoke Portuguese and understood that the gate had changed.

Eventually, the debonair desk man found me, smiled, offered his hand, and with his bossa nova accent whispered, "Come with me."

We walked for a while and finally reached a different gate, at which point he gave me a new ticket and directed me to my flight, which had been held for me and where he'd upgraded me to first class—the only conclusion to this story that pleased me almost as much as my other fantasy.

Another romantic adventure happened long before the "selfie" became a popular activity, but I think of this story as a precursor, as well as a warning about dating actors.

I'd just flown from New York to L.A. on my birthday for a week of concerts and teaching. I met a friend for dinner, a beautiful gal who was then eighty but looked sixty and acted thirty. Her given name was Jeffreys, but everyone called her Jeff, which she hated, so I called her Fred.

Fred took me to her favorite Beverly Hills haunt, a place she'd first gone with her parents, who were Hollywood scriptwriters in the '30s and '40s. It was one of those old-style steak houses with dark green walls, mahogany paneling, white tablecloths, low lighting, and portions the size of Texas. Fred knew the town cold and had fabulous stories about everything and everybody. I think she even dated Gary Cooper.

Our spectacular looking waiter—an actor, we surmised—took our drink order. As he walked away, I pointed at him and said to Fred, "That's what I want for my birthday."

"Ah, but is he available?" she rejoined, giving him the once over.

"What do you think—six-foot-two? Taller?"

"I'd give him six-three, and worth the climb. Never thought I could like a man in an apron."

He came back with our overfull martinis, spilling them a bit. Fred jumped in with, "Excuse me young man, you're a bit young for me but you're perfect for my friend. Are you available?"

He straightened to a military posture, flexing his well-developed pectorals, which bulged nicely through his tight black T, and said, "Available, heterosexual, and disease free."

Even knowing Fred's capacity for shenanigans, I was a bit surprised by this move. I did think it was a clever answer, although if he *was* an actor, he could have previously said this in a movie. Still, a good line, well delivered.

Our suspicions that he was an actor increased when he again splashed our drinks and forgot to take our order, something a real waiter could probably handle. Our guy had excellent hair and pithy patter though, so we took a leap.

Three drinks later I was plastered; Fred, not even tipsy. She enthusiastically suggested, "Give him your number! We'll wrap this up with one last drink and I'll scoot out so you can go home with him."

"Are you out of your mind? I just met the guy and all we know is we think he's an actor and know he's a lousy waiter."

"Yeah, but look at him! If only I were ten years younger." She sighed.

"Fred, that would make you seventy."

"Your point?"

"Listen, I just flew in and I'm tired. I've got concerts every night for the next eight days. I need sleep. And food."

"In my day we knew how to close a deal."

A compromise was struck: We stayed for dinner and I gave Sean (not his real name, also not his stage name) my number.

He and I met for a drink the next day. We had fun, and decided to rendezvous the following afternoon for some horseback riding atop the Santa Monica Mountains, he with romantic thoughts of the movie *The Horse Whisperer*, I hoping I wouldn't wind up too saddle-sore to sit on a piano bench.

By now I had learned that Sean was indeed an actor, and in the midst of a soul-searching crisis. He'd stopped going to acting classes, resentful of the fact that he wasn't getting the parts Brad Pitt was getting and angry that he had to struggle for money. The usual.

I revealed that I was in town for some concerts and would love to have him attend one. He agreed and things went so well that I asked him to stick around, which he did for the entire eight days. After five nights of concerts and lovemaking, I was happy but exhausted. I reported back to Fred, who was thrilled with this turn of events. She wouldn't listen to any of my complaints that Sean's IQ was on the low side. Yes, I was having a great time, but it was hard to feign interest in his struggles with Hollywood.

"I have a feeling he's a lousy actor. He couldn't even play the part of a good waiter, remember?"

"Well, he *is* so handsome."

"Snap out of it, Fred. They're all handsome. And I feel like he's playing to an imaginary camera at all times. We went to lunch and he had the loveliest expression on his face. I thought he was looking at me, but then realized he was admiring himself in the mirror behind me! I started to ask a question and he interrupted with, 'Forty-two!'

"I said, 'I thought you just turned forty.' And he said, 'Oh, I thought you were going to ask how many women I've slept with.'

"'You've *counted*?' I asked in horror.

"'Haven't you?'

"It was a turn-off, Fred. This guy has issues."

"Don't let him talk," she advised. "My generation knew how to let men go on and on and pretend to listen while planning our grocery list or some such thing."

I called my pal Ellen, who always has something helpful to say when I phone from the road for a bit of support.

"I'm exhausted, Ellen. We go at it nonstop and then he rests up all day while I go off to give master classes and concerts."

"You seriously want sympathy here?"

"I'm tired. I've got work to do."

"Judy, you're living the life. Buck up. Take some vitamins."

"And last night, in the middle of a particularly enjoyable moment, I had my arms around him and felt his incredible back muscles and said, 'Whew, you can't imagine how great this feels,' and *he* said, 'I know.' I said, 'What do you mean you *know*? You've felt your own back muscles?' He answered, 'No, I dated an Olympic athlete and she had awesome muscle definition.'"

(Men, a suggestion: When a woman compliments you at a time like this, don't bring up a former sweetheart whose body is superior to the one presently in your arms.)

"Ellen, I think I'm done. Sean says I'm patronizing. Am I patronizing?"

"Of course you're patronizing. He's a waiter."

"I have enormous respect for waiters. Some of my best friends are waiters."

"Yes, but they're *real* waiters, not an actor doing a bad portrayal of a waiter. What prompted this?"

"We were sitting in his living room, which looked like a college dorm room, small, dusty, very little in it except a couch, a TV, and a few old copies of *People* on a beat-up coffee table. He went on and on about a standing ovation he'd gotten in his acting class."

"What did he perform?"

"That's what I asked. He said he hadn't performed. He got the ovation just for 'having the courage to show up,' since he hadn't been there for a while. I said, 'That's where jazz musicians are different from actors. We have to perform something to get a standing ovation.'"

"Diplomacy was never your strong suit. Then what?"

"He said I was finally ready to see his bedroom. I thought it was a romantic move, but what he really wanted me to see were the walls covered from floor to ceiling with pictures of him in various macho poses."

"Hmm. With all forty-two lovers?"

"No, alone."

"Ah, come on. He's alone in *every shot*?"

"Yes, he's the only one in the picture. The last thing he sees before he nods off at night are walls covered with pictures of himself."

"You're right. Come home. Give him a mirror. He won't even notice you've left."

18

Anatomically Accessible

"Wow, Pat, this place looks like a spa! And everyone's so friendly and good-looking. Have you noticed?"

"Yeah. I feel like I've stepped into an episode of *Grey's Anatomy*. I guess Sloan Kettering not only gets the best minds, it gets the best faces."

My friend Pat had come with me on my first visit to Sloan Kettering in Manhattan to meet my cancer surgeon. I'd gotten my diagnosis in May 2003. My mother had had cervical cancer in her twenties, and even as a teenager I saw her neuroses reflected in the weird delight she took in her various illnesses. My fear of cervical cancer was one of my initial incentives to start therapy, in hopes of expunging any psychological similarities to my mother that might make me vulnerable to a similar fate. In 2001 my gynecologist had told me that research showed that cervical cancer wasn't hereditary. At the time I was relieved, but also found it ironic that my fear of inheriting this disease had been a positive motivator in facing many of my problems. Then, two years later, I got cervical cancer.

Pat had been through breast cancer, so she was the perfect big sister throughout my surgeries, chemo, and radiation. She's also detail-oriented, whereas I'm a big-picture gal, so I knew she'd ask all the questions I wouldn't.

The best warning Pat gave me was, "The bills will make you sicker than the cancer."

Thanks to that advice, I put all my medical bills in a folder and didn't look at any of them for two years. It took that long for the insurance company to figure out who paid what. I needed to focus on living.

— —

"Judy Carmichael! Judy Carmichael!"

"I'm here."

"I hate them announcing my name," I moaned. "I don't want anyone to find out about this. They're going to be shouting 'Judy Carmichael' a hundred times before this is over. Someone's bound to recognize me."

"That's the least of your worries, honey."

"Yeah ..."

"The doctor will see you now, Judy."

We were greeted by an extremely tall, fit doctor who looked like someone who saves lives all day. Dr. Barakat was the head of gynecological services and I was lucky to get him. I was told this repeatedly throughout my time at Sloan Kettering.

"Judy, after looking at your chart and seeing you now in person," he said, "I think we can do the surgery laparoscopically, which is much less invasive, so you'll heal faster. This is extensive surgery and not usually possible laparoscopically. Fortunately, you're anatomically accessible, which is perfect for this approach."

"Funny, I just had a date where someone wanted me to be *more* anatomically accessible."

"Ha! You're funny. That's great. What I mean is, you're thin, so we can get to what we need to with this method. We don't have to go through layers of fat."

Pat proceeded with her list of questions while I fantasized about my new surgeon being anatomically accessible.

"I'm hoping what's called a 'cone biopsy' will be sufficient, so I'd like to schedule that now. We'll know if we need to do more after we do this surgery and proceed from there. You won't have to stay overnight with the cone biopsy, but it is fairly extensive. You'll go under for a couple of hours, followed by a bit of recovery time."

Two weeks later, I was back for a cone biopsy.

"Hi, Judy, I'm Dr. Prud'homme, your anesthesiologist. I hear you're a jazz pianist. I'm a huge jazz fan. I looked you up and love your music. I've brought some CDs I thought you might like to hear during surgery. Ella, Duke, Basie—what do you think?"

I was already a bit groggy from whatever they had given me to relax me before the big dose to put me out. Still, I was cheered by this thoughtful gesture. "Perfect," I murmured. "Play Basie." She cranked up the music, which inspired everyone to dance around while preparing to dive into my anatomically accessible self.

And finally, there he was, leaning over me, my big, strong, life-saving surgeon.

He took my hand. "Are you ready? How are you feeling?"

"Basie's put me in the best mood," I said in my vaguely drugged state. "Wait!" I said with a jolt. "It's more important that it puts *you* in a great mood."

— ∽

I came to with my surgeon's lovely face looking down at me.

"We'll need to do the more extensive surgery, Judy," he said gently.

I think this is bad news, but I'd let this guy do anything to me.

A few hours later, I was dressed and out the door with Pat. I've always been loaded with energy, but even I was surprised that I felt so great after fairly major surgery.

"Let's eat at a little restaurant I saw around the corner," she said. "The weather is beautiful, and I thought it would be nice to sit outside, if you're up for it."

"A steak sounds good."

"Easy, girlfriend. Are you OK to walk? Are you woozy?"

"Actually, all I can think about is that steak."

I'd seen slim folk get even thinner when they got sick, and I was determined to keep some meat on my bones.

After lunch, Pat dropped me off at a friend's apartment, where I was going to spend the night. It was a spectacular June day and, while I was supposed to be tired, a long walk and a margarita sounded perfect. I wanted to stay positive and not sit around and worry. I called my friend Tanja, a fan of that lovely drink.

"Tanja, it's Judy."

"Hey," she said. "God, I'm in business hell. You can't get anywhere in this fucking company without a dick. I swear I hate it here."

"Where are you?"

"I'm at a convention in D.C."

"That's too bad. It's a beautiful day here in New York and I thought you might join me for a walk in Central Park and then get some margaritas. I've got cancer and just had surgery and will have to have more, plus chemo and radiation. I thought it'd be fun to go to that Mexican place we like and chill out. But it sounds like you have your hands full."

"Wait, you've got *cancer*? Oh, my God!"

"Yeah. I wasn't even going to tell you but you sound like you could use some perspective. And listen, you can't tell anyone. This is about me, not you. I don't want anyone to know about this. If they react in any way other than asking, 'What can I do to be helpful?' it'll piss me off, and I really need to stay positive.

"And Tanja, a little advice. It's best not to say to your coworkers, 'You can't get anywhere in this company without a dick,' since you're one of three women in your firm. You don't want to make it two. Just a thought."

It was a little harsh, but every now and then I indulged in hitting people with the verbal two-by-four of "I have cancer" when they were whining excessively. I've never liked whiners.

19

We're the Lucky Ones

I looked up at the friends who surrounded my bed as I awoke from my second cancer surgery on August 24, 2003. My mom's birthday was August 26, which was when I saw her for the last time. The closeness of these two dates seemed significant. My first surgery had been a breeze; this one, not so much.

"Did I get a lip job?" I managed to slur, through hugely swollen lips.

"I think the big lips are a good look for you," Ellen said.

"Apparently, this happens sometimes with the anesthesia, Judy," Pat explained. "You look like Angelina Jolie."

"I don't want to talk about my affair with Brad Pitt," I muttered drowsily before falling asleep.

My second surgery took longer than expected—four hours plus. I'd arranged for a private room, but woke up to find an older woman in the bed next to mine. I was feeling waves of terrible pain as my meds wore off, although my roommate seemed to be in much worse shape than I.

I drifted in and out of sleep, waking in the middle of the night to the sounds of moaning nearby. My roommate was moving fitfully. From her dream state, she cried out, *"Mommy! Mommy!"*

I had read about dying soldiers on the battlefield calling for their mothers. Still, this surprised me, coming from a woman of over seventy. I realized it would never occur to me to call out for my mother.

I continued listening to this woman's anguished sighs. I stared up to the ceiling through the low, gray light, which filtered through the gauzy curtains surrounding my bed. My cheeks were wet with tears.

Slowly, something in me shifted. I heard myself say, "It's all right, dear. Mommy's here. I won't leave you. You're safe. Go back to sleep now. I love you."

I didn't know I could still feel deeply and care for someone in pain, after so many years of ministering to my mother. I had thought that part of me was gone.

I continued to comfort her from my bed, until her breathing calmed and she drifted back into a deeper slumber.

The next day, I endured an excruciating walk around the ward. I was struck by the silence and palpable fear in every room I hobbled past.

When I was getting radiation five days a week, I received my treatments from a few technicians in their early thirties, all upbeat and encouraging. I offered to treat them to a hundred-dollar-per-ticket fundraiser I was doing a few months after my last scheduled radiation treatment. I wanted them to see me in an elegant setting, making music, to celebrate what they'd helped make possible.

"I can't believe you'd do that, Judy," said a member of my team.

"What are you talking about? It's a lovely event at Steinway Hall. I want you to see me in something besides a hospital gown and witness the results of your work to cure me."

"Most people say they never want to see us again because we'll remind them of their cancer."

People who have experienced life-threatening disease often talk about their lives changing because they've faced death. That was not my experience. I've always been a positive person, trying to keep negative thoughts and people away from me. Having cancer deepened that resolve.

The only appropriate response to someone telling you they have cancer or any serious illness is, "How can I help?" What most people say, in a sort of desperate tone is, "You've got cancer? But you're OK, right?" That means, "Don't tell me any more. I'm scared of this and don't want to talk about it."

What I've come to call the ugly cleanup of cancer is much harder than the initial surgery, radiation, and chemo. You get through the devastating diagnosis, the body-altering surgery, then side-effects remain that don't allow you to get on with your life.

I never say I'm a cancer survivor because it implies I've done something special. What about the people who don't survive? I also know too many people who get cancer again, years after they had "survived" the first time.

I had lymph nodes removed during surgery, which left me with something called lymphedema; it causes swelling in my legs and stomach and a susceptibility to staph infections. It was so severe in the first few years after my surgery that I would swell fifteen pounds or more from the beginning of a concert to the end. *Fifteen pounds in two hours.* I'd feel it happening and didn't know why, or how to deal with it. It was a tremendous assault to my vanity, a terrible distraction, and a constant reminder that I'd had cancer. I felt I could never move on; and since I perform for a living, it presented yet another obstacle in how I dealt with presenting myself on stage.

My surgeon barely addressed this. The others who treated me had little to add. I once mentioned the condition to one of my doctors and she responded, "I know, I have it in my arm from having had breast cancer."

"What do you do about it?"

"I cry."

I did research on my own and have improved over the years, but it's a continuing battle. I'm proud to say that my advocacy inspired Dr.

Barakat to apply and receive a grant to conduct the largest study ever done on gynecological lymphedema.

On one of my follow-up visits to Sloan Kettering, I got into the elevator, joining two others. I was followed by a man who moved in next to me as the doors closed behind him. He turned and smiled at me. With a shock, I realized he had lymphedema on his face that had disfigured it grotesquely, making one side hugely distended and lumpy. The couple with us in this enclosed space recoiled involuntarily. I forced myself to act natural, make eye contact, and smile back at him. He looked at me with warmth and said, "Just think: We're the lucky ones."

Around this time, my friend Jude did one of my road tours with me. I showed her my legs after a concert. She was the only person I'd allowed to see me in this state. I was always at my most swollen after a concert.

"Oh, Judy! I've never had good legs but you've always had great ones. If I had your beautiful legs and this happened to me, I'd kill myself."

After I'd been in therapy a few years, I was complaining about a particularly irritating run of career issues. My therapist George sat quietly for a minute, then slowly began to speak.

"Judy, we've been together a long time now. I'm been thinking about this for a while. I've seen people from every profession, businessmen, painters, poets, novelists, actors, everyone. After knowing you, though, I can honestly say that there's no harder way to make a living than as a jazz musician. Nothing. I deal in fantasy but your reality is as hard as you think it is."

Platitudes piss me off, but empathy comforts.

At the beginning of the cancer experience, the goal is to save your life. When you get through the various treatments, however, and your life is altered in enough terrible ways, you begin to wonder if it's all worth it. There are always new or lingering issues, so the bar is continually raised no matter how brave you are.

Dr. Barakat suggested I see a lymphedema specialist named Michael Alatriste, who educated me and worked with me and continues to do so. Dr. Barakat kept me from dying. Michael Alatriste gave me my life back.

Physical therapist Sinead FitzGibbon is another person whose sup-port was invaluable in making life worth living when I was feeling fairly hopeless. Not only did she help heal my post-surgery body, she kept me believing it was possible to move forward. To get me performing again, Sinead also enlisted her family in Ireland to arrange a concert in her hometown of Ross. And hip hop producer Tommy Coster hired me to play a concert in his studio in Santa Monica for his musical community, ostensibly for that purpose, but really to cheer me up, get me at the piano again and to make me some money. A handful of friends knew I was sinking emotionally and financially and did what they could to prop me up.

One of my great strengths is focus. After five weeks of radiation, I had "chemo fog" that destroyed my ability to focus for years. I played a jazz club in London during this period and in the middle of a tune, I couldn't coordinate my hands. It was frightening. The critic for the London *Times* was there to write a review and the room was packed. I felt completely defeated. I was tired of fighting for everything, never feeling like myself, having my body wrecked and not being able to play the piano the way I always had. The only thing that kept me from walking off that stage was a certainty that if I did, I'd never walk onto another one.

The recovery was long and hard, and the financial burden is with me still. I had almost no income for three years, since nearly all my time was spent in the company of doctors. Most entertainers I know who have gone through devastating illnesses go bankrupt. I managed to avoid that, but for years I fought against losing my house while trying to get my brain working again and my body and piano playing back on track.

—　～

I interviewed the great pianist Fred Hersch for my radio show *Jazz Inspired* a few years ago. Afterward I told him how much I admired his handling of his long battle with AIDS and his fundraising for AIDS research. I also told him a bit about my cancer experience, prompting him to ask what I'm doing now with my music.

"Believe it or not, I've started singing. It's wild, because I've had two vocal-cord surgeries and always had huge hang-ups about my voice. I never even sang in the shower, but now it's my new passion."

Fred nodded, not surprised. "Of course you're singing."

"What do you mean?"

"You're a new person since the cancer. Of course you'd do something unexpected and new."

Fred has faced far worse health challenges than I have, so this meant a lot.

＊　＊

One of the things no one warned me about was how swollen I'd be after surgery. I looked like a Teletubby. My friend Pat brought me some of her sweats because my pants didn't fit. I also had a catheter for a couple of weeks because my bladder had been nicked during surgery. Dr. Barakat had warned me that the catheter could get plugged, and if it did, that I'd have to get right to the ER to have it removed, since my bladder could burst or be damaged further if the catheter were not removed properly.

I was home only a few days when it plugged. A few days later it happened again. I went quickly from uncomfortable to extreme pain. The only person I could find to take me to the hospital was my fellow tennis-player Irwin, a lovely retired professor of eighteenth-century French literature. Irwin is the epitome of the absent-minded professor, and is basically useless in an emergency. I was desperate and deteriorating fast. He was scared to death, puffing like mad on his pipe, no doubt wishing I'd called someone else.

"Irwin, you've got to drive faster. If we don't get this catheter out, my bladder could burst. I could die. I feel faint and may pass out. If I do, you've got to remember my birthday and a few details or they won't admit me."

"*Don't pass out!*" he pleaded, speeding faster than he'd ever driven, probably thirty miles per hour. The car windows were fogging from my heavy breathing.

We finally arrived. Irwin ran inside, found a wheelchair, poured me into it and brought me to the admitting desk. The admitting nurse ignored us.

"Please, I'm in terrible pain," I pleaded weakly. "All I need is someone to remove this catheter and I'll be fine."

"What's your insurance?" asked Nurse Ratched as she yawned and continued with her paperwork.

Suddenly I was gasping for air, speechless. Irwin started petting my head, trying to comfort me as best he could.

"Why is she shaking?" he wailed to the admitting nurse.

"She's going into shock," came the bored response. "I need her insurance card."

After much back and forth, she finally told us to wait in the corner, which we did for thirty torturous minutes. Eventually a nurse walked by who recognized me from my being there two days earlier with the same problem.

"Judy, God, what's going on?" she demanded.

I couldn't speak, couldn't even lift my head.

"I've got this," she said to Irwin as she quickly wheeled me into the treatment area.

She called to another nurse, "Please take this patient to Room Three while I find the doctor. Hang on, Judy."

The nurse who took over wheeled me into a wall, smashing my left hand against it.

"Oh, I'm sorry, I was trying to be speedy," she said, laughing. "There goes your career."

Oh, God, she recognizes me.

"I know I've seen you in concert," she continued happily as we rolled along. "Let's see, was it Carnegie Hall? Guild Hall?"

I could barely speak. "I've played both," I whispered. "Please, I really need you to get the doctor so he can take care of this. I'm in terrible pain. Can you help me onto the table?"

"Now wait. Just sit there a minute. I want to figure this out. Bay Street Theater? Merkin Hall? I've got it! Tilles Center, right? I saw you with the Smothers Brothers. I loved that concert. Aren't they the best?

Are they as nice in person as they seem? I used to have such a crush on Tommy. Now what's going on with you here?"

———

A few weeks later I was back at Sloan Kettering for a follow-up exam. Supposedly they were going to do some probing, which I couldn't imagine because of the intense pain. I was still pear-shaped, and not an attractive pear. I sat freezing in a thin, inadequately sized hospital gown, waiting for the doctor, when in walked Rosie O'Donnell.

"Hi, I'm Doctor Blaga. How are you feeling?"

Wow, she looks exactly like Rosie O'Donnell. Try to act normal.

"I'm OK. Still very swollen and sore."

"The nurse who visited you at home to check on the catheter said you weren't taking your pain medication."

"I know pain pills can slow healing, so I'd rather muscle my way through."

"Judy, I know how much pain you're in. Suffering through it can slow healing too. Take the meds."

She turned around, reaching for something. When she turned back to me, I was stunned.

"Is that a dildo?" I asked with wonder.

She stuttered, obviously embarrassed. "No, it's a, a dilator. You'll need, uh, to start using this to, ah, um, stretch yourself and help get, everything, uh, working again."

"Are you out of your mind? I feel like my vagina is on fire and you're talking about rehab?"

"Use it or lose it."

"You don't seem terribly sympathetic."

"I'm sorry. OK, don't think about this now," the doctor said. "You do need to get started with these dilators as soon as possible, though. There's a lot of scar tissue from the surgery and the radiation will damage the tissue further so we have to get your vagina in shape. We'll give you graduating sizes to build you back up."

"I feel like Goldilocks, all these size choices until I get it just right." I was trying to stay positive but was feeling discouraged, edging toward hopeless, a place I didn't want to go.

"Seriously, you need to use the dilators or the tissue won't heal properly. It's going to be painful, *extremely* painful, but you have to start as soon as possible."

I carried my dilator with me when I started traveling again and was pulled out of the security line every time for carrying "sex toys" which I didn't realize were a security risk.

I was fascinated by the awkward approach from the TSA folks as they decided which one was going to ask me to open my bag and arrest me for sexual contraband. Before the reveal, I'd ask if I could say something to the official about to nab me. I would whisper in his ear, "I have cancer. This is part of my therapy."

That's when I realized the extent to which people are scared of the C word. None of these people knew what a sex toy had to do with cancer, but they couldn't have moved away faster if I'd said, "I have leprosy." After I'd mentioned cancer, I never had to open my bag.

Remember this if they roust you for your Rabbit.

20

And Then My Heart Stood Still

"Please come in. I'm Dr. Dupont, your new chemo oncologist."

God, yet another looker. Where do they find these people?

"How are you doing?" he asked.

"I'm OK. But I do have to tell you something. The only thing that's really making me nuts is how often my treatment protocol is changed. It's unsettling. Just when I get myself prepared for a specific schedule, without warning you all change your minds and figure something new to do to me."

He looked embarrassed.

"Ah, me," I went on. "You're about to tell me I'm not doing chemo once a week, as I was told, but some other plan, right?"

He looked me over in my sleeveless, cashmere black turtleneck, black leather pants and boots, looking like a girl about to go on a date, which I was.

"That's a great outfit. You have sort of an Emma Peele thing going on."

"You're an *Avengers* fan? You seem a bit young for that show, maybe just a couple years older than Doogie Howser."

He laughed. "I have the DVDs."

"Ah. Carry on. You're going to tell me there's been a change of plan. I can feel it."

"Well, yes. I've decided to admit you today—now actually—and put you on a continual chemo drip for a week, and then one chemo dose once a week for the following four weeks and radiation five days a week for five weeks."

"You're joking, right? I don't even have a toothbrush. I'm about to go to dinner and don't have anything with me."

"We can admit you tomorrow, but this really is the best plan with your situation. I'd like to start today. I've discussed it with Dr. Barakat. I need to tell you the possible side effects."

I was completely thrown off and stopped listening. No one knew I was here. I was about to break it to a close friend over dinner that I had cancer, and now I had to check into the hospital. I live two hours from Manhattan, so I couldn't run home for supplies. I left and wandered the halls, a bit addled, and ran into my radiation oncologist, Dr. Rengan, one of my favorites.

"Judy! I just heard what they did to you. I am so sorry. This has got to be a shock. What can I do? You look great, by the way."

"Thanks. I have a date and wasn't planning on checking in tonight, obviously. I'm kind of in shock. I'm trying to stay positive but these kinds of surprises bring me down. Can you tell me the possible side effects with this protocol? I couldn't concentrate when I saw Dr. Dupont and got this news."

"I'll get your chart."

He returned with my file.

"Let's see. The most common side effect from this type of chemo is loss of hearing and loss of feeling in your fingers."

"Good thing I'm not a concert pianist."

"Wait! You *are* a concert pianist. Let me think."

"I can't do this treatment, doctor. There has to be another way or I'll have to take my chances and not get the chemo."

"No, you should do chemo. We'll figure something else out. I'm so sorry, Judy. We discover new things every day, which is why we keep changing your protocol. Don't worry. I'm on it."

Settling into my new room, I met one of the most interesting people I'd ever encountered: my new roommate, Diane, a native New Yorker. Diane was a heavy-equipment operator whose multiple cancer surgeries hadn't lessened her amazing spirit. Diane had been in the hospital so often that she knew the ropes, and clued me in on everything. She'd had a double mastectomy, and bore an elaborate tattoo, from one side of her stomach to the other, that intricately covered the scars she'd gotten from her many reconstruction surgeries.

I was hooked to my chemo drip and multiple other things. Diane was on an intravenous antibiotic for an infection. Like me, though, she refused to see herself as a "cancer person" and was constantly unhooking herself to go across the street to get us a couple of Starbucks treats.

"It's just so great to get outside."

"I can't believe you unhook your drip yourself."

Periodically one of her doctors would come by.

"Is Diane at Starbucks again?"

"No, I think she went out for Ben and Jerry's. I'm not sure, but she said if you came by to tell you she'd be right back and she's bringing you something."

She was a lucky draw on my part.

— ⁓

I ate like a stevedore, trying to pack on some pounds.

"Another brownie sundae, Judy?" asked yet another doctor. "Are you having two a day?"

"I read that chocolate is good for cancer."

"Good to know."

I was doing great. I felt toxic but hadn't thrown up and wasn't losing weight. On my fourth day of twenty-four-hour chemo, I was chatting with Diane, having just finished a steak; I was about to plunge into another brownie sundae when suddenly I felt a crushing pain in my chest.

"Diane, I can't breathe!" I gasped as I clutched my chest.

Alarms went off and an overwhelming nausea hit me.

"Judy, hang on! You're having a heart attack. I've seen this before. It can be a side effect from the chemo. I'll get the doctor. Hang on!"

Diane unhooked her IV and raced out the door.

Shit! I can't breathe. After all this, I can't believe I'm going to die from a heart attack.

A few minutes later I looked up, realizing I was laid out flat. A nurse was wiping bits of brownie off my face.

"Judy, you passed out into your sundae. We're all quite impressed with your food intake, by the way."

"My chest feels awful."

"You're OK. We've stopped the chemo. There won't be any more right now. Rest."

I looked over at Diane and smiled weakly.

"Thanks for saving me."

"I knew you wouldn't die. You're a fighter. They heard the alarm, so they were on their way. And you still have your beautiful hair. All the baldies are rooting for you. You're our favorite."

"You're my favorite, Diane."

"Let's celebrate. I'll unhook myself and go get us a couple lattes."

21

Jazz Inspired

$\mathcal{O}$n 1995 I started thinking seriously about developing my own radio series. When I appeared on Marian McPartland's NPR series, *Piano Jazz*, in the late '80s, her producer liked my speaking voice and ease with spontaneous conversation and told me I should have my own show. Other radio professionals had said the same thing.

On *Piano Jazz*, Marian and her guests, most of them pianists, chatted and performed together; Billy Taylor, her fellow piano player, profiled other jazz artists in periodic segments on *CBS Sunday Morning*. I wanted to do something broader, something that would include all of the arts and sciences, celebrate inspiration and creativity, and also bring more fans to jazz.

The enjoyment of jazz increases with repeated listening and further understanding. I thought of hosting a show in which I talked with well-known artists who weren't necessarily jazz musicians, but who had found inspiration in jazz. I thought that such a series might bring people to jazz who hadn't previously given it a chance; it would also be an interesting platform for exploring each guest's creative process. I also felt that to talk with jazz musicians about the music that had inspired them would help listeners understand the music on a deeper level. I wanted to feature not only famous artists but others who weren't household names. The sad truth in the arts is that extremely young or extremely old artists are the ones most often celebrated, when most of life is the time in between.

A new public radio show usually starts in a local market, with sponsorship through a station; if it becomes popular, it will expand to other markets. I started *Judy Carmichael's Jazz Inspired* independently, without a sponsor or station behind me, which is unusual. I interviewed thirteen jazz lovers, celebrated creative people I knew personally who agreed to be my initial guests and help me launch the show. This gave me a thirteen-part "special," the fewest number of shows a station will take for a series. I couldn't afford to hire a full-time producer, so I taught myself to edit and produce by listening to a feature done on me by NPR's *Morning Edition*. In the first year I also worked with various NPR producers, including David Goren, Felix Contreras, and Tim Owens. I owe a lot to all three.

I hoped that someone at NPR or another of America's large public radio networks would hear the show, love it, and take it on as one of their sponsored shows. For a year NPR included it in its weekly series *Jazz Riffs*, but that show ended when NPR cut back on jazz coverage, so I've remained on my own.

Independence has its advantages. I choose the guests and produce as I wish. In 2017 I celebrated seventeen years on the air. I often carry my equipment with me so I can tape interviews while I'm on the road. My production engineer is Kurt Heidolph. I choose the guests, do the interview, gather the music and choose the edits; Kurt assembles it all. We pretend we're a staff of fifty, so please don't spread it around that we're just two people.

One of my first interviews was with the late novelist E.L. Doctorow. He and I met on a tennis court in the Hamptons in the mid-'90s and became a doubles team for a while—he the tall terror at the net and I the whirling dervish covering the rest of the court. One of my great thrills was to occasionally be included in his longtime weekly men's doubles game with the late writer Peter Matthiessen and other acclaimed authors; we played on a private court in Sagaponack. These men were great players but much older than I, so I was invited not for my riveting repartee—they provided plenty—but for my spry legs and forehand crosscourt.

I'd just moved to the Hamptons full-time and knew very few people, so this was a heady introduction to the scene. Doctorow was an early supporter of my idea for *Jazz Inspired* and generously agreed to be in my initial group of thirteen interviewees. Once the show took off and I was looking for other guests, he said, "Have you noticed you only have old white guys on your show?"

"All I know are old white guys."

"Branch out."

My guests are all committed to the artistic life and feel everyone should be creative. Billy Joel, who studied briefly with the jazz pianist Lennie Tristano, epitomizes the commitment of the kind of people I wanted on *Jazz Inspired*. He made a list of songs he'd written that were specifically inspired by jazz, and detailed his original concept for each of them, essentially producing the show for me.

Billy and I met in Sag Harbor shortly after we had tied for "Favorite Hamptons Entertainer," voted on by the readers of *Dan's Papers*, a popular local magazine. I approached him at a reception at Bay Street Theatre.

"Hi, Billy. I'm Judy Carmichael. We're both Steinway Artists and neighbors. I thought I'd say hello."

"Nice to meet you," he said as he shook my hand. Then, as I turned to leave he said, "Wait! Didn't we just win something together?"

It was a funny moment and I jumped on it, asking him to be on *Jazz Inspired*. Originally Billy had wanted to be a classical or jazz pianist, so he was a perfect candidate for my show. He said he'd be delighted, on the condition that we have the conversation over lunch at his favorite spot in Amagansett, an elegant place frequented by well-dressed ladies-who-lunch. He wore jeans, a T-shirt, and a baseball cap. I wore the same, without the hat.

We began our lunch like an awkward blind date, but three bottles of wine later we were two drunk musicians exchanging war stories. After a few more long interviews with other guests I realized I couldn't do this with everyone, but it sure was fun with Billy.

After Billy and I had chatted a bit, I said we should probably get started. Everything was fine, except I couldn't get the recorder working. I was beginning to panic. Billy watched me for a while and finally reached over to the machine, flipped a switch, and said, "I think you push this button that says 'Power.'"

We talked, we ate, we drank, we talked, we ate, we drank, finally moving on from the interview to discuss where we were both going with our careers.

"You know, Judy, you should do corporate gigs. I never did them, but Sting's doing them now, Paul, everybody. You should too."

"I've done a few, and they do pay well," I said, pretending we were vaguely in the same business.

"I'm doing one next week for some bank. They started by offering—" (a ridiculously big amount of money). "But, you know, Judy . . . I had to say no."

I reached for my glass, took a sip, and thought: *I could pay off my mortgage with that amount.*

"Then they offered—" (twice the ridiculously big amount of money). "And you know, Judy . . . I said no."

I choked a bit, but covered it and fantasized how that amount would pay off my mortgage and buy me a Lotus Elan.

"Then they offered—" (price of a small island in the Caribbean). "And you know, Judy . . . I said yes. You really should do corporate gigs."

New Year's Eve was coming soon, and Billy asked, "By the way, where are you playing for New Year's?"

"A little club downtown called Knickerbocker Bar and Grill."

"How late are you there?"

"Until two a.m."

"I love Knickerbocker. I'm off a little after midnight, so I can come see you. I'll bring the band. They'll love you."

"Thanks, Billy. That would be great. Where are you playing?"

"The Garden."

"Of course."

— —

After more than three hundred interviews, I continue to be inspired by the people I'm fortunate enough to have on the show. It's been thrilling to sit for an hour or more with smart, talented people and talk about art.

The actor F. Murray Abraham let me talk with him onstage before an off-Broadway play in which he was appearing; later he said that our discussion had inspired him in that evening's performance. He introduced me to his producer and director, knowing they'd spread the word on my new show.

The opera singer Renée Fleming squeezed me in between five other interviews she had scheduled and gave me an hour instead of the twenty minutes her publicist had allotted. Tony Bennett and Robert Redford each sat for two hours and Paul Prudhomme for three. Ed Bradley, Charles Osgood, and Leonard Maltin helped me relax and made me feel as if I'd been an interviewer as long as they had. Steve Allen entertained me and gave me new insight into comedy, Roy Scheider gave me input on an actor's approach to an interview, Frank Gehry talked about his early hiring of Oscar Peterson for a college dance, and Seth MacFarlane had me over to his house in Beverly Hills and brought Stewie and Peter along. Each guest took my goal to inspire our audience to heart and opened up in ways that brought our conversation to life.

The last thoughts Chevy Chase expressed on *Jazz Inspired* were not about his own work but rather words of encouragement to everyone to be creative and experience the joy it can bring to ones life.

My original goal with *Jazz Inspired* was to help listeners gain a better appreciation of jazz, learn how creative people are inspired, and to embrace creativity and inspiration in their own lives. I hope *Jazz Inspired* has done at least a little of that.

22

My Sister Shagged a Monk

I had always disdained the thought of playing on a cruise ship, assuming the great days of luxurious cruising were over. Then, in 2002, I was offered a six-day crossing from England to New York on QE2 and thought I'd give this experience a chance. I figured everyone should do an ocean-liner crossing at least once. I was hired to play two concerts; the rest of time I would have off, enjoying first-class accommodations with black-tie dinners every night. At that time, the pouring champagne was Veuve Clicquot, the caviar Beluga. QE2 was the largest consumer of caviar in the world, in large part due to me.

In 2003 I was diagnosed with cancer. The QE2 connection led to other cruise work when I especially needed it. I'd revealed my cancer to only to a handful of people and disappeared somewhat from the concert world during the first two years of my recovery. Sneaking a cruise in now and then helped me get back on my feet financially in a less-pressured environment.

The old QE2 on which I sailed was a classic ocean liner built to smoothly cross the Atlantic in any kind of weather. She is the only ship to survive a ninety-foot wave, the same size made famous in the movie *The Perfect Storm*. I was on this ship during a Force 12 hurricane in sixty-foot seas, and while it wasn't exactly smooth sailing, it was an impressively cool ride. I got to experience QE2's last gasp of full-on elegance before it all went downhill; thereafter many ships went for "elegant casual" or other euphemisms that allow for sloppy dress. I moved on to smaller ships, where I got to relive the atmosphere of my black-tie crossings on the QE2 and where an elegant experience continues to this day.

"Exclusive" is the operative word on these high-end excursions. Almost every passenger on the smaller ships is good-looking, healthy, rich, and one half of a happy couple. I've decided that no couple books a cruise on a ship with only three hundred passengers unless they *are* a happy couple, their happiness made easier, of course, by being good-looking, healthy, and rich. You don't see fat people on little ships.

It's easy to envy or dismiss these folks, but I've met great people who have worked hard for their money, marriage, and fitness. With the luxury of extended time together over drinks and meals, I've learned a lot about different cultures and points of view. I've also decided that while money won't necessarily make you happy, it sure can make you happier.

Interesting things happen in this environment, for the passengers are relaxed and privileged and feel free to say whatever they like. I was recently in the luxurious lobby of a fancy, historic hotel in Barbados. I lounged on an ornately upholstered couch beneath an exotic tree that drooped above me sexily, my thoughts drifting. The delicious tropical breeze blew through the open shutters as I waited for my transfer to the ship.

The ceiling above me was at least twenty-five feet high, with large, cream-colored bamboo fans hanging from it that revolved lazily in each corner. I sighed as I leaned back into the over-stuffed pillows and wondered if I could sneak my feet up on the antique rattan chair in front of me and not look like a heathen. A stylish woman of a certain age settled in next to me as I surreptitiously removed my feet from the chair.

"Are you waiting for the ship?"

"Yes, are you?"

"Yes, such a sweet little ship. I cruise a few months a year on her."

My new companion leaned in conspiratorially, glanced around, and said, "Have you noticed that there are an awful lot of black people here?"

"Well, we *are* in Barbados," I responded, a bit confused.

She glanced skyward, cocked her head thoughtfully, and added, "I just wonder then, how can they afford to come to this hotel?"

An interesting fact commented on by the ships' staff is that you get a sense of how the cruise will play out the minute you see the passengers embark. I find that the more unusual the itinerary, the more interesting the traveler. I've met great folks everywhere, but usually find more intriguing ones cruising around Cape Horn than I do when I'm drinking and sunning my way through the Caribbean.

On a particularly boring Caribbean excursion I decided to crash the "Friends of Dorothy" meeting, knowing that a group of gays had to have something interesting to offer. "Friends of Dorothy" is an old-fashioned code term for a gathering of gays; it's used as a signal for like-minded travelers to get together.

"Hi, my name's Judy," I said as I walked into the welcoming crowd. "I'm a *friend* of 'Friends of Dorothy.'"

"Thank God, another woman!" responded the only other female, an eleven-year-old named Emma who'd been adopted as a baby by two charming guys named Mark and Joe. "Aren't you the jazz pianist?" she continued.

"I didn't know you were gay," added a particularly fit, enthusiastic soul, a rabbi named David.

"I'm straight. You guys aren't heterophobic, are you?

Rabbi David was holding a service the next night and invited me to that as well.

"Aren't you the piano player?" asked one of the participants. "I didn't know you were Jewish."

"I'm not, but I'm trying new things on this cruise. I'm also a new friend of 'Friends of Dorothy.'"

"You're gay?"

"No, but I'm a big fan of *The Wizard of Oz*."

I've had some of my most interesting conversations on ships, where the mix of nationalities and travel experiences can result in fascinating exchanges. I once asked, "What's the most interesting travel adventure you've ever had?"

"Well, I once got lost in a condom factory in India."

And my favorite:

"So you're an identical twin?"

"Yes. And I'm still very close to my sister. That twin thing is true."

"Are you alike?"

"With most things, although we've taken a bit of a different path at various times in our lives."

"How so?"

"Well, I was married to an ambassador while my sister was shagging a monk."

"So she could honestly say that sex was a religious experience?"

"Actually, I don't think the sex was that good."

I've been to lots of fascinating spots on cruises, one of my favorites being Ephesus, the ancient Greek city near Kusadasi, Turkey, on the Aegean coast. Much of it is intact, so you get a good feel for what was originally there. It has two impressive amphitheaters that were still used for concerts until a few years ago, when damage from hoards of rock fans and vibrations from rock music started wearing down this amazing place. Everyone visited Ephesus: Cleopatra, Paul, the Virgin Mary, Sting, Ray Charles—all the biggies. This is where Paul wrote his letter to the Ephesians, discouraging the selling of idols. Idol-selling continues to this day, of course. I just saw Nunzilla, a fire-breathing wind-up nun doll, in our local toy store yesterday, so obviously no one listened to Paul. It's so easy to ignore a letter.

The ships that visit this spectacular site arrange a classical concert in the evening, presented either in the small amphitheater—two thousand seats, although we were around seventy-five for the performance—or in front of the larger 25,000-seat theater where everyone sits at white tablecloth-covered tables with candles on them. The weather is always nice because cruise ships go to the best places at the best time of year. A string quartet plays, and at the break tuxedo-clad waiters serve champagne. Every now and then, drifting across the jasmine-scented air you can hear the sound of bleating goats with their neck bells ringing softly, which complements the strings nicely.

Another favorite spot is Petra in Jordan; it was used in a chase scene in *Indiana Jones and the Last Crusade.* This is an ancient trading site where huge facades are carved into the sides of the mountains that are revealed after a long walk or a horse or camel ride along a narrow path framed by huge cliffs.

The first façades you see as you emerge from the shadowy path and high cliffs are carved into the mountainside facing you, front-lit by the sun. The contrast in light enhances the dramatic effect when you step out from the shade of the canyon path.

A close pal, the British violinist Peter Fisher, was on this trek with me. He insisted we ride some camels to get the whole experience. Peter speaks Arabic along with a few other languages, so he took charge of our camel rental. He argued, or rather negotiated, with one of the colorfully clad men in charge and scored us two droll-looking ungulates.

"I've done this before, Judy," said Lawrence of Arabia. "Follow me."

"Peter, they've only given us a left lead. Where's the right one? How are we supposed to steer these monsters? My beast doesn't look too friendly, either. He keeps spitting at me."

"We'll be fine. Kick with your heels like you do with a horse. Say *schweeeeeeeee* to get him to stop."

"Are you serious?"

"Yes. I know what I'm doing."

Peter is the epitome of handsome, dignified, English good form and looked it, in his Panama hat and white linen. Although it was roasting hot, Peter had the comfortable cool of a man sipping iced tea at an English garden party. I, however, was melting in cargo pants and a T, a California girl who should have been body surfing instead of riding a surly, stinky animal on stilts. The camel wranglers did not look happy trusting us with their long-legged friends.

We cantered along through the dusty, dry canyon, with spectacularly carved cliff faces surrounding us. Suddenly Peter's ride took off at a gallop, with mine following in hot pursuit.

"SCHWEEEEEEEEEEEEEEE! SCHWEEEEEEEEEEE! PETER! IT'S NOT WORKING!"

Peter yelled back, "JUDY! MAKE HIM STOP, MAKE HIM STOP!"

"WHAT AM I SUPPOSED TO DO WITH ONE LEAD? YOU SAID YOU KNEW HOW TO RIDE THESE THINGS!"

"JUDY, I CAN'T MAKE HIM STOP! HELP ME!"

"YOU'RE THE CAMEL EXPERT, PETER!"

"ARGHHHHHHHHHHHHHHH! JUUUDYYYYYY!"

I contemplated jumping off, but it's a long way down from atop these high-rise creatures. Peter was freaking out, as was I, and kept shouting for me to stop our runaways. His British cool had frozen.

A crowd of locals had started running after us, robes and dust billowing behind them, shouting a collective, "SCHWEEEEEEEE, SCHWEEEEEEEE, SCHWEEEEEEEE!" One of them finally jumped out from behind a boulder and grabbed our recalcitrant rides, screaming accusations of camel abuse; at least that's how Peter translated it later over martinis. I'm afraid camels are yet another example of the fact that while soulful eyes and long eyelashes can seduce, it doesn't mean they should be trusted.

Take note.

23

This Happy Madness

The Brazilian novelist, playwright, and journalist Fernando Sabino and his beautiful wife, Lygia, came to hear me at Hanratty's at least once a year during my time there in the 1980s. Fernando had thick, dark hair and shining eyes, and spoke an exuberant, unintelligible English that reflected his enthusiasm for talking and his refusal to admit that he couldn't actually speak the language. Not surprisingly, I missed a lot of what he said.

From repeated interaction with these two, I gleaned that Fernando worked for a Brazilian newspaper, writing a sort of gossip column about his travels abroad and his love for jazz. I assumed he was the Brazilian Liz Smith. Not until much later did I discover that he was more like a combination of Liz Smith, Harold Pinter, and Tom Wolfe.

Fernando's work has not been translated into English, so few Americans are familiar with it, but many others are. When American Express produced a commercial in which famous people say they've been card members for years, the two people chosen to represent South America were Fernando Sabino and Pelé.

Fernando kept insisting I should come to Brazil to perform. Eventually he arranged for me to give a private concert in Rio for some friends of his who were serious jazz fans.

Fernando and Lygia met me at the airport, and Fernando launched into a list of things he had planned. Seeing my confusion, Lygia handed me a sheet of paper with my itinerary on it. The first thing I spotted was:

1) Lunch with Tom Jobim

"Is that *Antonio Carlos Jobim*?"

Yes, said Fernando, who explained that he thought I would like to meet him—and that he wanted to meet me. We would gather at Jobim's house for lunch, and he and I would play for each other. Fernando conveyed all this as though meeting Brazil's most famous composer, the man who wrote "The Girl from Ipanema" and many other iconic tunes, were an everyday occurrence.

Jobim made classic recordings with Sinatra, Sarah Vaughan, Elis Regina, and countless others, delighting fans and influencing musicians around the world. Jobim's popularity brought Brazilian music to an international audience and was one of the contributing factors in marrying jazz and the sounds of Brazil.

I glanced at the second item on our itinerary.

2) Lunch with Oscar Niemeyer

"We're having lunch with Oscar Niemeyer, the architect of Brasilia?" I exclaimed. "This is amazing. I'm having lunch with Brazil's most famous composer and most celebrated architect my first two days in Rio. I can't believe this!"

"He's an interesting man and we thought Bill might like to meet him too," Lygia said. Bill Lacy, my sweetheart during this period, ran the Pritzker Architecture Prize, which is often called the Nobel Prize in architecture. One of Bill's tasks was to give the winners the good news in person to confirm that they would accept before the news was given to the press. When I told Bill I was going to Brazil, he jumped at the chance to accompany me.

"This is a wonderful coincidence. You can't tell a soul: Oscar Niemeyer was chosen for the Pritzker Prize this year. This is perfect timing. While you're running around with Fernando, I'll call Niemeyer and arrange to meet. I'll tell him I'm traveling with my mate to hear her perform, and since I'm in Brazil I'd like to meet him. He won't suspect I'm there because he won the Pritzker."

Now that lunch with Niemeyer was arranged, Bill wouldn't have to schedule a separate meeting with him. Instead, he would get Niemeyer alone sometime during our afternoon together and tell him he had won architecture's most prestigious prize.

The afternoon with Niemeyer was memorable, especially the Steinway grand he had put on his outdoor balcony as an objet d'art. It had been ruined by the elements, but was quite beautiful as a piece of sculpture.

Tom (pronounced *tone*), as everyone in Brazil calls Jobim, was a gracious host and enthusiastic about meeting the young stride pianist Fernando kept raving about.

"I've been looking forward to hearing you, Judy. No one plays stride anymore."

I played a few tunes as he stood and watched over my shoulder, making appreciative comments.

"Why don't you do one of Tom's tunes?" said Jobim's much younger wife, who had no idea who I was.

"I want to hear what Judy does. I hear my tunes all the time."

"Tom, I have to tell you something. A tune of yours I particularly love is 'This Happy Madness.'"

The melody and lyric capture the mood of Brazil and the joy of love in a special way that any songwriter would envy. The song's English lyrics were written by Gene Lees, who also wrote my first liner notes.

I sat next to Tom as he played for me. I'm not exactly sure how he managed the sound he did. He laid his hands on the keys like beanbags. They were soft and sort of squished out flat in a delicate, non-pianistic way, yet he achieved a groove that was exact and swinging. I've never seen or heard anything like it. I was hypnotized by the music and by his beautiful, soulful spirit. It all seemed understated and casual, yet intense and poetic.

Jobim's house was artfully strewn with magazines, books, and various interesting objects. Light streamed in through huge open windows. Large, colorful bowls filled with various styles of reading glasses were placed throughout the house. When the mood struck to write, or read, Tom was never far from at least thirty pairs of specs.

A few years later, I went to hear Tom's concert at Carnegie Hall. I was determined to get backstage afterwards and say hello, although I was prepared for him to not recognize me.

"I'm Count Basie!" I announced to the backstage guard with feeling.

He burst out laughing and said, "Well, Mr. Basie, I don't see you on the list but of course you're welcome to enter."

I spied Jobim on the other side of the backstage area with a sea of people between us.

"My JUD-gee! My JUD-gee!" Tom called out, waving to me over the heads of his fans.

I worked my way to him.

"Tom! What a thrill to see and hear you again."

He took my hands in his and gave me a quick kiss.

"It's so good to see you, JUD-gee. How's that magnificent left hand of yours?"

⌣ ⌣

Fernando was determined to make me known to the Brazilian public. Everywhere we went on this first visit of mine to Brazil, a crowd of press followed us like movie stars.

Fernando had introduced me to a brilliant woman named Ana Te, who positioned herself as my assistant/best friend/translator and anything else I needed. Ana Te worked in media so she knew the ropes.

Fernando set up a number of TV interviews for me before my concert.

"I'm going to be interviewing you and want to give you the questions in advance," said yet another beautiful *brasileira*, this one a TV commentator.

"That's OK," I replied. "I'd rather keep it unexpected and fresh."

"Let me give them to you so you can think about how you'd like to answer," she said with a hint of concern.

She told me twenty questions she was planning to ask. They were the usual, so I didn't think much about it.

"This will be live, Judy. I'll be off-camera asking the questions. The focus will be on you as you answer."

"Great."

She dove in. For the next twenty minutes not a word of English was spoken. Every question was asked in Portuguese, a detail the interviewer had neglected to mention.

I think the interview went something like:

"When did you start playing piano?

"Such a beautiful country. Everyone has been so friendly."

"What is your impression of Brazil so far?"

"Since I was around four or five."

"Your performance will be at Ritmo. Are you looking forward to playing in that famous club?"

"It's not primarily what I do."

"Will you play Brazilian tunes in your concert?"

"No, I'm single."

Ritmo was a late-night dance club owned by the forty-year-old fanatical jazz fan who had financed my concert. He set up tables covered with navy tablecloths and surrounded them with gold-painted chairs, transforming the room from a mildly tacky disco into an elegant cabaret. The event was for his close friends, all dressed to the nines, and his mother, who brought to mind Patti LuPone in *Evita*. She had given him his first introduction to jazz. This was his elegant thank-you.

Brazilians appreciate music in a way I haven't seen anywhere else in the world. The great American guitarist Gene Bertoncini explained it this way: "If you look closely at a sonogram of a pregnant Brazilian woman, you'll notice a tiny guitar right next to the fetus." I'm not sure that's true, but I have witnessed the uninhibited joy Brazilians display when they hear music.

My next trip to Brazil was a tour for the State Department, one of many such tours I've done in my career. The audiences were responsive like none other in the world. I'd just played two weeks at a club in Toronto, where the most I'd gotten was polite applause followed by long discussions about my playing and how great it was.

I'd say with frustration, "Really? You enjoyed it? No one seemed that into it."

"Because we didn't applaud? We're not very demonstrative in Toronto."

No kidding.

Brazil is the anti-Toronto. My first concert was in Brasilia, Niemeyer's architectural experiment, which worked spectacularly well or didn't, depending on your point of view. The audience responded with clapping, foot-stomping, and dancing in the aisles.

Last year, a major magazine in Brazil did a feature on me in connection with an appearance of mine in the country. We talked at length about my film and TV appearances in Brazil, my many festival performances, and my friendship with Jobim, Niemeyer, and Fernando. A month after my last chat with the writer I got a follow up email. "I'm just finishing your feature and had one more question: Did you have an affair with Tom Jobim or Fernando Sabino?"

When I told the journalist I hadn't slept with Jobim or Fernando, I asked if she was disappointed.

"No, but I had to ask."

"Why?"

"Well, why do you think they were interested in you?"

"Believe it or not, because of my music."

— ⌣

Just as John S. Wilson of the *New York Times* had championed me back home, so had jazz critic Leonard Feather of the *Los Angeles Times* gotten behind me on the West Coast. Shortly after the release of *Two-Handed Stride*, Leonard recommended me for a television music series called *America's Music*."

"This is going to be big, Judy," he said. "All the old-timers are on it, all the New Orleans guys. Al Hirt will host, and you'll be the only young person in the entire series."

My appearance included two solo tunes along with some witty exchanges with Al. I thought this was my big break, until time passed, it never aired, and I wasn't paid. I checked in with Leonard.

"Leonard, I never got my money for *America's Music*. What's going on with that?"

"I wasn't paid either."

"What are we going to do?"

"Not be paid."

Stories of musicians not being paid abound, but I've managed to mostly avoid that. Still, I've had a few battles. Mike Hashim, Chris Flory, and I were booked at a well-known club in Washington, D.C. for a week. The day before we were set to leave, Mike called me.

"Judy, I just heard from two different musicians who've worked the place that their checks bounced. Do you still want to do it?"

"Well, it's too late to book something else. I'll call and confirm that they're going to pay us cash every night, as I stipulated in the contract. We'll hope for the best."

The owner came to hear us our first two nights and paid me the promised cash.

A night later, I was told I'd be paid in cash for the rest of the week on Saturday, our closing night. Saturday arrived and the owner was nowhere to be found. I went to the bartender, who'd been friendly during the week and seemed sympathetic to the situation.

"Where's the owner? He's supposed to pay me the balance of what's owed me tonight."

"I have a check for you. Something came up." He rolled his eyes in sympathy.

Clubs I've worked often use the excuse, "Everyone paid with a credit card tonight, so we don't have any cash." They're usually lying, which I'd anticipated might happen here. I was angry but cool.

"Where's the kid?" I asked, referring to Craig, the assistant manager, who was probably twenty-seven but looked seventeen.

"He's downstairs in the office."

I'll never know exactly what came over me as I descended the stairs, but I had my Carrie Mathison moment: strong, determined, and a bit insane in the pursuit of my man and mission.

I walked into the office, closed the door behind me, and locked it. I stared down at Craig, sitting behind his desk in the cramped, dreary space. I also noticed a safe.

"You owe me some money, and we're not leaving this office until I get it."

"Everyone paid with credit cards tonight so we don't have—"

"Don't give me that tired excuse. The safe is right there, and you're going to open it." I pointed to the iron box holding my dough. "I know you have cash and you're going to give it to me."

He cringed. Excellent.

"I'm waiting."

"I don't have any cash, honest."

"Well, then, you won't mind opening the safe and letting me see that it's empty."

He sighed.

"OK. I'm going to get in a lot of trouble for this."

"Like I care? Open the safe."

Not surprisingly, it was loaded with cash.

— —

I did a few more State Department tours of Brazil after my Fernando escapades, then didn't visit the country for years. Finally, in 2004, I got an interesting email.

> Dear Miss Carmichael,
>
> I run a festival in Brazil and would like to have you be a part of it. I have been a fan of yours ever since I saw that TV series you did with Al Hirt called *America's Music*.
>
> Sincerely,
>
> Marcelo Teixeira da Costa

Marcelo had become a jazz fan when he was seven. He'd asked his very hip grandmother to play him a recording of "Itsy Bitsy Spider." She refused, saying, "No, that's a silly song. I'm going to play you something better, 'Potato Head Blues,' by an American trumpet player named Louis Armstrong."

Thanks to his grandmother, Marcelo became a trumpet player himself and a serious jazz fan. He recently told me that when he starts dating a woman, one of the first questions he asks her is if she's a Louis Armstrong fan. "And if she doesn't know who Armstrong is, I don't ask her out a second time."

My first Marcelo trip for his "I Love Jazz Festival International" was in August 2005, two years almost to the day after my cancer surgery. I was just starting to get myself together physically, and Brazil was a perfect place to start. After that first year, Marcelo asked me to be the artistic advisor for the festival. To the original two cities, Belo Horizonte and Brasilia, we added five more: Belém, Rio, São Paulo, Curitiba, and Recife. We worked together for ten wild, wonderful years.

America's Music had been taped in the early '80s, which led me to conclude that Marcelo was my age or older. But when I got to Brazil I was greeted by a handsome, sophisticated, smooth-talking thirty-year-old— think a young Marcello Mastroianni. His right-hand woman, Duda Gruppi, was a curvy five-foot-ten beauty in her twenties who epitomized all the fantasies one has about gorgeous Brazilian women. Marcelo and Duda had seen a video of *America's Music*. Unbeknownst to me, the series had been released in Europe and South America with the profits never making it to the musicians who appeared in it.

Brazil is the least ageist country I've visited, and having fun is a major priority. I've had Brazilian men and women of every age spontaneously tell me I look wonderful, whether I know them or not. Once a woman slapped me on the rump and said, "You have a great ass for an American. American women usually have wimpy asses, but yours is nice." (My musicians refer to Brazil as "The Land of the Ass," so this was a serious compliment.)

I was at a post-concert dinner, in conversation with a good-looking chap who practiced Capoeira, a martial art that combines elements of dance and acrobatics and gives the practitioner grace and an amazing body. He was trying to convince me to try it.

"You would enjoy the movement and what it does to your body. You are a musician and an athlete, so this is a natural for you. I could practice with you if you'd like to get together tomorrow."

He turned to order another drink from the waiter. The woman next to me leaned over and whispered, "He wants you, JUD-gee, I can tell. He and I were together for a while and still occasionally hook up, but I don't mind sharing. He's as good as he looks."

"Good to know."

— —

I taught master classes during the I Love Jazz Festival, and had done so the day before a concert I gave with sax man Harry Allen and guitarist James Chirillo in 2009. The concert in Marcelo's hometown of Belo Horizonte was for an audience of ten thousand. There were huge screens around the stage, projecting our performance from the five cameras filming us. The audience had been exuberant and appreciative. By now I'd done the Jô Soares show, the Brazilian equivalent of the *Tonight Show*, appeared in a documentary about Fernando Sabino, and performed in Brazil often, so I had a big following.

After we'd finished playing, Harry and I went to the VIP area to get a drink and meet the upper-crust Brazilians who'd paid large sums to mingle with the festival musicians and the local celebrities who'd come to hear us.

Harry and I were surveying the scene—I sipping a caipirinha, he holding a glass of something non-alcoholic and green—when I spotted a soulful-looking lad with a mesmerizing gaze. He came close and put his arm around my waist and pulled me up to him in a move George Clooney would admire. I placed my hand gently on his abdomen, mildly pushing him away. Well, not really, but I feel obligated to say that I showed some resistance.

"*JUD-gee!* It is so good to see you and wonderful to hear you play again. What are you doing after the concert? Maybe we could slip away."

I glanced at Harry, who was looking on disapprovingly as the hunk with his arms around me moved in for a kiss. Suddenly I realized, to my horror, that this debonair devil was a student from the master class I'd given that day—my *high-school* master class. I gently extricated myself and said Harry and I had somewhere we needed to be. As we walked away, Harry couldn't resist a comment.

"Judy, tsk, tsk. I knew you liked younger men ..."

"Don't start with me, Harry Allen! That guy looked at *least* thirty. And he acted older. So smooth."

Harry and I are still in disagreement on this particular episode.

— ⌣

I took Mike Hashim with me for the first incarnation of the I Love Jazz Festival, which was then called Festival Brazil. The other bands were from South America, except for the one other "American star," Bob Wilber, who went on at length in English during his performances, confusing everyone. I had decided to learn a bit of Portuguese, which the audience appreciated. Mike was baffled but encouraging.

"Judy, I've seen you speak Italian, German, French, Chinese, and now Portuguese. I happen to know you speak none of these languages. How do you do it?"

I was a German major, after all.

The writer James Gavin, who is fluent in Brazilian Portuguese, tells me I speak this lovely language with a Mexican accent, no doubt a result of my Southern California roots. My Mexican friends tell me my Spanish has a vague Italian flavor, probably a result of that affair with ... oh, never mind.

— ᴗ

Since I performed at the festival every year, I brought different size ensembles for variety. I was also responsible for hiring musicians from England and the States to fill out the festival, while Marcelo focused on the ones from the rest of Europe and South America.

Many crazy things happened in my ten years with Marcelo, but one adventure, which reflects the insanity of it all, occurred with my septet in 2008. We arrived at a little town, the name of which escapes me. I remember that it was historic and important politically for Marcelo's family, which is highly placed in Brazilian society. Marcelo once asked if I would do a special concert for his mother's charity because "the vice president is a big fan of yours and he'll be there." I thought he meant the vice president of the charity. He meant the vice president of Brazil.

We arrived in the town and I asked to see the promised Steinway grand I was to play that night. As usual, when there is a problem in Brazil, explanations are copious and confusing. Finally it was admitted that the Steinway had been in storage for some time, and when it was brought out for this impending concert, it was discovered that the interior had been eaten by rats.

The governor of the state would be in attendance along with other important people, so a good piano was especially important. Having a septet meant I needed an instrument that could be heard above this large group. All they could find was a beat-up upright, a small, quiet, piano-shaped object I'd have to play with my back to the audience because of its orientation.

The crowd of five hundred elegantly dressed sophisticates were seated cabaret-style under an open-sided marquee surrounded by endless greenery and flowers. The concert was at sunset, and a golden glow filled the tent as the sun shone through the fabric.

Bodyguards were on hand because of the many political figures in attendance. The band and I walked on stage to enthusiastic applause and charged into our first tune. I was so angry thinking about the demolished Steinway that I attacked the poor instrument in front of me like a lumberjack sawing an oak. I'd turn around to introduce the tunes, an awkward move with the orientation of piano. My back was to the audience, which left them staring at my bouncing bottom throughout the concert, as I played like a madwoman.

Suddenly, while in mid-tune, I sensed someone next to me. I looked to my left and saw the very drunk governor leaning down and whispering in my ear.

"*What are you doing?*" I yelled over the music. "*Get off my stage!*"

"You are so beautiful, *JUD-gee*," he murmured in my ear.

The band was romping on "I Got Rhythm." They witnessed my plight but couldn't get past their music stands to rescue me, although jazz musicians aren't exactly known for their physical bravery. "What if I hurt my hands or my lip?" Mike Hashim once told me his idea of danger is finding a new way to get from Eb7 to Ab.

"Brazilian music like jazz, no?" said the governor into my cheek, the wine-soaked smell of him making me queasy. Finally, one of the bodyguards rushed onstage and dragged him away as we completed the tune and finished the concert.

"Come on, guys, we're done," I said as I stomped off the stage. "They don't deserve an encore." We made our way to the back of the tent and found a table. I ordered three bottles of Veuve Cliquot. They owed us. Meanwhile, the drunken governor started making his way to our table. He took a swing at a nearby woman. Incredibly, Marcelo, our festival director, stepped up and threw a punch, then looked at his hand, surprised it hurt from the hit. Another woman screamed. A chair flew through the air, then another. Instantly we were in a bar brawl in a John Wayne movie.

In unison, my musicians and I picked up our table and moved it farther into a corner. We settled back in to watch this amazing scene as I reached over and topped up the guys' champagne. The sun was just setting, casting a dramatic, blood-red glow that backlit the scene and added to the cinematic feel.

"Judy, you really know how to throw a party," my clarinetist commented.

My drummer, Eddie, stood up and my musicians joined him, all turning toward me and raising their glasses as the fight continued beyond us. Eddie waved his arm with a sweeping gesture toward the room and looked at me. Solemnly, he said, "In the 'Land of the Ass' it took Judy Carmichael's ass to start a fist fight!"

I love it when men sweet talk me.

24

I'm Happy

"Hi, Judy. Dr. Barakat is running late. He'll be with you shortly."

"Thanks, Beth. Nice to see you."

I hugged the gown around me and shivered.

It's always freezing in these hospitals. This robe is nice and comfy, though, sort of a flannel material. It fits well, too, more like a hotel robe. Funny how I thought Sloan Kettering seemed like a spa the first time I visited.

Dr. Barakat charged in, smiling and in command. I imagined this was how Teddy Roosevelt entered a room.

"Judy! It's so wonderful to see you. How are you?"

"I'm good."

"You look wonderful!"

"It's this stylish robe I'm wearing, by a designer named Sloan Kettering."

He laughed. "Tell me what's going on with you."

"A lot is going on."

"There's always a lot going on with you." He gestured to a woman at his side. "Judy, this is Shelly, a new nurse here at Memorial. Shelly, Judy's a jazz pianist. My wife and son and I went to a concert she gave in the Hamptons. She's always running around the world performing. I can't keep up."

"You're always running around the world, doctor. So what's new with you?"

"I went back to school and got my M.B.A. at Columbia in hospital administration and I'm still working on the lymphedema study. You were a big motivator for that, as you know. I'm going back to China next week to show some surgeons a new technique."

"And saving lives in between. I see you're slacking as usual."

"And you?"

"This year, 2014, is the fourteenth anniversary of *Jazz Inspired*, my radio show. I was just getting it up and running when I got cancer, so I'm proud that I kept that going. It's now on a lot more stations and it podcasts, as well, of course. Also, I'm singing now, which is new. I've always had vocal issues so I didn't attempt it. Plus, I've started writing music and lyrics on my own, and writing lyrics to Harry Allen's music."

"He's the tenor player I heard with you in Sag Harbor, right?"

"Yes. When I started playing again, after all the treatment, I thought I had to up my game. I'd always played with the same musicians because I've never felt part of the jazz community and have been intimidated by most musicians. I stayed with a small group of guys I used repeatedly. I've changed all that and have been playing with lots of new people. Harry's one of them. He says he's been coming to hear me for years and claims I ignored him. He and a few other great musicians have changed my music and my attitude about playing.

"And I'm finally performing ballads. This is possibly the biggest surprise of all. I've always loved ballads but seldom played them.

"Why not?"

"I've never been happy enough to play ballads."

"And now?"

"I'm happy."

He smiled. "Listen, I could talk to you forever, but we need to get to your exam. Everything looks good. And Judy, it's been *eleven* years."

"I know."

My surgeon superhero looked at me and grinned. He leaned over and whispered in my ear, "You're cured."

25

Listen

After having known Count Basie for a few years, I asked him if there was a secret to life. He smiled that sly grin of his and said, "Listen."

"Yes?" I countered, waiting for something more.

"Just … listen."

Someone once complimented Miles Davis after a concert by saying, "Man, Miles, you played great tonight." Miles responded, "Maybe you just listened great tonight."

Many of the older musicians I met had a subtle delivery. Had I not been "listening great," I would have missed their nuances. This was especially true with Basie, whose sentences evoked his playing—spare, exactly right, and loaded with meaning.

While I was still working at Disneyland and Basie was appearing there, I went backstage to say hello. I was wearing a tight T-shirt and tighter white jeans that left nothing to the imagination. I was overcompensating, no doubt, for my Coke Corner costume.

Basie was sitting, so his eyes were about at my butt level. I had my back to him as I chatted with Freddie Green. As I turned to face Basie, he gave me a slow scan, top to bottom, focusing mainly on my spray-on pants.

"Well, Stride, I have to tell you: Those ... pants ... fit."

I was horrified. I was the girl who wanted to be taken seriously, not to look like a twenty-something groupie trying to hit on one of the band members. I'll never know if Basie meant to give me a particular message, but I heard what he was saying and changed what I wore from then on when I went to hear music.

━ ━

People tell me they envy my ability to play the piano. What I think is the great gift of my life and that of other artists' is the focus on listening, seeing, and paying attention. The designer Ray Eames was a friend and mentor when I was in my early thirties. (Ray and her husband and design partner, Charles Eames, had created the famous Eames Lounge Chair.) Whereas Basie told me to listen, Ray taught me to see. She made me stop the car once when we were winding up the canyon to her home in Pacific Palisades because she'd spotted a beautiful rose.

"Judy, stop!"

I screeched to a halt, thinking an animal was in the road. Ray jumped out of the car and beckoned me to join her.

"Come here, look at this rose! Isn't this the most delicious color? See how its hue is a bit dusty? It looks like an Old Masters painting."

Another time, Ray and I were driving in Manhattan when I had an inspired thought.

"Have you ever been to a carwash, Ray?"

"No. Would it be fun?"

Back in 1952, Ray and Charles had made a short film called *Blacktop*, inspired by a time when Charles had watched a janitor wash down a schoolyard across the street from their office in Venice, California. The result is a visual feast of water and soap mixing together as they move across the blacktop, illustrating how Ray and Charles's keen eyes could make something common look profound. Going through a carwash would be like as an acid trip to Ray.

~ ~

I agreed to do a State Department tour of India in December 1987 because I knew Ray would also be working there. The chance to see India through her eyes was an opportunity I couldn't miss.

India is a complicated place, dense with population, ideas, cultures, and visual stimulation. The people are the landscape. My tour covered many cities, but Calcutta was by far the most overwhelming. The juxtaposition of our modern age with what was essentially the Dark Ages was hard to comprehend.

There is still prejudice around jazz piano, but it was even worse in late 1980s Calcutta. The operators of the auditorium thought my playing might damage their precious Steinway, so they replaced it with an ancient piano that had strings and *keys* missing and hadn't been tuned since the British left. After playing the beast, I told the presenter that I could not perform a concert on it. Through various machinations, I managed to have a better one sent over from a nearby music school.

I returned a couple of hours later and found the new instrument onstage; the unplayable piano was on its way out, carried off by four undernourished Gandhi lookalikes, all of them wearing diaper-like dhoti. Their arms hung straight by their sides as they balanced the piano on their heads and moved slowly toward the door. An instrument this size weighs around a thousand pounds; these men could not have weighed more than a hundred and ten pounds each.

I was a bit light-headed from the intense heat, and couldn't immediately focus on the piano moving past me. The hall was poorly lit and the walls were a smoky mustard color so the men's bodies were almost invisible. All I could see easily were their white dhoti and the black piano above them. Ray was there as well, and delighted at the scene unfolding before us. "Judy, look! Your piano is floating past you on their heads!"

I inhaled the heavy air with a sigh and turned toward my emaciated piano movers, bowing in thanks as I absorbed the mystical scene. I sat down to test the piano on loan. After I'd finished my first song, I heard applause. I looked up to see that the four men had paused to listen. You'd think they would have been in a hurry with a thousand-pound piano on their heads, but apparently, they were serious jazz fans. They stood facing me for twenty minutes, clapping enthusiastically after each song. Finally, I told them I was through practicing so they would move on. My neck was aching in empathy.

I left the stage to hold the door for my new friends. They filed into the dust-filled street, arms still at their sides, piano on their heads, negotiating their way through bustling crowds, brightly colored buses, wandering animals, cars, beggars, and horse-drawn carts. The late-afternoon sun sparkled through the cloudy haze, creating an orange glow around the silhouetted grand piano, gliding along on human legs, fading into the sunset.

The last time I saw Basie, we spoke backstage before his concert at the Ambassador Auditorium in Pasadena, a place I would play years later. His arthritis was advanced by then and walking was difficult, so he used an electric scooter to move around.

"My arthritis is bothering me, Stride. I'm not sure I can still stretch a tenth," he said as he held up his left hand, expanding his fingers away from each other. "I may have to call you out to finish my concert."

"How you do go on, Mr. Basie."

"If anyone knows who could take over for me, it's me—and I say it's you."

26

Climbing the Wall

One of the nicest things anyone has ever said to me came from my great friend Mike Hashim: "Judy, I've always admired that you refuse to suffer."

I may refuse to suffer, but I seldom do things that have nothing to do with work, unless it's a dinner out or a sport. So it made sense that the person who would entice me to some non-work-related adventure would be my old gourmet eating and sports buddy Jim, he of the 1992 miniature golf challenge. I hadn't seen Jim in years, so we met for a reunion dinner at our favorite hangout, the American Hotel in Sag Harbor.

"Jim, whatever happened to that beautiful sister of yours? I always figured she'd marry a rock star."

"She did. Roger Waters."

"Who's Roger Waters?"

Who hasn't heard of Roger Waters, you ask? Remember my Rod Stewart evening? To put this in perspective, I'm also the girl who once heard music I particularly liked in a bar and asked the waiter, "Who's that?"

"His name is *Elton John*," answered my server with loud, perfect articulation, like I might be from another planet or maybe just a bit slow.

I am, however, not completely without rock cred. I've been to two rock concerts—one, a high school date to hear Three Dog Night, the other, a foray into the world of *NSYNC for a *Jazz Inspired* interview with David Cook, Taylor Swift's music director, back when he was playing with *NSYNC. And yes, I hung out a bit with Justin Timberlake.

Years later I played a concert in Europe, and my new, young bassist said, "Do you mind if I have my picture taken with you? (Flattered.) My dad's a big fan of yours. (Less flattered.) He won't believe I got to play with Judy Carmichael! He's a musician, too. He used to play with a rock band called Three Dog Night."

— —

Jim encouraged me to come to London for one of the final performances of Roger Waters's record-breaking tour, *The Wall Live*. "It's unlike anything you'll ever see," Jim enthused. "Roger's turning seventy and won't tour like this again. You really should experience the show. It's spectacular."

Jim introduced me to Roger a few weeks later, thus reinforcing his campaign for me to come to London for the extravaganza. I decided to clear my schedule and go for it. I'd have backstage access, VIP treatment, and get to be a rock groupie.

Arrival

In September 2013, I and sixty thousand others arrived at Wembley Stadium in Northwest London, and were smoothly directed to our respective areas. Not even Disney does herding better.

Brits dress more stylishly than others for outdoor events, with the possible exception of the Italians. I've seen this at English picnics, where they're all linen and champagne to our ants and bug spray. Their chic approach to stadium wear is even more impressive. And their bag inspectors are the most civilized in the world. As I waited in line at Wembley, one of them opened the bag of the man in front of me, pulled out his bottle of wine, complimented the vintage, and offered to open it for him. He produced a corkscrew, did the deed, wished him a lovely evening, and sent him on his way.

Downton Abbey meets *Reverb Nation*.

Pre-Concert, VIP Lounge

For a moment Jim stepped away, leaving me alone. Champagne in hand, I asked a fellow VIP, "Do you go to lots of rock concerts?"

"Oh yes, hundreds! At least one a week. How about you?"

"No. I don't go to rock concerts."

Aghast, he sputtered, "Never?"

"Well, I did go to one in high school."

"Really? Who was it? The Monkees?"

"Do I really look that unhip? No, not The Monkees. Three Dog Night. I also saw *NSYNC and hung out a bit with Justin."

"Yeah, he's always been into older women. You have that Cameron Diaz thing going on."

Un-hip and old.

Another guy saw me standing alone and shot over, slowing to a saunter when he got closer in an effort to look cool.

"Is this your first time?"

In a VIP lounge? At a rock concert? Receiving a bad pick-up line? WHAT?

Not knowing his meaning, I faked it and said, "Yes."

Inexplicably, he deepened his pitch and said, "Surprise me."

"I'm a man."

The Stadium

Massive. The pre-concert music was a surprise: Billie Holiday. Maybe these were my people, after all.

The Concert

A big wall at the back of the stage kept getting built up and torn down. Various things were projected on The Wall: goose-stepping hammers, sexy, near-naked women, mind-blowing graphics, pictures of a younger Roger. From a distance, Roger looks like Richard Gere. Excellent hair.

Loads of special effects; Fireworks; a machine gun; an airplane; and a helicopter flying through; a huge, evil-looking pig floating, blimp-like, over the audience; gigantic, slow-mo puppets that towered above Roger. Think Julie Taymor's *Juan Darien* on steroids.

Pulling a Seth MacFarlane, Roger did all the voices for the various cartoon characters projected on The Wall. Impressive.

The masses screamed unintelligibly.

I shouted to Jim: "WHAT ARE THEY SAYING?"

Jim shouted back: "ROGER, ROGER, ROGER!"

Me: "THAT'S WHAT I WAS SHOUTING A FEW WEEKS AGO AT THE U.S. OPEN."

Afterparty

It was loaded with lots of beautiful people in black. Very civilized and British, with no drugs or craziness like my hang with Justin. (Kidding.)

A tall, handsome, famous British soccer star approached me and smiled, "I thought I'd check out Wembley and see what they do here besides soccer." (He said "football," but I'm translating, since I speak British.)

Suddenly, he blurted out, "Wait! Aren't you Judy Carmichael, the super-famous, super-fabulous American jazz musician?"

"Well, gosh ... yes."

"I can't believe it! I *love* you. This is the highlight of my night! You're even hotter in person. How would you like to slip out of here and see if we can break down some walls?"

(Maybe kidding ... maybe not.)

A very special thanks to Elisabeth Scharlatt for the initial suggestion to write this book and to Frank King for the key to making it happen.

Thanks to my dear friend Chris Flory for being my first reader and for keeping me honest and accurate about our lives as jazz musicians, and to Tom Spain and Jane Andrews for invaluable feedback on my early efforts.

Thanks to Mark Naison for his endless positivity and to my editor Connie Rosenblum for her enthusiasm, encouragement and thoughtful guidance. Thanks to Jim Gavin for his belief in this book and his suggestions to improve it.

And thanks to all the fascinating, talented, inspiring people I've been fortunate enough to meet who have made my life a fabulous adventure and given me these wonderful stories to tell.

About the Author

Steinway Artist Judy Carmichael is one of the leading interpreters of classic swing and stride piano. She received a Grammy nomination for her first recording, *Two-Handed Stride*, and has been featured on numerous TV and radio programs including *Entertainment Tonight*, *A Prairie Home Companion*, NPR's *Morning Edition*, CNN's *Business Unusual* and CBS *Sunday Morning* in the U.S. and shows for the BBC, Australian Broadcasting Corporation and Brazilian film and television. In 2000 Judy created and launched *Judy Carmichael's Jazz Inspired*, which she continues to produce, host, podcast and broadcast on NPR and SiriusXm. Judy talks with everyone from Billy Joel to Seth MacFarlane about their love for jazz and how it inspires them. Judy continues to tour internationally over 200 days a year and when she's home, which she seldom is, she's usually on a tennis court in her beloved Sag Harbor, NY

www.judycarmichael.com

10791838R00164

Made in the USA
Lexington, KY
01 October 2018